the body eclectic

the body eclectic

evolving practices in dance training

edited by

melanie bales
rebecca nettl-fiol

university of illinois press
urbana and chicago

Manufactured in the United States
of America
1 2 3 4 5 C P 5 4 3 2

∞ This book is printed on acid-free paper.

Library of Congress Cataloging-in-
Publication Data

The body eclectic : evolving practices in
dance training / edited by Melanie Bales
and Rebecca Nettl-Fiol.
p. cm.
Includes bibliographical references
and index.
ISBN-13: 978-0-252-03262-2
(cloth : alk. paper)
ISBN-10: 0-252-03262-4
ISBN-13: 978-0-252-07489-9
(pbk. : alk. paper)
ISBN-10: 0-252-07489-0
1. Dance—Study and teaching. I. Bales,
Melanie. II. Nettl-Fiol, Rebecca
GV1589.B65 2008
792.807—dc22 2007035935

contents

part i: bricolage

part ii: deconstruction

part iii: training stories

preface

This book arose primarily out of our experiences as professors in large and active American university dance programs. Our many conversations about changes in both university and professional training began to reveal several recurrent themes. In our milieu, many dancers arrive with unformed notions about what they want to do with dance. They may go through several phases, migrating from style to style, forming and re-forming their body-minds along the way—a process unlike the more linear progression of an aspiring ballet dancer, for example. This process is reflected both in our curricula (multifaceted, open-ended) and over the lifetime of contemporary dancers. Professional training for ballet dancers has been developing for hundreds of years and is well defined through academies, as well as taught in other settings. Modern dance classes are taught in New York and other urban centers but, increasingly, universities are the centers of training for dancers who eventually join companies. A cursory look at the biographies of dancers in leading contemporary companies will show that university and conservatory programs are, in a sense, parallel structures to the ballet academy for aspiring professional modern dancers.

This suggests a shift, whether fully acknowledged by a given dance program or not, in the mission of university dance training toward professional preparation. Many programs, like ours, the departments of dance at The Ohio State University and University of Illinois Urbana–Champaign, began as adjuncts to physical education programs and grew out of the philosophical tenets that put dance inside the broader liberal arts curriculum.[1] In other words, the idea of dancing to learn has shifted toward learning to dance. Another reason for this professionalizing has to do with the continued presence of active performers and choreographers on university dance faculties. Change is also a result of the growth of American modern dance, despite shrinking public support. There are simply more companies to join, more choreographers, and more dancers than at the time when dance departments first emerged. Perhaps also thanks to the economic downturn, dancers have flocked to the universities because of the stability and continuity they have to offer.

A continuing shift in dance company structure over the past forty years may reflect larger societal trends. The idea of "going Hollywood" in the American business culture refers to the direction from large companies to smaller, less permanent organizations that mobilize around talent, as big Hollywood studios gave way to independent producers and film makers.[2] This idea is reflected in the shift in American modern dance from earlier periods—where companies sought to produce and preserve the repertory of the founder-choreographer through a stable, hierarchical structure much like a ballet company—to today's more fluid and unstable pick-up company. Both models exist at the present time. The larger modern dance companies such as the Cunningham company, the Ailey Dance Theater, the resurrected Graham company, Pilobolus and its offshoots, and the Mark Morris Dance Group are relatively stable, although all dance organizations are in constant financial peril and continue to exist alongside the less stable pick-up groups. Many large companies started as small bands of the choreographer's friends and although some pick-up companies aspire to big company status, all do not. Similarly, all dancers do not aspire to be in large or stable companies, or to work with only one or few choreographers, even if that would be the only way to earn a living wage in dance. The entrepreneurial dancer is a counterpart to the independent choreographer.

Beyond the issues of how the university is situated in the dance world and how the structure of dance companies has changed, we agreed that our field lacked consideration of other aspects of the training question. If this relatively new art form—roughly, modern dance from the early twentieth century and postmodern from the early 1960s—has at its core the will to discover or originate, what are the methods for inventing and developing vocabularies that support the artistic urges? Instead of centering on the making of dances, or the dances themselves, we focused on training, acknowledging that the studio is where dance both preserves and discovers its language.

From the onset, we intended to focus on the inclusion of body-mind, or somatic, techniques into dance training. Both of us have invested deeply in somatic practices, as well as dance: one is a certified Alexander teacher who has also studied the Laban material for many years, the other a certified Laban/Bartenieff Movement Analyst who also practices yoga. Our own experiences reveal the impact of this work on our dance technique teaching and perhaps even our aesthetic responses. The burgeoning of literature on somatic education in the past ten years by writer-educators such as Sylvie Fortin, Jill Green, and Martha Eddy also indicated a growing interest in the field as it relates to dance training. Also, it seemed that over the past twenty years, our guest artists, who come and leave deep impressions, were all involved in some movement technique outside of dance per se. The ways these professionals used the information varied; sometimes yoga or floor exercises simply became the warm-up, at other times the influence was less direct and more subtle.

As a way to introduce some ideas and generate responses, we presented a roundtable discussion at the *Dancing in the Millennium* conference held in Washington, D.C., in the spring of 2000. From the general consensus among participants at the conference, who came from universities and the professional world, we identified some of the main issues. At that time we used "postmodern," admittedly a vague term, like "release technique"; no one was sure if his/her definitions really matched anyone else's. The postmodern term served to distinguish the kind of training we eventually labeled post-Judson from more traditional, or earlier forms; our colleagues seemed to know what we meant. Three things kept resurfacing as either on the increase or fully established: the use of alternative movement practices in dance technique or *as* dance technique, with various ones in and out of favor (can anyone say "Pilates"?); ballet as an adjunct technique for most modern dancers; and the eclectic, self-styled approach to training. It also became clear that virtually all thematic paths led back to a certain point in time in one way or another: the period of experimentation in dance known as the Judson era, which refers both to the performances at Judson Church in New York City from 1962–64 and to the figures who were its progenitors, many of whom are still active in the field. After that, "post-Judson" seemed a more fitting label for our playing field.

Since that kick-off experience at the conference, we centered on the practices themselves that thread through the jumbled collection of experiences that comprise late twentieth- and very early twenty-first-century dance training. We wished to know what people were doing, why they were doing it, and how it fit into their view of dance and themselves as artists. Although we knew the outlines of many training stories from over the years, interviews provided the needed detail and context for the ideas that had surfaced. A template for the interviews in this book came from a 1998 interview with dancer Rebecca Hilton and Bryan Smith.[3] Hilton, who danced with Stephen Petronio, showed that when given the chance a performer has quite a bit to say of interest to other dancers, choreographers, writers, as well as artists or scholars in neighboring fields. Hilton's comments reiterate several motifs of this book. She names eclecticism as the training method of choice, values retraining or repatterning as methods necessary to staying open and ready for emerging forms of choreography, and notes that the choreographer/dancer border has become more fluid, and less defined.

No one person exemplifies all of the themes or trends that flow through the territory at hand. Almost all the interviewees were guest artists who came through our departments for amounts of time ranging from a few weeks to a few years, a fact we openly acknowledge. They represent artists who are highly sought after, nationally and internationally, as choreographers and dancers. Most divide their time between managing pick-up companies and teaching at festivals and colleges. Our roster is also weighted toward the New York scene; a more West Coast collection would presumably offer slightly different profiles.

This approach might be termed "ethnographic," as it loosely inscribes a circle around members of a larger tribe, gathering identifiers such as "downtown dance," "the release community," and "contact improvisors" as they also intersect and overlap. A dancer can belong to several circles concurrently, each circle having its own pattern of training, however idiosyncratically or fleetingly constructed. People who dance with so-and-so take ballet in the morning, study with a particular Alexander teacher on occasion, and drop into contact jams with other groups of dancers who dance with someone else. It was apparent in speaking with the vast majority of dancers interviewed that choreographers are no longer training dancers, at least not in the traditional sense of giving technique classes that train the dancers in their personal movement style separate from the rehearsal process. The rehearsal replaces training for many; dancers are expected to come to rehearsal warmed up. Choreographers are often interested in, and in fact inspired by, the idiosyncrasies of their dancers. Dancers work to become more themselves rather than strive to mirror those they work for. Dancers become their own guides in putting together their training packages, according to their needs and interests at a given time.

Since 1980, the proliferation of dance literature by critical theorists has been particularly fruitful, producing a heady profusion of books and articles focused on dance in its cultural context. Writers such as Jane Desmond, Helen Thomas, Ramsay Burt, Ann Cooper Albright, Susan Foster, and Ann Daly, to name only a few, have helped to place dance research on the agenda of the wider field of cultural studies/theory, with occasional forays into identity politics. Some of these same scholars, with others, have begun to lament the dearth of writing that offers qualitative movement description and a closer analysis of form, style, and meaning.[4] While we wish to bring the discussion back to the culture of dance we do not see our desire to do so as reactionary in nature.

The complaint has been that, outside of some excellent writing by critics, pre-1980 dance research was skimpy or shallow and consisted mostly of biographies and discussions narrowly framed. That situation has changed, and it is time to come back to the field with our minds expanded by so much recent exciting work. The fact that training itself is at the core of this inquiry is unique in dance scholarship and, to our minds, essential for future understanding of our discipline.

Dance technique, like other parts of the whole of dance, has been furthered through oral and physical histories; teachers and students are not always cognizant of the sources of their own material. Collecting training stories and reflecting on changing training practices are steps toward an eventual and more comprehensive view of dance technique. Toward that history, this book is one very small chapter in it. Further studies involving training issues might include an examination of cross influences between dance figures, such as Margaret H'Doubler and Anna Halprin, Susan Klein and Trisha Brown, Ruth St. Denis and Joseph Pilates, even Twyla Tharp and her boxing teacher. Another study could focus on technical-choreographic complexes such as Ailey/Dunham/Horton or Limón/Humphrey/Weidman. As dance scholarship grows, it seems vital that so-called insider knowledge be integrated into the fabric of our field. We hope that studies such as ours describe a "middle way" between dance subjugated to other disciplines and dance hermetically sealed. It is also our hope that readers from other disciplines will benefit from the considerations below, learning more about our field while drawing comparisons to their own.

Melanie Bales
Rebecca Nettl-Fiol

notes

1. See Janice Ross's book, *Moving Lessons: Margaret H'Doubler and the Beginning of Dance in American Education* (Madison: University of Wisconsin Press, 2000), for excellent insights into the practical and theoretical tensions that have existed since dance entered the university. See also Thomas K. Hagood, "Moving in Harmony with the Body: The Teaching Legacy of Margaret H'Doubler, 1916–1926," *Dance Research Journal* 32, no. 2 (Winter 2000).
2. See Richard Florida, *The Rise of the Creative Class: And How It's Transforming Work, Leisure, Community and Everyday Life* (New York: Basic Books, 2002), 28.
3. "A Dancing Consciousness," from *The Routledge Dance Studies Reader,* ed. Alexandra Carter (London: 1998).
4. See Dialogues section of *Dance Research Journal* 32, no. 2 (Winter 2000).

acknowledgments

The editors would like to acknowledge the help and support of the following individuals: colleagues Ann Dils, Karen Eliot, Candace Feck, Penny Hanstein, Scott Marsh, Bruno Nettl, Phyllis Richmond, and Desiree Yomtoob for their advice and suggestions, and to Marcia B. Siegel for listening to early ideas, for her writing workshop and her presence in the OSU Department; interviewees not included in the book but who gave their time and ideas, Anne Bluethenthal, Janet Charleston, Kristina Isabelle, Ted Johnson, Carolyn Lucas, Tiffany Mills, Shelley Senter, Wil Swanson, Luc Vanier, and Sara Wookey; our transcriber and manuscript assistant, Christina Providence, who worked on early drafts; the other contributors for their patience and knowledge, Glenna Batson, Wendell Beavers, Veronica Dittman, and Joshua Monten; and all the artists who shared their stories with us, including Natalie Gilbert and Martha Myers.

We also acknowledge our debt to these individuals and institutions: the libraries of The Ohio State University and the University of Illinois Urbana-Champaign, the OSU College of the Arts Faculty Research Grants program, and the UIUC College of Fine and Applied Arts and Research Board; the Laban/Bartenieff Institute of Movement Studies Certification Program and Vera Maletic; and the American Society for the Alexander Technique and its teachers Joan Murray and Alexander Murray. We recognize the fine scholarship in the dance field, both recent and past, which has inspired and paved the way for our research, including that of Sally Banes, without whose work this book would not be possible. We are especially grateful to our families for their support and understanding throughout a long but rewarding process.

melanie bales

introduction
deconstruction and bricolage
and other themes of the post-judson era

The following chapters contribute to the assertion that contemporary dance training since the Judson era of American modern dance is distinct from earlier approaches in several ways. One way has to do with the apparent disjunction between technique training and performing or choreography. Increasingly, the former does not necessarily dictate or follow from the latter in a direct way. Other ways recent training practices are distinct from earlier eras emerge through particular themes mentioned in the Preface and are reiterated within the essays and interviews in this book. Such recurrent themes include: an eclectic approach to training; the incorporation of somatic and other physical practices into or as dance technique; the inclusion of ballet as an adjunct to other more contemporary forms; and shifts in both the dancer/choreographer boundary and in company structure, with an attendant rise in the agency of the dancer to determine his or her training. The chapters within the book identify challenges and offer solutions to questions facing dancers in the current climate, over a range of styles and approaches, including critical articles, teaching perspectives, considerations of dance science and somatics, and personal accounts.

During the Judson era of the 1960s, views on technique training both expanded and broke down, prompting the exploration of other movement arts and a critical stance toward dance technique itself. A choreographic preference for the nondancerly took artists from the 1960s to somatic practices as a method for identifying movement principles and eroding dancerly habits, in much the same way earlier dance educators like Margaret H'Doubler searched for "natural" or normative movement. Many did not reject technique altogether, as Deborah Jowitt notes: "[T]hey viewed class as a way of staying in shape, not as a system for designing bodies or a factor in the finished work" (Jowitt 1988, 323). The boundary between training and performance/choreography is both blurred and overlapping in post-Judson training. The following chapters and interviews, along with the authors' own experience, attest to the many ways in which that fact is played out.

Often in seminal writing on the Judson era and its aftermath, paradoxical or opposing phenomena are expressed in terms of conceptual or descriptive dualities. Prominent Judson historian Sally Banes makes reference to choreography in terms of the division between more analytical, minimalist work in *Terpsichore in Sneakers* (1987), as opposed to the more playful or outrageous ("ludic" as used by Best and Kellner in *The Postmodern Turn* [1987]). Writer Deborah Jowitt refers to two notions about performing during that period: a so-called task-oriented, often more austere persona and a more exuberant, raw, or rowdy version (Jowitt 1988, 327). The coexistence of opposites is also an aspect of post-Judson training: an overt interest in practices from the past (both recent and ancient) while also appreciating the newly born or highly idiosyncratic, all in the spirit of non-mutual exclusivity.

In "Women Writing the Body: Let's Watch a Little How She Dances," Elizabeth Dempster ties together choreography, performance, and training with an overarching thematic motif under the terms "deconstruction and bricolage," noting that "[t]he processes of deconstruction and bricolage commonly associated with postmodern dance also describe an attitude to physical training. The development of what might be termed the postmodern body is in some sense a deconstructive process, involving a period of detraining of the dancer's habitual structures and patterns of movement" (Dempster 1995, 32). As Dempster indicates and as the reader will see reflected in the chapters that follow, analogous expressions for deconstruction are repatterning, stripping down, getting back to basics, debriefing the body of unwanted habits of movement. Bricolage, on the other hand, connotes the layering of disparate practices upon one another within the dancer-body, such as a classic Western form (ballet) with an ancient Eastern practice (yoga), reflecting postmodern "radical juxtaposition" through a training agenda styled and structured by the interests of the independent dancer. Another extrapolation of the deconstruction/bricolage dichotomy draws lines between choreographic approaches: whether looking back or going inward (related to deconstruction), as in work of Deborah Hay, Anna Halprin, Kei Takei, or early Steve Paxton; or whether going outward towards new forms, combinations, augmentations (bricolage) as in the work of Bill T. Jones, Alvin Ailey, Elizabeth Streb, or Twyla Tharp, to name a few.

Dancers also express similar juxtapositions in their desire for balance, as in alternating something slow and contemplative (somatic technique or yoga) with dancing where they can let go and get sweaty (jazz dance class or a rigorous improvisation). Although these examples may not correspond directly to deconstruction and bricolage, there is correspondence on some level: quiet self-examination can lead to reviewing old ideas and forming new ones (deconstruction), while studying certain dance styles "just for fun" implies a sense of open inclusion (bricolage). These two main theoretical concepts can overlap in practice, as in studying a dance form to expand one's range of movement possibilities (bricolage) and then eventually using that practice in a deconstructive way. However, the terms do provide a system for identifying dominant themes and organizing the chapters that follow.

This project aims to sort out and present a few threads in the complex fabric of contemporary American concert dance, with its broad mix of movement styles (judged alternately as hybridity or appropriation), by examining training practices. The central assumption is that the studio often acts as a conduit to dance/movement ideas, as well as being a place to ready the body for performance. By tracing certain themes through a collection of voices we demonstrate how class-taking practices and choices both guide and reflect the art of dance.

works cited

Barnes, Sally. 1987. *Terpsichore in Sneakers: Post-Modern Dance*, 2nd ed. (Middletown, Conn.: Wesleyan University Press).

Best, Steven, and Douglas Kellner. 1987. *The Postmodern Turn* (New York: Guilford Press).

Dempster, Elizabeth. 1995. "Women Writing the Body: Let's Watch a Little How She Dances." In Ellen W. Goellner and Jacqueline Shea Murphy, eds., *Bodies of the Text* (New Brunswick, N.J.: Rutgers University Press).

Jowitt, Deborah. 1988. *Time and the Dancing Image* (New York: William Morrow and Co.).

part i

bricolage

The contributions in Part I reflect in some way the idea that post-Judson dance training is described by a lively and ever changing multiplicity of resources. The range of those sources can also be seen in the interviews that make up Chapter 12. As stated in both the Preface and Introduction, postmodernism, with its simultaneous references to old and new, high and low, Eastern and Western art forms, is also reflected in the training practices of American contemporary dancers. Along with a brief description of each article and a suggested reading list, this introduction to Part I will consider the special role of ballet since it makes frequent appearances on the menu of self-styled training agendas, which is the subject of Chapter 6.

Although the reader finds the role of ballet technique in post-Judson training under the heading of bricolage, it should be noted that many dancers use ballet training in a more deconstructive way: examining basic technical problems such as alignment by taking classes designed to allow them to hone in on certain movement principles, finding more efficiency and less destructive tension. In other words, they pursue ballet with the eventual goal of applying the knowledge to nonballet performance or choreography rather than becoming ballet dancers. However, as with other forms, ballet may also cross the borders of technique training and become part of a choreographic vocabulary or be just one of many techniques studied.

For the majority of dancers performing today, studying ballet—however intermittent, familiar, ambiguous, useful, frustrating, or irrelevant—has been part of the training history. Nearly everyone interviewed in the course of writing this book had studied ballet at one time or another. The range of attitudes toward ballet as a form of training spans from deep gratitude to hardened rejection, from informed appreciation to nearly complete ignorance of its history or repertory. From the objections to and rejections of ballet held by the early moderns, as with Isadora Duncan, there has certainly been a noticeable warming-up. We might say postmoderns, or post-Judsons, have been sleeping with the enemy. Certainly, there are choreographers and dancers today who do not study ballet and have no interest in it on any level. However, ballet as training may be hard to avoid. In the professional world, modern/postmodern classes are mostly taught in workshops or at a very few company schools, whereas ballet classes can be easily found. In any case, with the increasing blending of all forms of dance (and nondance for that matter) that comes with a shrinking world, ballet is still very much in the mix of things.

The first chapter in Part I, "A Dancing Dialectic," gives examples from the experience of dancers navigating the complex waters of post-Judson training. Melanie Bales asserts that a process of thesis/antithesis/synthesis underpins the madness that is method in training that may only seem haphazard. In Chapter 2, "A New York Dancer," Veronica Dittman, who lived and worked in New York, offers a "day in the life" account and defends the position of a dancer who plays the field. "Training as the Medium Through Which" (Chapter 3) progressively narrows its scope from a more general consideration to the special concerns of post-Judson practice, and culminates in a list of influences culled from dance writers, the stories of other dancers and their own experiences in the field.

In Chapter 4, musician Natalie Gilbert shares with Melanie Bales her perspective as a dance accompanist. Gilbert's experience in the university and as music director of the American Dance Festival allows her a unique overview of a vast number of technique teachers spanning the post-Judson time period. Joshua Monten's "Something Old, Something New, Something Borrowed: Eclecticism in Postmodern Dance" draws a historical sketch of eclecticism and provides some colorful suggestions for recognizing its various guises. "Ballet for the Post-Judson Dancer: Evil Stepsister or Fairy Godmother?" (Chapter 6) considers issues, both problematic and pragmatic, surrounding the choice to include ballet as part of eclectic training. Bales draws from recent literature, the voices of her students and other dancers, and her experience as a ballet teacher.

The following readings are recommended, along with those listed after each chapter, especially for those who may be rich in studio experience but less well traveled in the writing territory.

—Melanie Bales

suggested reading

Banes, Sally. *Democracy's Body: Judson Dance Theater 1962–1964*. Durham, N.C., and London: Duke University Press, 1995.

———. "Sibling Rivalry: The New York City Ballet and Modern Dance." In Lynn Garafola, ed., with Eric Foner. *Dance for a City: Fifty Years of the New York City Ballet*. New York: Columbia University Press, 1999.

———. *Terpsichore in Sneakers*. Hanover, N.H.: Wesleyan University Press, 1987.

——. *Writing Dancing in the Age of Postmodernism.* Hanover, N.H.: Wesleyan University Press, 1994.

Bull, Cynthia Jean Cohen. "Sense, Meaning, and Perception in Three Dance Cultures." In Jane Desmond, ed., *Meaning in Motion: New Cultural Studies in Dance.* Durham, N.C., and London: Duke University Press, 1997.

Carter, Alexandra, ed. *The Routledge Dance Studies Reader.* New York: Routledge, 1998.

Copeland, Roger. "The Objectivist Temperament: Post-Modern Dance and the Rediscovery of Ballet," *Dance Theatre Journal,* vol. 4, no. 3 (Autumn 1986): 6–11.

Daly, Ann, ed. "What Has Become of Postmodern Dance?" *The Drama Review* 36, no. 1 (Spring 1992): 48–69.

Driver, Senta, ed. *Choreography and Dance,* vol. 5, no. 3, *William Forsythe.* Harwood Academic Publishers, 2000.

Foster, Susan. *Reading Dancing: Bodies and Subjects in Contemporary American Dance.* Berkeley and Los Angeles: University of California Press, 1986.

Johnston, Jill. *Marmalade Me.* Hanover, N.H.: Wesleyan University Press, published by the University Press of New England, 1998.

Jowitt, Deborah. *Time and the Dancing Image.* New York: William Morrow and Co., 1988.

Novack, Cynthia. *Sharing the Dance: Contact Improvisation and American Culture.* Madison: University of Wisconsin Press, 1990.

Paskevska, Anna. *Ballet Beyond Tradition.* New York: Routledge, 2004.

Warren, Gretchen Ward. *The Art of Teaching Ballet: Ten Twentieth Century Masters.* Gainesville: University Press of Florida, 1996.

Writings of critics/authors: Arlene Croce, Ann Daly, Brenda Dixon Gottschild, Jennifer Dunning, Deborah Jowitt, Marcia B. Siegel.

On-line review sites: www.danceviewtimes.com and www.danceinsider.com.

melanie bales

1 a dancing dialectic

Two current overlapping debates in the dance field particularly germane to the topic of training practices will provide an introduction to the discussion below. While the emphasis here is to offer a few examples and suggestions as to how some contemporary dancers craft themselves into the material of an art form, I am aware that training is situated among the same issues that affect choreography, history, and criticism. Further, I find that by examining some aspects of how dancers train—since often the training is the medium through which movement ideas are born, transmitted, and transformed—movement can be identified as a conveyer of meaning and placed in relationship to other parts of the whole.

two debates

The first of the debates revolves around recent dance scholarship that seeks to place dance within a larger arena of study, particularly cultural studies. Positing a spectrum of sentiment on how dance is best framed, we might find on one end those who see dance as a cultural artifact produced by political and identity struggles or, disparagingly, as an art practice unable to be seriously considered apart from other structures or fields of study. On the other end of this construct would be those who feel dance, like art with a capital A, should be seen as the artistic expression of an individual or a spirit, capable of transcending, or at least transforming, some of the very issues at the core of cultural studies. I suspect that few dance scholars and artists would be located at my artificial end points but somewhere nearer the confusion and complexity of the middle ground.

One example from this debate can be found in Marcia Siegel's critique of Susan Foster's 1986 book *Reading Dancing*, entitled "The Truth about Apples and Oranges." Citing several flaws in Foster's methodology, Siegel states that, in any case, she "would still object to the idea of 'reading dancing,'" because it "gives no account of the actual process of looking at dance, which is fundamentally intuitive, visceral, and preverbal" (1992, 88). Another example further toward center comes from Ann Daly in her brief but pithy 1991 article "What Revolution? The New Dance Scholarship in America." Daly concludes that "[i]t could be true, as alleged, that interdisciplinary thinking may potentially do damage to the field, but *only* if the specificity of dance is lost at the expense of theory" (1991, 50).

Jane Desmond's book *Meaning in Motion: New Cultural Studies of Dance* begins with her essay entitled "Embodying Difference: Issues in Dance and Cultural Studies," in which she addresses, through many examples, the topic of movement style transmission across various boundaries. Of particular interest to me is the frequent mention of the importance of analysis "at the level of the body," while also making the important distinction between "the body" and the body in movement. She goes on to say that cultural critics must become more movement literate and suggests looking to Laban's system of Effort/Shape for help[1] (1997, 50). Presumably, increased movement literacy via Laban Movement Analysis (LMA) or otherwise would add to the scholarly infrastructure comparatively lacking in the dance field, and shift the emphasis to bodily *movement* rather, or along with, bodily *representation.*

As a dancer trained subsequently in LMA, which continues to inform my view and understanding of movement and dance, I concur that it can form a basis for inquiry into a variety of topics across styles and eras. As to how the study of training can enrich our field: what richer place to mine the specificity of the dance language than in the studio, where movement invention and transmission is foregrounded, and where we dancers and choreographers have spent the bulk of our dancing lives?

The second current debate among scholars, critics, and dancers gathers around a word that is alternately rejected, celebrated, ignored, and overused:

postmodernism. What is it, who is it, and how does it move? Does the *post* mean after or against? Is it over or just starting? Is it a good thing to be, or a bad thing? One somewhat contentious argument at the end of the 1980s revealed some of the complexities and challenges that arise when that word comes to the fore. Susan Manning, in her article "Modernist Dogma and Post-Modern Rhetoric" (1988) took issue with the designations and terms of inclusion that Sally Banes uses in her important book *Terpsichore in Sneakers.* Banes, in turn, argued for a historical use of the term (Rainer had called what she did postmodern) in preference to what she saw as Manning's essentialist use of the term. Banes's expertise on the period of dance-making arising from the Judson Church group prompted her to locate postmodernism within that era. Manning offered other markers and cited certain artists as exemplary of her definitions.

In another example of the postmodern conundrum, a collection of essays from several outstanding writers, titled "What Has Become of Postmodern Dance?" appeared in the *Drama Review* in 1992. In that journal volume, Marcia Siegel provides a succinct description of her position at the time: "New dance now has inherited traits from all its postmodern predecessors: the objectivity, nonlinearity, and nonrepresentation of the 60s; the formalism and physicality of the 70s; the eclecticism and parody of the 80s. The 90s new dance already looks like something different from all of these. Is it still postmodern? Do we care?" (1992, 92).

Cynthia Novack's essay, in the same volume, summarized her views on postmodern dance as distinct from modern dance "not only in the particular techniques associated with the new dance . . . but also in the changed political and social context in which performers and spectators lived" (Novack 1992, 54–55). Novack agrees that a "qualitative change" occurred at the time after the political movements of the 1960s, and she is "not at all certain that we're at another such crystallizing point" (56), referring to the time of writing, which I would extend to the present.

I raise these issues for two reasons: first, to state my position in regard to believing, with Banes, Novack, and others, that there has been indeed a "sea change" in the dance field owing in great part to the Judson period. Therefore, I am interested in examining training practices that took particular shape at or after that time. Second, I suggest that a closer look at training practices may circumvent or suggest new categories or definitions of movement style not forcibly tied to the all-powerful, yet perhaps increasingly meaningless, p-word.

As to the borrowing from other fields, dance could be likened to Germany during the Industrial Revolution. By the time Germany joined in, the technology of the forerunners was already dated, and so Germany, the yokel of Europe, acquired the newer machinery and was suddenly more updated than its neighbors. I will not stretch an already tenuous analogy to say that this gives us any real advantage, but we do have other art forms and fields to look to for comparison and contrast, as dance scholarship develops. Dance has the possibility of drawing on historical and theoretical discussions that took place earlier in art, architecture, and linguistic circles. Given the relative dearth of documentation and dissemination of dance artifacts in comparison with art, music, and literature, things have tended to move slower and have remained a bit more "local." I think of how shockingly underexposed most of our graduate students are. Unless a video or film exists of a particular dancer or choreographer, and is reasonably available, they must rely on written accounts often lacking in movement description.

Certainly it is clear that preservation—whether in written, notated, or visually recorded form—is a key component toward a future in dance studies. These last points may be a digression but may also offer yet another opportunity to suggest that the studio, the class, the teaching, and the learning of movement are all also essential substances of an ephemeral art form. In the class, a dancer or choreographer may come to know about his or her dance predecessors on a movement level, even if often the source remains unarticulated.

judson as marker

One of the main markers of the Judson period has to do with the introduction of quotidian or pedestrian movement into dance during this era; the very definition of dance was overtly tested. This changed not only the content and context of dances but also questioned who was a dancer and how the dancer related to his or her body, especially when the body was a dance-trained body. It is one thing to be an untrained dancer performing in a dance piece and quite another to be a former ballet student or a Merce Cunningham dancer performing "pedestrian" movement.

In eschewing the "taut, charged body" (Banes 1993, 45) of the ballet dancer, or the heavy dramatics and rigid limbs of Graham dancers, the Judsonite substituted walking, running, and climbing. Often this involved simultaneously rejecting dance movement—that is, the actual vocabulary or the steps—along with what is known in LMA as the "body attitude" (carriage) of the dancer-body.

No! they said, echoing Rainer's famous manifesto: no more the uplifted back and extended verticality of the ballet dancer, and no more of the full-chested Limón presence or tightly contracted abdomens of Graham. They were after the relatively slack and more loosely mobile torso of the guy on the street, never mind that most guys on the street are not really all that mobile. The importance here is that it wasn't a matter of having a different technique, it was a matter of technique versus *non*technique, challenging the border between the two.

Along with the cultivation of the everyday, whether ultimately successful or desirable, came changes in technical training attitudes and practices that have persisted. One outgrowth/solution was for the training to be the dance, as with the form of engagement eventually known as Contact Improvisation. On the other end of the spectrum were instances of complete disjuncture between performance and training. A quote from Lucinda Childs in Banes's *Democracy's Body* illustrates this disjuncture in the early phase of Judson: "Everybody seemed to be going to Slavenska, so I went, too. You had to keep your body together, even though there was a dichotomy between the discipline of that technique and the actual activity you were involved in" (Banes 1993, 99).

That noticeable space between training and choreography is still negotiated in creatively individual ways today. Returning to the consequences of pedestrianism or human-scale elements, and to the shift to a more released Body Attitude, interesting paths can be traced and connections drawn. I might situate the shift within the Africanist "aesthetic of the cool,"[2] which would relate certain dance styles or dancers to each other in that way. I could relate the urge to cast off the artificiality of trained movement with its telltale torso historically to Isadora's hatred of the ballet and the corset.

I could cite differences in Body Attitude in making distinctions between two dancers. In a recent performance of American Ballet Theatre (Autumn 2000), two different Twyla Tharp pieces were presented. In one, a duet, Ethan Stiefel wowed the audience and, to my mind, had absorbed or captured the essential statement of her style. In the other piece, the leading man, José Carreño, a beautiful classical dancer, didn't quite get it right, and it was in the Body Attitude where he failed. There could be other reasons why he couldn't tap into her line, but what I saw was too much formality in that crucial area of the body, so that the (post-Judson) Tharpian juxtaposition of *haute*-technique combined with casual offhandedness was missing. Although both men were primarily ballet-trained, one seemed better able to absorb what I would identify as a significant remnant of Judson's play with pedestrianism. Recognizing the movement and training implications of Judson's legacy, I will turn to focus on more current training issues.

deconstruction and bricolage

The doctrine of rejecting technically honed dance phrases in favor of movement "found" in daily life carries with it the notion of letting go, peeling off, getting back to *something*: nature? the basics? the functional? the real? The process remains as the milieu changes: in the 1960s people let go of hang-ups; in the 1990s and beyond, they released tension. I propose that two major trends in training since the Judson period have emerged for contemporary dancers—practices that allow dancers to engage in a dialectical relationship with oppositional body-mind phenomena.

The first trend might be termed *eclecticism*, or the process of appropriating various movement practices, existing dance traditions, or training methods from other art forms. The second trend related to the Body Attitude factor can be identified as deconstructive, or the process of "debriefing" the body or clearing away unwanted debris. Accordingly, Elizabeth Dempster, in her article "Women Writing the Body: Let's Watch a Little How She Dances," from *Bodies of the Text* states, "The processes of deconstruction and bricolage commonly associated with postmodern dance also describe an attitude to physical training. The development of what might be termed the postmodern body is in some sense a deconstructive process, involving a period of detraining of the dancer's habitual structures and patterns of movement" (1995, 32).

The idea is often to pare down, not build up (muscle, habits); to get out of the way (of nature's better decision), to allow rather than to make something happen; to "listen" to the movement impulse before acting. There is something of the Zen not-doing mentality here, and yet also of the modernist stripping down to essentials. Elaine Summers, who later originated Kinetic Awareness, weaves together the debriefing idea with the yen to clear out and start over in a passage describing constructive criticism of a piece Judith Dunn showed in a Judson group meeting: "Another point is that we weren't saying to her 'You shouldn't point your toes.' We wanted to know whether she really did want to, or whether she shared the struggle many of us were having about training and mannerisms. I personally had a lot to shed to get down to what I wanted in movement" (Banes 1993, 81).

Although some dancers today may still practice only one "pure" style, such as Graham technique, or take classes derived directly from some other style originated in the period before Judson, this phenomenon is becoming rare. In fact, there is just about any kind of "training package" you could imagine going on these days, and therein can be found one of the major descriptors of contemporary dance training. Especially outside of the university where a curriculum, even if quite eclectic, has been formed by the faculty, training among professionals at the millennium is self-styled.

However, certain groups of dancers share methods and types of training and form a kinship or commonality of taste and preferences. Many members have direct ties back to Judson (as Stephen Petronio via Trisha Brown) or base their work on improvisational structures of some stripe, since during Judson, improvisation emerged strongly and in various guises. In several of the kindred circles, the inclusion of somatics, which includes a wide range of body-mind practices, is an important element in readying the self to respond to choreographic demands. An example would be the so-called release community, the subject of two consecutive 1999 volumes of the *Movement Research Performance Journal* (18 and 19), in which somatic practice and improvisation is embraced as, or in, dance training. When some part of a technique class incorporates yoga, or Bartenieff Fundamentals, or Body-Mind Centering, and so on, the resulting experience can reflect both bricolage and deconstruction in that the somatic practice is added as an element of the whole training package (bricolage), but the *process* of examination and re-visitation during the practice may be deconstructive.

practical matters and matters of choice

Since the dance boom of the 1970s subsided most American modern dancers are no longer members of stable dance troupes that offer company classes, and they may dance with several companies simultaneously. Therefore, they can or must pursue their own training. This is often offered as yet another reason why training has become so eclectic: that dancers engage in a wider range of styles and classes in order to be technically and stylistically viable to more choreographers. In any case, the way the dialectical engagement functions, in terms of how the training elements are structured and how intensively or intermittently each element figures into the whole, varies with each individual, and hinges on practical matters like convenience, finances, and the like.

A typical menu over a year-long period might include ballet classes several times a week, study with an Alexander teacher over a period of time, a technique class with someone who is both trained in Alexander Technique and a former dancer, a workshop for Contact Improvisation, or occasional lessons in West African Dance. All these may be studied simultaneously, overlapping or in a sequence, and may shift and adjust depending on whether the dancer is performing and with whom. One form that is highly codified (ballet, African) may be offset by one that may not be dance at all, such as a somatic practice, Pilates, or workouts at the gym. Often the rehearsal experience will prompt the dancer to balance him/herself out through training choices. Anthony Phillips, dancing with choreographer Bebe Miller, spoke of an intense time rehearsing a Miller piece, "Going to the Wall":

> Recently, I get as far away from dance as I can when I am not dancing. As far as training, I do work that is based on trying to get force efficiently through my body. I am constantly trying to figure out what is not

mechanically functioning or what is holding within my body that is not allowing energy to drop down through. That practice of trying to clarify my skeleton, my body . . . so the energy moves efficiently is what prepares me to have a clear slate to move in the studio and then let emotional tension and energy enter my body to express itself. To survive physically, my training needs to be really clear and pure and without much complication. (NIPAD, 7)

Here, the deconstructive, or debriefing, process is evident. He goes on to say that the work with Klein Technique—a very slow, introspective, and meditative practice developed by Susan Klein based on principles of Bartenieff Fundamentals—gives him what he needs and is "pretty much all I can do at this point because the work is so complicated. To take a ballet class or some kind of stylistic class is too much information" (ibid.).

In these statements, the dancer describes several processes: he balances out complexity with simplicity; he complements the activities operative in rehearsal such as high physical output, generation of material, and interaction with other body-minds with a slowed-down, contemplative practice like Klein Technique; he consciously positions the experience of a "stylistic class" against a more anatomical approach to movement. Perhaps after the rehearsal process of this particular piece, he will choose to go back to taking ballet for any of a number of reasons. In any case, the fact that he has agency in his training, and that he crafts it according to his changing needs, is obvious and emblematic of this approach to training.

a working list of oppositional pairs

Talking to dancers and being in that milieu for many years, I can say that Phillips's expressions are very typical, not exceptional, although Klein Technique might be substituted with Chi-Kung, Alexander Technique, or yoga. Drawing from these perspectives, I distilled several word pairs that reflect juxtaposed complementary or oppositional ideas. An entity could be found on either side of the virtual fence, depending on the context in term of the dancer's former experience, rehearsals, or other classes. For example, a Contact jam session can be all about risk and virtuosity when compared to a more static form, *or* a chance to find an easier, full-bodied indulgence if alternating with a rigorous ballet *barre.* I hope the list, offered in a spirit of creativity, will invite examples from the reader's experience:

— anatomy-centered vs. image-centered
— articulate, separate vs. full-body, holistic

— artificial or constructed vs. normative
— attention to inner impulses vs. "shape oriented," imitating form
— dynamic vs. uninflected
— effortless of expertise, automaticity vs. "beginner's mind"
— emotive vs. "deadpan" (performance attitude)
— extremes vs. averages, norms
— familiar vs. foreign
— forced, muscled, planned vs. inevitable, liquid, spontaneous
— held body attitude vs. mobile torso or dropped weight
— highly structured vs. improvisatory
— highly stylistic vs. generic
— hyper-personal vs. impersonal
— ironic, campy, put-on vs. sincere, earnest
— meditative repetition vs. discovery through invention
— muscle vs. bone
— musical, rhythmic, aural vs. kinesthetic
— ornate, baroque, decorated vs. minimal, simple, spare
— playful vs. serious, disciplined
— principles of movement vs. culturally distinct forms
— restrained vs. free
— schooled, trained body vs. pedestrian, "anybody"
— soft vs. hard
— struggle, hard work vs. allowing, accepting
— traditional techniques vs. nondance movement
— visual vs. tactile

dialectic within a practice

There is also opportunity for synthesis through engagement of opposites *within* the practice of single class or training experience. As a life-long student of ballet, a former professional performer, and teacher for the past twenty years, I have become aware of the multiplicity of roles this form can play in the body-mind and training practices of the post-Judson dancer. Within one class, several modes coexist: contemplative self-reflection through shedding excess tension and avoiding mannerisms (deconstruction), gathering new skills and strengths by adding challenge (bricolage), and exploring different performative personas.

Susan Foster, in her article "Dancing Bodies," states that "[t]raining thus creates two bodies: one, perceived and tangible; the other, aesthetically ideal. . . .

Both bodies are constructed in tandem: each influences the development of the other" (1997, 237). Then she goes on to identify "[a] third kind of body, the demonstrative body, [that] mediates the acquisition of these skills by exemplifying correct or incorrect movement" (238). The three bodies—perceived, ideal and demonstrative—relate also to the dancer's body past, future, and present. He or she considers or relives past experience critically, and recognizes present information or knowledge in order to render a technically transformed future. Also, Foster's training triumverate reiterates dialectical processes: oppositional pairs (perceived body versus ideal body) and the idea of thesis-antithesis-synthesis (ideal, perceived, demonstrative).

Despite some post-Judson dancers regarding ballet as either irrelevant for them, or having negative feelings about some aspect of it, ballet training has been enjoying a Renaissance of sorts over the past twenty-five years or so, across many boundaries. Teachers like Marjorie Mussman, Nadine Revene, Jocelyn Lorenz, Janet Panetta, and Maggie Black to name a few, have been instrumental to the rise in popularity, attracting modern/postmodern dancers, many who wouldn't be caught dead dancing *Giselle.* Besides including ballet in a training program as bricolage, I have seen how dancers recognize the predictably well-ordered, systematic development of the *barre,* and enjoy that in a meditative sort of way. They can release their minds from learning new patterns, and at the same time layer that experience with stylistic play.

Although Anthony Phillips's example above identifies ballet as something he avoids when feeling overwhelmed with complex choreography, many dancers turn to it *because* it is a known entity (familiar vs. foreign from my list). Of course, this stance depends on how familiar ballet is: a "first language" or a recent acquisition. I have seen dancers in ballet class try on aesthetic ideas or work on technical challenges that they have decided are useful; for example, finding the long spine without over-reaching or holding tension in the chest, acquiring speed through quick joint release instead of tensing the whole body.

Many who studied ballet as children are also grappling with the familiar and the unfamiliar in a different sense: how ballet used to feel, how it feels now—the past body and present body in dialogue. They may introduce relatively newly developed sensibilities about momentum and follow-through to the class, and struggle to resolve those movement choices with the shape-orientation of the style. Sometimes, they see how far they can go one way (too much release and lose the form), and end up finding new solutions to old problems or limitations. In any case, investigating the complex and individualized ways contemporary dancers take ballet class gives an example of how other practices may function within the larger scope of eclectic training and how any individual technique can have multiple facets.

Another example of dialectical engagement within a practice can be seen in yoga study. Playing again the word pair game, several for consideration of yoga practice are: passive versus active (the stable body parts vs. the mobile parts, the strength vs. the stretch); the repetition of the poses versus finding something new each day; focus on group practice or spatial awareness versus focus on the self, or "inner space"; a sense of the universally human (yoga as a spiritual practice that unites people) versus the hyperpersonal (experience of one's individuality in flexibility, body shape and tone, strength, and perseverance).

In conclusion, the idea of dialectic is only one of many such investigations possible in considering training as an integral part of dance research. Body metaphors, for example, are heavily peppered in somatic study and improvisation techniques and provide a source for further study. In a 1987 article "Body Metaphors: Some Implications for Movement Education," Carol-Lynne Moore describes five bodily *Weltanschauungen:* body as beast, machine, *objet d'art,* child, and chimera, and suggests some ways they figure into sports and dance training. Though each can have positive and negative ramifications (body as machine can be mindless drilling, body as child can be self-indulgent preciousness), "in reality, the body may be a chimera, a mythological creature composed of the parts of several different animals" (Moore 1987, 36–37). Although Moore does not make the connection in her article, the post-Judson dancer may be drawn on a chimera of body concepts, techniques, styles, and approaches. Post-Judson body as chimera, or patchwork quilt, can be construed as a healthy eclecticism or a jack-of-all-trades, master-of-none failure. In any case, body metaphors, such as those suggested by Moore, provide a framework or starting point for investigating how training interacts with historical periods and artistic values, through changing attitudes and assumptions.

My particular interest in aesthetic ideas and artists related back to the Judson era delimits my personal tastes and experiences. Undoubtedly, an examination of training practices of other periods in dance would prove as revealing. Training post-Judson is characterized by a freedom of choice that echoes the precepts inherent in the artistic investigations of the time. Rather than being haphazard, unconsidered, and irrelevant, I believe that dancers and choreographers show purposeful and reflective creativity in exercising their right to choose, even if it is often more complicated, sometimes frustrating and confusing. Because seemingly disparate physical practices and concepts have come into the mix, the dialectical process describes one way to structure and order information and self-knowledge. The subject of training in dance generally is certainly underrepresented in the literature and scholars both inside and outside of dance would benefit from any research addressing the region most densely traversed by the dancer.

notes

1. Desmond's use of this outdated term for Laban Movement Analysis is balanced out for me by the positive endorsement she gives to the study of LMA as a tool in dance research.
2. For the appearance of this term in reference to art and dance, see the writings of Robert Farris Thompson (1993) and Brenda Dixon Gottschild (1996).

works cited

Banes, Sally. 1993. *Democracy's Body: Judson Dance Theater, 1962–1964.* Durham, N.C.: Duke University Press.

Daly, Ann. 1991. "What Revolution? The New Dance Scholarship in America." *Tanz International,* Köln, Jahrg. 2, no. 1 (January).

Dempster, Elizabeth. 1995. "Women Writing the Body: Let's Watch a Little How She Dances." In Ellen W. Goellner & Jacqueline Shea Murphy, eds., *Bodies of the Text.* New Brunswick, N.J.: Rutgers University Press.

Desmond, Jane C. 1997. "Embodying Difference: Issues in Dance and Cultural Studies." In Jane Desmond, ed., *Meaning in Motion: New Cultural Studies of Dance.* Durham, N.C.: Duke University Press.

Foster, Susan Leigh. 1997. "Dancing Bodies." *Meaning in Motion: New Cultural Studies of Dance.* In Jane Desmond, ed., *Meaning in Motion: New Cultural Studies of Dance.* Durham, N.C.: Duke University Press.

Gottschild, Brenda Dixon. 1996. *Digging the African Presence in American Performance: Dance and Other Contexts.* Westport, Conn.: Greenwood Press.

Manning, Susan. 1988. "Modernist Dogma and Post-Modern Rhetoric." *The Drama Review* 32, no. 4: 32–39.

Moore, Carol-Lynne. "Body Metaphors: Some Implications for Movement Education." *Interchange* 18, no. 3 (Fall 1987).

NIPAD project, "Going to the Wall," a multi-media DVD-ROM documenting the process of creating Bebe Miller's work." Directed by William A. Smith, Roberta Shaw, and Vera Maletic. Interview of dancer Anthony Phillips on page 7 of the transcript text of dancers' interviews.

Novack, Cynthia J. 1992. "Old Forms, New Meanings." *The Drama Review* 36, no. 1 (Spring).

Siegel, Marcia B. 1992. "Is It Still Postmodern? Do We Care?" *The Drama Review* 36, no. 1 (Spring).

Thompson, Robert Farris. 1993. "An Aesthetic of the Cool" in *Arts of Africa, Oceania and the Americas: Selected Readings.* Edited and with critical introductory essays by Janet Catherine Berlo, Lee Anne Wilson. Englewood Cliffs, N.J.: Prentice Hall.

veronica dittman

2 a new york dancer

It's 2002, and I am a dancer living in New York City. Like most dancers I know, I work for independent choreographers on a per-project basis. I train according to my own whims and interests; I train to become the type of dancer I would want to watch. Ballet class currently underpins my schedule, augmented by Contact Improvisation when I can get it. In other phases, I seek out favorite modern (which I mean to include "postmodern" here) teachers when they are available. When I have access to studio space, I will gladly forego class in favor of working by myself: honing technical skills, improvising, composing little phrases, doing whatever feels good.

The dancers I know maintain similarly personalized and eclectic training regimens. Some take ballet, some take Klein Technique; for a few, the only time they dance is in rehearsal, otherwise they practice yoga. I think this particular phenomenon—dancers who create their own curriculum in the service of a unique dancing identity of their own design—is specific to this time and place in the evolution of dance. It has come into being because of recent events and trends, and in turn is shaping the direction of the field. I would like to look at two of the influences that gave rise to this phenomenon of the self-styled dancer, and then consider some of the questions it raises and trends it fuels.

I venture that the biggest factor contributing to the rise of dancers like us is the collapse of the modern dance economy in the early 1990s. *The Village Voice* now has only one page of dance classifieds where once there were three or four, and audition listings there are rare, with most of them seeking dancers for a single gig. There are barely ten modern dance companies in the city of New York that offer their dancers forty-eight weeks of work with a salary you can live on and health insurance; that's steady, viable employment for perhaps two hundred modern dancers. Below that very narrow top tier, dancers are all working for more than one choreographer and/or holding down outside jobs to fill in the gaps financially. Even choreographers who have heaps of artistic accolades cannot get the funding to offer their dancers steady work at a living wage. Individual situations range from paid rehearsals and performances for a few weeks a year to unpaid rehearsals and a two- or three-digit stipend for an annual "season" of four nights of performance.

It is still possible to move to New York, train diligently in the school of Paul Taylor, Merce Cunningham, or Trisha Brown, serve an apprenticeship, and eventually become a member of the company, but that only happens for a handful of people each year. It is still possible to follow around a Doug Elkins, Stephen Petronio, or Iréne Hultman and eventually dance for them, but the payoff will be an artistic, personal one. You'll still have to keep your other job. In addition, choreographers at this level on the food chain may need to accept lucrative choreographic commissions or university gigs that don't involve their dancers at all.

The changes in arts funding during the 1990s resonate further down the spectrum as well. There used to be the possibility of catching a rising star, getting in on the ground floor with an unknown choreographer and staying with them as their reputation and ability to offer employment grew. The ceiling on success in modern dance is so low now that it's almost impossible for "emerging" choreographers to make the next step toward paid work for their dancers. Choreographers right out of school, with no shortage of talent, brains, or hard work now need almost impossible quantities of luck and personal connections to break through to the next level. The Joyce Theater's "Altogether Different" series, which spotlights "fresh" new talent, now sometimes features the same choreographer more than once over the span of a few years. This is testimony simultaneously to these choreographers' artistic chops and their inability to make the jump financially from a shared program format to their own season.

That a dancer's devotion to and hard work for a particular choreographer can seldom be returned in kind—either with reasonable compensation or an ongoing, long-term artistic relationship—contributes in large part to dancers' free rein in shaping their artistic identities rather than defining themselves by their work for a single person. There is no longer the question of which choreographer I want to dance for, with an appropriate course of training to achieve that goal. Instead, the question becomes, which choreographers do I want to dance for? Or more broadly still, what do I want to do with my dancing? Here is the trade-off inherent in this crappy millennial arts economy: while I can't sustain myself on my work for a single choreographer, I feel free to explore any avenue that interests me. This gives rise to much more interesting questions: What are my strengths and movement tendencies? How do I want to grow as a dancer, and what rehearsal/performance situations will encourage that growth? What feels good to me now, and is there a way to work my kinesthetic interests into my professional life?

This sense of broad artistic and creative possibilities brought on by economic circumstances is further fueled by the fact that most of us came through good university dance departments within decent liberal arts programs. For the most part, we don't come from a single-track conservatory mind-set anymore. On one level this means we're used to collaborative, interactive choreographic processes, and we have a broad experience improvising and choreographing ourselves. On another, we have exposure to writing, technology, history, kinesiology, and somatics from within our departments as well as other strong interests we may have developed elsewhere in the university.

For those of us dancing outside the security of a job with Mark Morris or Paul Taylor, this breadth of experience and interests, combined with the economic necessity of second and third jobs, makes us more likely to define ourselves as "slash" artists—dancer/choreographer/teacher, dancer/lighting designer, dancer/computer programmer/graphic designer, dancer/writer/masseuse are just a few—than to remain within a narrowly proscribed dancer identity. Many of us are already assuming the roles of choreographer and teacher even while we're still dancing, and some choreographers' creative processes call upon us to wear all those hats within a single rehearsal. As such, we don't fit anymore into the traditional dancer/choreographer relationship, wherein we are a tool or vessel for the choreographer's ideas; the paradigm of dancer as child/student and choreographer as adult/teacher is decimated as is any pre-ordained course of training or development that may have implied.

So circumstances have given rise to this new breed of vaguely maverick dancer who belongs to no one. Rather than trying to become a particular type of dancer for Choreographer X, I'm trying to become my best self: wholly unique. What are the implications for this multitude of individualists? An obvious resulting challenge is fitting oneself into a group situation. One solution is to make my own work, to craft my own venue for my dancing. So many dancers go this route that New York is rife with solos and collaborative duets, the product of talented dancers with no full-time gig and at least one choreographic impulse.

Not every dancer can choreograph. There are endless evenings of solo after solo, performed for an audience of the performers' friends. The flipside, though, is exciting. Dancers are empowered to create dance for themselves, rather than having to wait for the magic moment when a choreographer chooses you, allowing you to do your thing. And, there are so many people creating work (despite the rehearsal space crisis) that it's a bit of a creative free-for-all. Through curated and uncurated showcases and self-produced concerts, anyone can get their work out. Not only can any movement be dance but anyone can make it: the Judson edict spun out a bit further.

How does all this empowerment and autonomy affect how we work in a group for a particular choreographer? What does it do to the process of making a dance together? The first challenge is assembling the group. With no uniformity of training, and the likelihood that the group is together only for a finite project, we can only look for common ground, to some extent in our dance training, but also in our expectations of the process. Then the challenge of balancing choreographic power must be negotiated anew in each rehearsal process. Not only are we individualist dancers but it's also generally acknowledged that we bring some choreographic savvy to the process as well. Far from the traditional black and white situation in which the choreographer tells the dancers what to do and the dancers do it, there are now infinite gray permutations of shared choreographic responsibility. Often dancers are asked to generate phrase material that may then become a solo or may be taught wholly or in part to the group. Dancers are asked to manipulate elements of space, time, weight, or intention in movement phrases that the choreographer has created. Dancers are asked to improvise.

While these types of processes allow a significant creative voice for the dancer, they can also be a significant source of frustration. The dancer has input, but in most cases the choreographer maintains the artistic reins of the work, making executive decisions on how it is ultimately shaped. It can be difficult to measure out creative freedom, to be asked to create a phrase of movement but have no control over what happens to it, whether it is excerpted, rearranged, or discarded. The more dancers are called upon to participate in the choreographic process, the more choreographers must be sensitive to the vulnerable position that results from being asked to generate authentic, interesting movement but surrender it to the will of another person.

Although this situation is trickier, subtler, less clear-cut than a traditional dancer-choreographer relationship, I now find it more satisfying. Attending an open audition for a big wheel—a David Parsons or Bill T. Jones—is starting to seem slightly ludicrous; I'm not sure I want to or can work in a product-oriented, single-ego-centered atmosphere anymore. I've become too accustomed to rehearsals wherein, possibly because no one is getting paid, there is a respect for the dancers' input into the process. These rehearsals that I used to see in terms of their unprofessionalism—the lack of pay, the lack of ongoing commitment, the exploratory nature of the process—now have spoiled me for more "professional" situations in that I've come to expect a certain egalitarianism in rehearsal. I've become so used to rehearsals in which I am valued for my particular Veronica-ness that it's become difficult to work for choreographers who I perceive to be dictating my role too narrowly rather than engaging me in a dialogue.

With this type of collaboration the norm in many circles now, we can also look at its effect on the product, on the dances being made. As already mentioned, there is a plethora of solos and duets to accommodate so many independent dancer/choreographers. What characterizes the group work that emerges from a company of self-styled, highly individualized dancers who each may have some hand in the choreography?

The extent to which the group has a shared dance vocabulary of course influences the texture of the work that eventually shows up on stage. Once we find ourselves in a group dance situation, a certain symbiosis occurs. We contribute to the dance in all the ways described here, but in turn we begin to assimilate the other styles and energies in the room. This happens because we often are asked to learn material that the other dancers have created, but also because our contact with this particular group may influence the way we are training. The dance vocabulary that emerges may inspire us to pursue some element of it—contact improv, hip-hop—outside of rehearsal, or the other dancers may recommend a class or teacher they are really enjoying. In this way, our area of overlapping dance vocabulary expands.

Still, I doubt we can achieve the type of bone-deep unison that comes naturally to a company of dancers who share both a uniformity of training and a long, consistent history together. Much of the group work created in the situations described here celebrates (albeit sometimes secondarily) the individuality of the members of the group, a choreographic characteristic that springs naturally from the process. It becomes less and less likely that you will see a group dance in which all the people on stage can "breathe with one breath," as with companies that adhere to one mode of training, such as Martha Graham's or José Limón's. That magical unison is a powerful thing, and not to have it as a tool at our disposal is a loss, but I'm not prepared to say that the current state of the group as a collection of individuals represents a degeneration or downturn. It's just a change, a phenomenon that marks this particular time and place in the evolution of our field.

Similarly, I'm reluctant to pass judgment on the fact that we're all more diluted, more generalist than dancers who are steeped in one particular school or style. Although we don't have that strength or clarity in a single technique, the trade-off is that we each have more tricks up our sleeves, a greater range of movement possibilities at our fingertips.

These characteristics—diffusion, decentralization, the prevalence of solos and duets, the group as a collection of discrete entities rather than a single idea magnified, the mixing of many styles in a single work—all color the dance we're making. They spring from the way in which we create, from who we are, from the social and cultural world we inhabit. They are the simple, probably inevitable evidence of this artistic environment, and are not inconsistent with the general feeling in turn-of-this-century America. The rise of zines, independently produced rock and film, even open-source software development, points to the decline of powerful monolithic institutions that define and dictate any field. With the usefulness of these institutions in the American modern dance world so weakened, it may well be this do-it-yourself attitude at the grassroots level that pushes the field forward into whatever the next era may be.

melanie bales

3 training as the medium through which

Dance artists, even those who study well-honed traditional techniques, know intuitively that "learning how to dance" is not a straight path traveling forward. It is more a journey of discovery, of trial and error, two steps in one direction, then one step another way. As with other cultivated talents, dance draws upon one's inherent abilities and other movement experiences in creating the dancer-self. Since the advent of modern dance (as distinguished from traditional forms of dance), the point has been to come up with something that was not handed down in one big piece but shaped by an individual following his or her instincts and preferences. Modern dance pioneers Isadora Duncan and Ruth St. Denis left their ideas behind through other dancers, legacies that continue, not just through accounts of their dances or their lives, but in the movement ideas passed on through dance training. Both individuals and eras have different purposes for making dances. My aim in this chapter is to center on some particular modes and practices in dance training as delimited in my introduction (see pages 1–3). I do not think that the training practices or techniques of one era were any more purposeful or rigorous than any other but that if today, for reasons both artistic and economic, the training process seems haphazard, overly eclectic or disjunctive, it may actually reflect more closely the process as it is experienced.

a paradigm shift and technique as critique

Dance training of all kinds simultaneously preserves or generates movement ideas, provides a network or forum for artist interaction, and shapes or is shaped by choreographic and theatrical intent. Therefore, noting differences in aesthetic and theatrical approaches across certain eras in dance will point to distinctions between the training practices that support those differences. Reflecting on how training, like choreography, seems to go through various transformations and phases, I was interested to read an article by Noël Carroll in which he points out how a turn toward theatricalism since the 1980s contrasts with the "antitheatrical bias" of much of the dance of the 1960s and 1970s and might, at first glance, seem like just another swing of the pendulum—a view that he calls cynical. He then develops the argument, drawing from artists and critics spanning Jean Georges Noverre to Trisha Brown that, despite its reputation as a laggard, the art of dance has really always been in alignment with "the most influential, often successively reigning theories of art" (Carroll 1992, 326). Further, this new theatricalism in dance joins with other art forms and theories in conceiving of itself as pluralistic, "antiessentialist, nonisolationist, semiotic and concerned with representation" (327). While appreciating the main persuasion of Carroll's article, I was drawn to some statements he made in reference to the Judson era.

Carroll's article also links Yvonne Rainer and her NO manifesto to several different theories and movements. One link, through the fact that the manifesto banished certain theatrical conventions from dance, recalls the "Gautier-Mallarmé-Valéry-Levinson" line of theory, the proponents of which championed the power of pure dance and located the expressive properties of dance in the movement itself. Rainer's particular brand of antitheatricalism, Carroll goes on to say, also joins her with the theory of Greenbergian modernism, which "conceived of art as a form of critique." Her "minimalist tendencies" recall yet another theoretical link, namely anti-illusionism, and in "applying this model of critique to the dance, Rainer again identified movement as its essential feature" (325).

Although Carroll argues that Rainer's antitheatricalism and the "new" theatricalism are enough unlike theories through history that they suggest dance stays in line with current, rather than antiquated, theory, I am still more compelled by the implications for dance training that these theoretical alliances pose.

For even though dance (choreography) may align itself with this and then that theory of art, the practice and technique of dance goes on in a more subterranean way, preserving and extending some things and throwing away other things—which, in turn, influences choreography. Every new generation since the advent of modern dance has tried in one way or another to connect the performative and choreographic aspects of the dance art with training practices, but the Judson period produced a solution that was different enough to signify a paradigm shift. It was that generation in particular who, rather than endeavoring to establish a more or less direct link from training to choreography, actually tore the two asunder in a deconstructive process that changed that relationship ever after. Further, that process made it possible for dancers to eventually embrace the paradoxical view of technique as a critique of technique itself.

In *The Structure of Scientific Revolutions,* Thomas Kuhn made a distinction between pre- and post-paradigmatic science and recognized that often developments in science are not incremental but happen in sudden, relatively radical jolts. After the jolt, things go off in a new direction, there is a flurry of activity while scientists absorb the new theory and readjust to it (1962, 12). The changes leading to the Judson (pre-paradigmatic) shift formed the groundwork for the experimentation that would follow. Merce Cunningham asked questions about how dance could be presented and perceived but continued a line begun by the early moderns in his process of crafting a cohesive technique and vocabulary (while acknowledging sources ranging from ballet to computer programs). Other figures also contributed to the eventual shift, like Anna Halprin (vocabulary not at all central), Alwin Nikolais (dancing body one of several focal points), and Erick Hawkins whose Eastern-infused technique rejected previous premises about bodily tone and tension (Celichowska 2000, 2). Paul Taylor, whose early career was contemporary with Judson figures,[1] but whose roots were solidly planted in second-generation soil, boldly allowed each dance to differ radically in theme and tone, and, to some degree, vocabulary.

During the Judson period, questions about what constituted a dancing body, a dance vocabulary, or a dance style elicited many suggestions depending on who answered and is one reason why it is nearly impossible to pull any handful of artists together under one stylistic roof. Also, several different established vocabularies could be "radically juxtaposed" within one piece, so no one training practice could be thought of as supporting or underlying the piece as performed. Despite the irreverence, the anti-intellectual intellectualism, the disdain for furnishing entertainment, the casual-to-the-point-of-boring attitude in some dances, the Judsonites were involved in rigorous inquiry. One part of the inquiry effected a disruption of flow between dance vocabulary and dance making and, as

I stated earlier in this chapter, relieved training from its role as direct feeder to, or repository for choreography.

eclecticism and its relations

Also and significantly, the fact of eclectic training (which was always practiced in some form) emerged fully exposed. The flurry of post-paradigmatic activity led in many different directions choreographically, from the development of Contact Improvisation to the beautifully flouncy style of Trisha Brown to the inclusive circle dances of Deborah Hay. Not only were there vast differences in the movement vocabulary but also differing solutions to the boundaries between audience and performer, dancer and choreographer. Just as the inquiry allowed a freedom of choice in what was allowed on stage, the dancer's view of training was shifted, echoing the postmodernist admission that there was "no there there,"[2] no center or one central technique that could do it all. This allowed for the burgeoning of investigation into somatic techniques and continued investment into eclectic training practices.

I wish to make an essential point here that should erode the sense that our dance training paradigm shift included all aspects of training or impacted all dancers and choreographers at the time; some of them barely noticed a ripple. Here, my nifty Kuhn analogy breaks down, unless we equate dance makers who extend quasi-direct lines from Martha Graham or Doris Humphrey with people who believe the earth is flat. Also, several vital streams of interest have continued from the early modern era but have either widened during and after the early sixties or surfaced to become more blatant or accepted. For example, American modern dance's attraction to Eastern philosophy and movement forms has shifted from relatively more superficial or subterfuged to a deeper, more overtly valued one, a view espoused in Mark Wheeler's dissertation (1984), entitled "Surface to Essence: The Appropriation of the Orient by Modern Dance." After Judson, with the ensuing post-paradigmatic proliferation, it should be expected that the pieces of the composition/training/vocabulary/artistic viewpoint puzzle would be investigated and rearranged in a multitude of ways. Therefore, it is often more enlightening and accurate to note distinctions among the various puzzle solutions on a case by case (artist by artist) basis, instead of asking assignations like *postmodern* to suffice.

Drawing from physical practices outside the dance circle is also not new, as some excellent recent scholarship reminds us (Ross 2000; Tomko 1999; and Ruyter 1999), although again, after Judson, such influences were more openly acknowledged.[3] One woman's François Delsarte is another woman's Susan Klein.

Since the 1960s and 1970s, study of both relatively contemporary theories of body and movement (Awareness Through Movement, Alexander Technique, Bartenieff Fundamentals, Body-Mind Centering, or Skinner Releasing Technique, for example) and ancient or traditional (yoga, Chi Gung) has escalated to a point of prominence among certain tribes of professional dancers, and is strongly reflected in the academy, summer workshops, and more or less overtly in some choreography.

The desire to throw off the old and uncover something either new or essentially human, or even universal, remains a continuing theme. Early moderns were throwing out and off anything that seemed too staid, over-cultivated or European. Randy Martin contrasts the muscular contraction of Graham technique (torque) with "release technique," a term that encapsulates for Martin "approaches to movement initially associated with Judson Church and then finding dissemination in a range of modern dance practices from contact improvisation to the work of Trisha Brown." Despite other differences between torque and release, he notes that "release technique is still part of the heritage of modernism insofar as it emphasizes transcendence of the deformities that culture has wrought" (Martin 1988, 172). Part of the appeal of somatic education, whether in the early part of the twentieth or twenty-first centuries, stems from the rhetoric of healing, paring down to the essentially human or individual, offering a path to self-discovery or growth.

the hired body and other misnomers

As the Judson legacy spawned a dizzying range of movement resources for dance makers, it also unleashed creative solutions to the broken-down (or liberated, depending on how you see it) dialogue between choreography and training. Furthermore, if a workshop led by a nondancer could serve as a composition class to the New York avant-garde in dance, while the dancerly stepped aside for the quotidian, why shouldn't training get into the spirit of things? Some innovators eventually took on the project of developing highly technical vocabularies that required custom-designed combinations of rigorous physical practices (as with Tharp dancers who maintained consistent, serious study of ballet, yoga, and other individual interests).

Others let training as we knew it drop away entirely, an attitude reflected in Deborah Hay's statement, "Every day the whole day from the minute you get up is potentially a dance" (Foster 1986, 6). This shows an extreme conflation of life and art. An approach or practice Hay uses,[4] where the dancer draws his/her consciousness to the cellular level of experience to create a dance, provides an example for making a crucial distinction that I feel is often overlooked. In this example, the cellular consciousness process functions as the way movement is resourced (an improvisational tool), the training, the performance, and the choreography all rolled into one. This kind of approach is way off to one end of a spectrum. At the other end would be found a process where a choreographer/director teaches ready-made phrases to the dancers, subsequently arranging the material for the stage with other theatrical elements. How that director finds material can vary: improvising and capturing through video; borrowing or splicing in something beloved, familiar or hackneyed; using music to elicit visions of movement, to name a few. It all comes under the modern dance rubric for now. Hay's approach, along with other improvisatory projects, can lead to a decidedly nontheatrical end product—which is often exactly the point as with dances no one sees, except the performers themselves. The performer's experience is valued over the interaction with (or presentation for) an audience. At its best, the result is a transcendent or rewarding sense of communion or new insight; at its worse, a self-indulgent disregard for the audience or the discipline.

There is a vast distance between the primarily improvisatory approach (no other training practiced, although the improvisation may be specific, rigorous, and structured) and training in one vocabulary or style of dance as determined by the choreographic project. Paralleling this is a contrast between the role of the dancer as same-as-choreographer (Contact Improvisation, for example) to one with little or no voice in decision-making (which is so rare as to be almost wholly theoretical). Therefore, it is also much more difficult now, barely post-millennium, to assign ready categories to style, vocabulary, or choreographic method. Three examples from the writings of Susan Foster, who has made valuable contributions toward the consideration of dance and technique, reveal some problems with arranging training under prefab headings.

Significantly, Hay is the Judson artist who Susan Foster chose as one of four exemplars in her weighty 1986 book, *Reading Dancing.* In one of many tables delineating distinctions, Foster ascribes a word to each of her subjects under a heading called "The Meaning of Art" (42). Hay is Communion, Balanchine is Celebration, Graham is Communication, and Cunningham is Collaboration. What comes up missing for me is another C-word: Critique. If she had chosen Yvonne Rainer, the word might have surfaced unavoidably. The gap shows up in the other parts of the table too, as under "The Purpose of Dance Technique," which for Hay is "to attain harmony by performing the dance." Where is "to examine or investigate movement in its relationship to the creative project, the culture, the individual"? The other three purposes—"to attain control by acquiring prescribed skills (Balanchine), to express the subject by training the body (Graham) and to become articulate by doing the movement

(Cunningham)" (42) could all apply generally, but her point is well taken in terms of emphasis.

Perhaps, despite Foster's brain-stretching ideas and copious notes, some things are necessarily excluded in drawing thematic categories. I don't believe she means to be conclusive in the category-forming.[5] However, the very trope that crystallized the practice of training as research and critique, and also allowed for the direction that Hay took as an individual artist, is only represented narrowly as applied to Hay's particular direction. In the chasm created between codified-technique-learned-then-performed and movement-improvised-in-response-to-the-experienced-moment lie so many unmentioned approaches and projects that relate if not completely then partially. What about using Cunningham vocabulary, or some improvised variant thereof, in a non-Cunningham piece? What about intuitively inserting a phrase from *Giselle* into a solo improvised dance? If these suggestions sound like what was done during the Judson concerts, that is the point. Likewise, training practices falling into the chasm between the codified techniques of Balanchine/ballet, Cunningham, Graham, and Hay, or even Hay-like techniques, are legion. All in all, I do get the distinct message that Foster is uncomfortable with or not particularly interested in dance that is not *either* fully codified in its technical training *or* fully spontaneous, improvised movement.

In Foster's 1997 article "Dancing Bodies," she begins by drawing both a connection and a distinction between body philosopher Michel Foucault's "instructable body" and the three bodies of dance training that she conceives to examine several practices. The three bodies—perceived, ideal, and demonstrative (the mediator of the other two)—are explicated in the techniques of classical ballet, Duncan, Graham, Cunningham, and Contact Improvisation. Actually, the ideal/perceived/demonstrative model is not visited upon Contact and downplays the fact that mastery and expertise is a part of that form despite the lack of fixed, circumscribed vocabulary.

Returning to gaps and chasms, following the description of Contact Improvisation there is a sharp and precipitous drop-off, but those who disappear over it are at least considered, if derogated. In fact, the author seems to blame the eclecticism of artists of the 1980s and 1990s, whose roots she traces back to the Judson era, for failing to create other unique vocabularies instead of blending or sampling existing ones (Foster 1997, 253). While that is a clear bias and recalls for me students who have asked what "brand" of modern we teach in our program, Foster makes another leap that I find strange. Because the "independent choreographer" (like the independent performer) is reliant on managers and presenting agencies rather than established academies for his/her livelihood, the body that participates is labeled as "hired" and "exists alongside others that remain more deeply involved in, and consequently more expert at, the techniques I have outlined" (255).

This particular hired body is "homogenized" and prompts me to speculate who she has in mind with this jack-of-all-trades, master-of-none body. There are some clues perhaps: first, there is the photo of Mark Morris with two of his dancers between the pages about the hired bodies. Since the other photos in the article directly relate to the other techniques (one each for ballet, Duncan, etc.), am I to assume that dancers in Morris's company are more financially motivated, less expressive, and only half-heartedly devoted to Morris's work, unlike dancers in Cunningham's or Limón's? Are Ailey dancers exempted from the hired status because they have a school and solid funding base, even if their training is eclectic? Some dancers go through long stretches with no training at all other than rehearsal—where are they in her scheme? The article introduces the idea of dance training stooping to the level of bodybuilding, aerobics, and video dancercize and briefly separates such practices that represent the "scientization of the body's needs" from normative or natural theories. Although I am not clear on exactly who Foster had in mind when she assigned the label, I do know that there is more to their bodies than being for hire.

The fact of the messiness may be off-putting, but being hard to label doesn't necessarily make anything lower quality or less valuable. My main purpose here is to show how easily post-Judson training can slip into something more uncomfortable and resist closer examination of the kinds of processes dancers and choreographers work with creatively or purposefully. Also, if a dancer or choreographer strays from time-proven methods or practices (or styles), it requires a very rigorous questioning of what material will be used and why. Some kinds of training will be haphazard and unconsidered, some choreography will be derivative or bric-a-brac. But let's not castigate the eclectic, the synthesist, or the borrower but instead follow the process where it may lead. It remains to be seen as to whether discrete styles or choreography or training may reach codification in time.

In another part of his article on technique that addresses the sociopolitical roles within the class, Martin notices how the dancer must negotiate his/her way through by assuming various roles—observer, actor, student, teacher—in matters both technical and aesthetic. He frames his discussions within a university Graham-style class. Graham classes are notoriously authoritarian, so issues of "domination and authority" may be more pertinent than in many post-Judson classes where the interaction is usually more informal. In any style of training, the teacher-student dialogue is actively negotiated if only within the same person, as Foster's idea of the three bodies—ideal, perceived, demonstrative—reveals. Sociologist Martin is most interested in finding analogies between dance technique and political entities, but in making his distinction between torque and release notes that many university dancers take both styles, that "the residues of one technique may collect even in the midst of another" and that "one form of training may come to interfere with another" (174). I find it important that neither experience is presented as a permanent or irreversible state. Also, I agree with his statement that "[i]n this process of self-governance, a technique for regulating techniques, the dancer must generate her own authority" (175), in that it appreciates the nature of the challenges of post-Judson training with its burden of freedom on the (entrepreneurial) dancer.

of babies and bathwater, and one grecian urn

Given the fact that dancers considered here are working under the assumption that they are "responsible" for exploring a range of physical practices as free dance agents, they also have the luxury, or curse, of endless reconfigurings of their dancer identity. This phenomenon on an individual level finds a parallel on the dance culture level. The post-Judson dancer physically sifts through techniques and practices in complex processes of inclusion and exclusion (see Chapters 1 and 12). The artists of the Judson period deconstructed the dancing body in order to see what was there to be discarded, played with, embraced, laughed at, or simply experienced. Further, both dancer and era acknowledge the underlying notion that at any moment "starting over" is not only allowed but may be necessary or desirable, and that to shed, uncover, or strip down can be as valuable as creating and building. The "negative space" of the body-mind, the place where things forgotten, dormant, peeled off, or not yet born reside, meets up with the newly created, arrived at, discovered, or reconsidered.

Lecturing in the 1970s, Deborah Jowitt notes: "It is interesting when you think of the purity and high-mindedness with which any radical starts out: they throw out baby, the bathwater, the tub, everything; and then bit by bit they bring them back" (Livet 1978, 138), From my perspective in the university, one of the first reactions of a dancer to what she encounters in our midst is to reject what has been familiar in order to embrace the new (out with ballet, in with pushing and falling). Eventually, she may reincorporate aspects of earlier training into her repertoire. The Judsonites got a lot of press over what they threw out (the NO manifesto) and perhaps less about what emerged gradually as various elements were added back in (music, facial expression, virtuosity). In both cases, for the student dancer and the Judson artist, the initial step of rejecting is followed by a phase of selective choice.

Interestingly, the very things that have stepped in as modern dancers shed learned dance techniques (whether temporarily or permanently) expose both what unites and divides individuals or periods from one another. Further, the continued investigation into somatic practices, Eastern forms, and improvisation in both choreography and training, with a concomitant emphasis on starting over, ironically begins to form a tradition or a lineage of practice. It is outside the scope of this chapter or this book to attempt a comprehensive comparison of how those practices were embodied over the course of American modern dance history. The forms above were present since Duncan and Genevieve Stebbins but have assumed different guises along the way depending on the individuals and their environment.

Also, there has been a progression in that by now, the modes of eclecticism, somatic practice, investigation into Eastern forms, and conscious improvisation have reached the point of fullest exposure and most open acknowledgment in terms of dance technique. This progression may have several reasons, including the fact that exposure itself is a value of the postmodernist attitude that prefers juxtaposition to synthesis (salads, not melting pots) and to show the individual in context rather than in isolation (it takes a village, not Howard Roark). What was sublimated or subsumed, even colonized (as Martin would term it) by earlier artists, is now eagerly offered as part of the artist's "package." No one tries to hide study of yoga, or African dance, or Alexander work as elements that could diminish artistic individualism. Perhaps because of this increased exposure and given the fact that modern dance, including our subset of post-Judson, welcomes polemic into the aesthetic experience of dance, ethical and aesthetic values surface with particular resonance, if not clarity, in the consideration of training.

Two recent texts represent some post-Judson views and provide examples of how aesthetic values interact with technical ones. They also expose another theme in modern dance since its inception: the science-art, nature-culture interplay as it pertains to dance technique. Each era, from Duncan to Humphrey to Hawkins, had its own way of approaching the border tension of those binaries.[6] The first is Louise Steinman's *The Knowing Body* (1986), an ode to several "philosophers of the body" and "art/science investigators" (3) who engage in work that is "low and slow" (13). The artists include Simone Forti, Barbara Dilley, Suzanne Hellmuth, Dana Reitz, Ruth Zaporah, and Steve Paxton as members of the Grand Union. Among the practitioners mentioned are Irmgard Bartenieff, Moshe Feldenkrais, F. M. Alexander, Bonnie Bainbridge Cohen, Lulu Sweigard, and Irene Dowd. Steinman identifies herself as part of a community for whom healing is the dominant metaphor, referring, for example, to the rift or wound created by the severing of the inner experience from the unity of body and mind (2).

Throughout Steinman's book, the world of the senses and "mythical thought" are placed clearly above the Descartian body-as-machine as exemplified by some aspects of modern medicine and science. Resources for the practitioners she describes come from "an understanding of developmental movement, as well as from the healing powers of dream and visualization" (3). She also encapsulates what I call the debriefing mode in acknowledging that "relearning is undoing" (16) and situates her subject within the "turning inwards" that came out of the Judson era and resulted in improvisation as a performance form. The emphasis is on self-discovery through somatic techniques, improvisation or meditation; there is no real separation between the making of the self and the making of art.

In a paper she presented for the International Association for Dance Medicine & Science, Susan Klein outlined some of the main precepts of her practice, described as "a way for people to work through individual injuries, to understand the workings of their own bodies, and to heal themselves" (1993, 1). In her diaspora of students mentioned are several well-known artists of the post-Judson ilk: students of Bonnie Cohen, company members of Trisha Brown Company and Brown herself, Stephen Petronio, Bebe Miller, Ralph Lemon, Phoebe Neville, Yvonne Rainer, David Gordon, Douglas Dunn, Neil Greenberg, Rosalind Newman, David Roussève, Twyla Tharp, and Lucinda Childs. The mode revealed in the tract is very much the debriefing one, a paring down, getting to the center of things: she speaks of the "level of the bone" versus building muscle strength, and reminds that in Chinese medicine bone is related to the will.

Even in Klein's writing there is a sense of power and movement, and "working with the bones to connect the body and create clear, simple, and direct lines of movement and energetic force." Several dualisms crop up: internal knowing versus external shaping (2); teacher demonstration versus student self-discovery (4); analyzing versus integrating (4, 7); conscious repatterning versus instinct (7) and energy (movement) versus matter (structure) (10). She places Trisha Brown's technique on the energy end of the continuum, along with Tai Chi and Contact Improvisation, disparaging some ballet and "many modern techniques that have slipped over to this held, formalized posturing." Klein sees her work "in the middle of the continuum, on the interface between energy and structure, where they are equal" (11).

I hope it becomes obvious to the reader that these two texts have underlying ethical and aesthetic values. The Steinman book shows a clear preference for right-brain associations and favors self-direction and individuality, framing dance as personal growth, not as entertainment. Klein's tract also follows the healing mode but is comparatively more concerned with the dancer's technical expansion; however, good technique, efficient or healthy body use, and beauty are seen as one entity. As dancers continue to engage in and increasingly draw from practices outside dance technique per se, they are surely absorbing the values and concerns inherent in those studies. Of course, often that is exactly what leads someone to Alexander or Bartenieff or Cohen.[7] Then there is the larger question of what it means when the physical practice experienced by a dancer contains explicit or implicit information beyond dance or even art (that is, human values). Do the ideas of movement theorists whose main interests were not the art of dance make up more and more of the "medium through which"? Or are those ideas simply more compatible with the post-Judson body-mind and have tended to overlap as a matter of course? We can also distinguish between being conscious of allowing a physical practice such as Alexander or Tai Chi to inspire new perspectives or creativity, and becoming "all about" any such practice. In the latter case of nearly full personal alignment with a system, however humanistic or fulfilling, the relationship can become strangely like that of a religious conversion where everything is seen through one lens. The art of dance with its attendant powers of transformation may become merely a backdrop.

A chapter on physical training systems of the late nineteenth century in Linda Tomko's *Dancing Class* (1999) prompted me to reflect on the similarities between the turn of this century and the last. The last of four physical culture bodies described, the "relaxed, harmonious body" as exemplified by American Delsartism and especially as espoused by Stebbins, uncannily echoes the features of current "release techniques," the term Martin uses interchangeably with post-modern and is closely related to the present term of post-Judson (see Chapter 11). Tomko points out three of Stebbins's fundamental activities: decomposing or learning how to relax, establishing poise or equilibrium, and energizing or learning how to efficiently mobilize for action. A further purpose was the importance of deep breathing (18). Further, she notes that those trained in Delsarte "aimed to selectively contract the necessary muscles and to invoke specific quantities of desired energy, efficiently leaving other muscles and energies relaxed and untapped" (19). Tomko's interest is in relating the values inherent in the various physical culture bodies to issues of class and gender, and surely the upper-middle class striving to be cultured finds a comic apotheosis in the stilted, faux-Delsartian tableau of the ladies of *The Music Man* performing their "one Grecian urn"!

This brief example points several directions. First, the influence of these sorts of practices within the American dance continuum is probably underestimated and deserves further study. Second, looking at things in terms of characteristics helps to unhinge and call into question certain set associations and form new ones, as in the comparison of release technique and American Delsartism. Finally, it reminds us how the dancer, when moving through various physical practices, also moves beyond the role as dancer and joins with other communities, both foreign and familiar. One downward dog!

In conclusion, I suggest a summary of what defines post-Judson training:

1. conflation and hybridization of styles across modern vocabularies, ballet, vernacular dances; explicit borrowing from dances of other cultures, acknowledgement of *pastiche* versus synthesis;

2. investigation of Eastern/Asian philosophy, art and physical practices both ancient and modern;
3. disruption of prior ideas about the roles of training, rehearsing, performing, composing, and the interrelationships among them (study X, perform Y);
4. de-professionalization of the performer from the idea of the "anybody," blurring of the dancer/nondancer division, cultivating other kinds of moving bodies in dance;
5. reconfiguration of boundaries between choreographer and performer, collective methods of choreography, shift in valuation toward dancer, a "buyer's market" where performers craft their training from what suits them;
6. proliferation of styles, performance techniques, teaching methods; increasing number of choices and possibilities as time marches on;
7. exposure of theoretical tensions such as between science and art, nature and culture; emphases on efficiency, versatility, the wisdom of the body; somatic and other alternative practices playing a substantial and fully acknowledged role in dance training;
8. primacy of movement over musical or theatrical structuring, separating movement from music in the classroom, privileging touch and kinesthesia over the auditory and visual (or "optical");
9. shift in tone or attitude after the 1960s echoed in more passive body attitude, concepts like "allowing," more weightiness or resilience in quality, culture in class more collegial, less authoritarian;
10. investigation of and faith in methods of improvisation including Africanist principles as expressed through jazz, chance procedures, authentic movement, Contact Improvisation, and structured performance improvisation.

notes

1. An amusing account of their snobbery appears in his autobiography *Private Domain* by Paul Taylor (New York: Knopf/Random House, 1987).
2. Referring to Gertrude Stein's comment on Oakland, California: "There is no there there." *Everybody's Autobiography* by Gertrude Stein (New York: Random House, 1937).
3. See Twyla Tharp's autobiography, *Push Comes to Shove* (New York: Bantam, 1992), 50, for her recollection of Martha Graham commenting on Ruth St. Denis and yoga.
4. See page 9 of Susan Foster's *Reading Dancing,* as well as her introduction to Deborah Hay's book, *My Body the Buddhist.* Deborah Hay, with a foreword by Susan Foster. Hanover, N.H.: University Press of New England: Wesleyan University Press, 2000.

5. See Foster's "outlines of paradigmatic approaches," *Reading Dancing*, 259.
6. Martin tackles these dualisms from several angles, including how modern dance has appropriated Orientalist and other tropes into it and then claimed to have "transcended" difference by making universalizing statements about recapturing the primitive (1988, 170) or naming nature as the only source of movement invention, as in St. Denis's statement quoted in Martin's article: "'All the motions one needs for the study of dancing can be found in nature'" (169). Although when Martin states, "It is in the claims to be a set of movement principles for any occasion, transcendent of any given situation, that the repressed figure of science returns through modern technique" (170) in reference to the early moderns, it is easy to attach the idea to later figures like Erick Hawkins, for example, who found scientific substantiation for his aesthetic leanings and organized his technique around what his study of kinesiology told him. In this way, Hawkins completely conflated science and art. He also openly applied Asian philosophies and practices to his dances and to his technique, preferring what he considered Eastern values of noninterference and quiet contemplation to "Western" values of mastery and extroverted display. These values were reflected further in Hawkins's soft, rounded, evenly flowing phrasing, as opposed to the muscular verve or jagged attack of other movement styles.
7. For an inclusive view of the many faces of dance, see Sondra Fraleigh's introductory article in *Researching Dance: Evolving Modes of Inquiry*, edited by Sandra Horton, Fraleigh and Penelope Hanstein. Pittsburgh, PA: University of Pittsburgh Press, 1999.

works cited

Carroll, Noël. 1992. "Theatre, Dance and Theory: A Philosophical Narrative." *Dance Chronicle* 15, no. 3.

Celichowska, Renata. 2000. *The Erick Hawkins Modern Dance Technique*. Hightstown, N.J.: Princeton Book Company Publishers, A Dance Horizons Book.

Cunningham, Merce, in conversation with Jacqueline Lesschaeve. 1985. *The Dancer and the Dance*. New York: Marion Boyars, Inc.

Foster, Susan Leigh. 1986. *Reading Dancing: Bodies and Subjects in Contemporary American Dance*. Berkeley and Los Angeles: University of California Press.

———. 1997. "Dancing Bodies." In Jane C. Desmond, ed., *Meaning in Motion: New Cultural Studies in Dance*. Durham, N.C.: Duke University Press.

Klein, Susan T. 1993. Paper presented to the IADMS International Association of Dance Medicine & Science (unpublished manuscript). © 1993 Susan T. Klein.

Kuhn, Thomas S. 1962. *The Structure of Scientific Revolutions*. Chicago: University of Chicago Press.

Livet, Anne, ed. 1978. *Contemporary Dance: An Anthology of Lectures, Interviews and Essays*. Edited transcript of a lecture by Deborah Jowitt. New York: Abbeville Press, Inc.

Martin, Randy. 1988. "Between Technique and the State: The Univers(ity) in Dance." In Randy Martin, ed. *Critical Moves*, Durham, N.C.: Duke University Press.

Rainer, Yvonne. 1965. "'No' to Spectacle" from *The Routledge Dance Studies Reader*. Alexandra Carter, ed., *Tulane Drama Review*, vol. 10, no. 2. London and New York: Routledge.

Ross, Janice. 2000. *Moving Lessons: Margaret H'Doubler and the Beginning of Dance in American Education*. Madison: University of Wisconsin Press.

Ruyter, Nancy Lee Chalfa. 1999. *The Cultivation of Body and Mind in the Nineteenth-Century Delsartism.* Westport, Conn.: Greenwood Press.

Siegel, Marcia B. 1979. *The Shapes of Change.* Boston: Houghton Mifflin Company.

Steinman, Louise. 1986. *The Knowing Body: Elements of Contemporary Performance & Dance.* Boston and London: Shambala.

Tomko, Linda J. 1999. *Dancing Class: Gender, Ethnicity and Social Divides in American Dance, 1890–1920.* Bloomington: Indiana University Press.

Wheeler, Mark Frederick. 1984. "Surface to Essence; Appropriation of the Orient by Modern Dance." Ph.D. dissertation, The Ohio State University.

melanie bales

4 a dance-musician's perspective

an interview with natalie gilbert

The following interview was conducted by Melanie Bales with Natalie Gilbert in July 2002.

mb From your vast experience of accompanying many different kinds of modern dance classes, could you give some really broad categories or classifications from the accompanist's perspective?

ng Yes, from a musician's standpoint, you could group the classes into three general areas. One would be the more "traditional-modern" model, where the music and the phrasing of the movement material are together in a precise rhythmic structure that's repeatable. But there is a broad range of what's possible in this model, from something very specific as in a Graham class, with someone like Pearl Lang who really wants an almost literal reflection of what's going on in the movement. If the movement's going down, she wants the music to be down, and if it's going up, she wants the music to rise. Not that all Graham teachers do that, but certainly she does. If there's a five-count followed by a three-count and a one-count, a one-pulse, then that's exactly reflected in the accompaniment, and a musical phrase is made of that odd situation. In some Limón classes, there can be what we call "threes disease": a majority of the exercises are a swing rhythm or a fall-and-recovery rhythm of *one*-two-three *one*-two-three—that really reflects the rhythm of the weight of the particular phrase or choreographed movement. In this traditional model, the musician is creating energy in that context, in whatever style of music. The style of music can be quite broad, from Baroque to Jazz to atonal. It can be percussion, it can be piano, it can be cello, it can be voice, it can be electronics.

A second model that's related to that, but different in its outcome somewhat, is what I call a Cunningham model, where what happens in the class is very much counted and with this precise rhythmic phrasing again. However, the teachers seem less concerned with what the musician is doing. Most musicians who play for Cunningham classes play in the traditional model because that seems to be the easiest thing, especially for beginning classes. But in the back of your mind as a musician is the thought that this is training for a performance—a Cunningham performance—where the music has nothing to do whatsoever with what's going on. So when the students are established in their precise rhythmic phrasing, you can prepare the piano and just plunk around and see if they can hold the rhythm, and give them more of an experience that relates to what's coming in the performance.

mb And you have played Cunningham-style classes outside the Cunningham studio, for students who just want to learn more about the style, or add that to their movement repertory.

ng But again it's counted and not so much concerned with a movement style or quality, that's not the thrust of it, but rather the rhythmic precision with the mood being less important. I think in the traditional model the mood is usually quite important.

mb Do you ever play for Cunningham classes where the warm-up part is as you described and then there's something at the end of class that's different?

ng Some of the teachers do sort of event-type things at the end of class, but more often it never gets to that point. It's simply repeating phrases that are capable of being counted, with the changes of direction and the changes of accent that are very much a part of that training.

I think then a third model emerged where, for a while, the teachers wanted no accompaniment whatsoever.

mb When was that, do you think, or when did you notice that?

ng At ADF [American Dance Festival] I started noticing it in the mid-80s. It was very big right around 1990. Now it seems to have found a balance in that often teachers don't want any music for the very first twenty minutes or half-hour of class. But then they do, as the class progresses. There was a huge movement to not have any sound whatsoever, because people were searching for breath phrasing, where it wasn't important for everyone to be in synchronicity, and it was more about exploring the impulse and where the movement was coming from and how long it would take to get where it was going, and less about any kind of rhythmic underpinnings. The rhythmicity of it was *way* at the bottom. In fact, missing, pretty much. That led into what's going on more today, where teachers really do want to have rhythmicity in their actual choreographic phrases, which they present after the dancers are warmed up. Many teachers—I think of Mark Haim, Heidi Latsky for a while, Tere O'Connor—don't particularly want the music to follow a rhythmic phrasing, even if it really could be counted. But in fact, when the class starts going across the floor, the phrase really starts falling into its own rhythm, once it materializes and the dancers find what it is.

mb Could that maybe reflect a choreographic process in making a phrase the teacher/chorographer starts with material based on improvisation that doesn't really have a set metric pattern but eventually evolves into something more solid?

ng Yes, I believe that's exactly the process that's going on. I believe it's an exploration by the choreographer to find out what it is that he or she is making in the first place, and what is the potential of going this way or that way with this weight and that weight, and then seeing how it reads on various bodies and then coming up with what's interesting. But there is a wide range of what people are willing to explore in terms of sound with that kind of model. It depends a lot on what the teacher's musical training and musical interests are. Some people come to the choreography at this point from a theatrical sensibility; the music is purely a backdrop.

mb It just collides in the moment.

ng It collides in the moment of performance, and it doesn't really matter. Tere O'Connor will do this to experiment. He'll say, "Just give me whatever," or, "What do you feel for this?" or "I definitely want no pulse in this" or "I definitely want dissonance in this." Tere happens to be very musically informed, so he has a lot more vocabulary to talk about what he wants. An exchange like that can be an interesting issue for some of us, in terms of how we develop a relationship with a working choreographer.

In another recent experience at ADF, the teacher, a sought-after emerging choreographer, felt that whenever he counted something he was falling into the traditional model, which he didn't want to do. We had an interesting conversation where I pointed out that that wasn't necessarily true, that counting something, or putting a pulse underneath something was not going to make it traditional in any way. A pulse can provide energy for a phrase, an uncounted pulse but a pulse nonetheless, and changing the rate of that pulse underneath a phrase can change how the phrase feels to the dancer and how it's perceived to the viewer. Many choreographers seem to be afraid of the music because they don't want it to flavor their work too much or overpower it.

mb Does the phrase "release" have any resonance for you as a musician? Do you think of certain classes as being, quote, *release* or not? And if so, how would you describe them?

ng Well, I think the release technique is certainly at the top of the list of this third model. I think a lot of us who have played for release technique classes realize that there is a rubato required. It's not about the rhythmicity of the movement in general, although again, as I said, a pulse underneath a released phrase can still provide energy that would not be there otherwise. But it certainly has affected classroom teaching in terms of how one relates to the musician, because there are fewer things counted and again the precise rhythmic phrasing is not at the top of the list anymore.

Iréne Hultman is really an interesting case in point because she does not count her material, and yet she has very rhythmic ideas and musical qualities. She has really made a huge job for herself in that she is the accompanist and the choreographer in that she uses her voice to convey the accent and the phrasing of the material that she's teaching, in a very personal way, and a very effective way. She is happy doing that and doesn't need a musician. It's wonderful but very tiring, I imagine, to do that because it's two jobs. Toward the end of class she would bring in a recording and teach the class a piece of choreography to the music that she had worked with, which is more of a repertory situation, where she's working on a phrase with a particular piece of music that brings the kind of quality and texture and energy to what she's developing. Rather than to try to get an improvising musician to replicate that, she simply brings the recorded music so she can continue on with her choreographic ideas.

mb Under this broad aegis of post-Judson or post-Cunningham, or since the 80s, or however you want to say it, there seem to be subcategories of approaches. I am thinking of many classes where the warm-up is something decidedly non-choreographic and then after that, phrases or repertory is explored.

ng There are some teachers who don't mind if you provide some relaxing, noninterfering atmosphere or sound as in a yoga class, while the class is going through explorations of breathing or personalized movement experiences, based on something that's going to come later in the class that the teacher feels is important in training for a specific movement. Later in the class when dancers are standing and doing phrase material, the class goes back to more of a collaboration between the musician who is there as composer-in-residence. And at that point I think it's kind of exciting, because nobody really knows what's going to happen and there's a spirit of exploration. They may have a commission in four months and need to start generating movement material, and they're exploring something. Also, the dancers become part of the exploration. The dancers are the real materials of the choreographer's eye. What the music can do for that process is to clarify some aspect of the movement-music relationship. I might be playing something extremely pulse-driven with a lot of quick, energetic, rapid, rhythmic energy. And the movement has a certain energy and a certain flow with that. When you switch to something much less intrusive, much more atmospheric, with no pulse, with no real sense of phrasing, the movement can take on a whole new meaning, in terms of where it should go, or what it is in terms of the context of a larger piece.

mb What seems to be also interesting about that is that the class is a place where something that we normally or generally think of as choreographic is happening, so that there's not so much of a model of "we train now, we dance later."

ng I do believe that is true, and I think part of it is because dancers come already trained in both senses, warmed up and with a certain level of expertise. I always talk about the model of NYU Tisch School of the Arts, where everyone has a ballet class every morning, and then they have a modern class. What immediately became obvious was that the modern teachers didn't have to do *tendus* and *pliés*. Everyone was warmed up on that level, so the modern teachers would do a few particular back exercises or something that might be specific to their movement and go right to the phrases, right to the choreographic process. And I think that more and more that is somehow the hidden model. Dancers are supposed to come prepared, warmed up, more or less ready to go. Again, it depends on the level of the class. I'm not talking about beginner classes here. I'm talking about more advanced work. At the Dance Festival, it certainly happens. People take either a yoga class or a Pilates class early in the morning, and maybe one technique class. Some people take ballet, some people take a movement class, and then from noon on, everybody's doing what we call repertory classes.

mb You have been playing at ADF since 1981 and you lived in New York from '73 to '90 playing classes all over the city. Could you say something about how, from the musician's viewpoint, the influence of somatics or body-mind study has influenced classes that you have seen or played for? I recall some comments from a brief meeting with the International Guild of Musicians in Dance group, many of whom complained about the awkward transitions, musically and otherwise, from the floor work to choreographed phrases.

ng In terms of warming up, I think the main difference is the fact that everyone doesn't have to be moving at the same time at the same rate, in rhythmic synchronicity. That takes away the sort of metronomic responsibility of the musician that comes from the ballet tradition as well—it changes that a little bit. Now I think there may be some of that coming back again. I mean, whenever you give something up you realize you're missing it and then people go back to it or find ways to reintroduce it. They realize when they look around in the choreography that it all looks the same, and one of the reasons it looks the same is because no one has rhythmic synchronicity any more. And so they go back and they try to get that again and I think that a little bit of that is going on. But certainly in the 80s and 90s there was a pulling-away from some of that precise rhythmic training. Some contemporary choreographers might have taken a ballet class, but then when they left the ballet class they wanted nothing to do with anything rhythmic. I think a lot of the improvisers are that way—in particular, Contact Improvisers. Those people really aren't interested in any kind of rhythmic counting.

I wanted to say one thing about the release classes, where there's sometimes no accent and no down beat, but I really believe there is phrasing. Dancers can be cued into how thinking of a phrase musically can help them access what it is they're trying to do. Sometimes when I think back about young choreographers who were working with vocal music, which became a big thing for awhile—making dances to operatic-type music, or to music with a lot of melody—one of the things that I always suggested was that the dancer really sing the phrase, sing the music as they were performing it, so that they could feel that particular phrasing that they were trying to access. Whether you choose to mimic the music or not, I think connecting to the inherent musical phrasing can help show you what it is. If it's with the music, then you can let go of that connection and have something more contrapuntal against it. There need not be a direct connection with rhythmic precision to have musical phrasing. I just wanted to emphasize that before we go on.

mb I'm going to change the subject a little bit, just because you're somebody who has played for professional choreographers teaching at ADF, and you've also played in New York studios where the students are mostly professional dancers.

The other branch of your experience is in the university. Given the fact that boundaries between university dance activity, including training, and professional activity have blurred in the period we have been talking about, the last twenty years, I am interested in what you have noticed there.

ng I believe that what's happening more and more is that dance is taught with a historical reference now. At the Dance Festival this is done because of the history of the dance festival and because of the age of a lot of the people who are teaching there. There are traditions: there's the Horton tradition, the Limón tradition, the Graham tradition, the Slayton-Farber tradition, the Paul Taylor tradition. And these things have very specific music ideas that were developed with them. Not that everyone who played for those classes played the same way or even the same instrument, but the people who track these traditions have a historical understanding of the relationship of the music and the movement, or the timing and the movement, or the phrasing and the movement, the weight and the movement. I think when you walk into a studio to take one of the few modern classes that there are in New York, that's not the case at all. There's *no* reference to history. That experience is about coming up with material and exploring sound that might be innovative and might make someone's work different from everybody else's, or might get someone onto a choreographic track that will lead to some exciting performance possibilities. This is also where technology comes in—the use of technology in class and laptops and computers—almost flipping into a Cunningham idea again where the music and the movement are definitely part of the performance but not necessarily following form and rhythmic phrasing, more the way you would think of lighting enhancing a dance. The sound-score enhances what's going on and inspires what's going on. I think that is happening with many of the young people that are teaching now. There is a trend now, too, away from the improvising composer in the classroom to having a DJ in the classroom who is sampling prerecorded music at his or her whim. Then there are some people—I think of Ron Brown—who will start with a live musician in class, or maybe start with recorded music for a while for the warm-up, then go to live drummers later on in the class. In the professional circles, they're looking at music in a more of a collaborative way.

There is a split in that regard because the universities are playing a very important role in keeping that historical information available, and also making sure that the dancers are able to not only do release technique, but also to perform a rhythmically set phrase or in a different movement style. At places like Ohio State, where work is reconstructed from notation, this is totally necessary, because the students have to perform works from early eras. It's not something you can just do at the drop of a hat if you've never done it before. That process differs from that model of studying with one choreographer, learning their technique, training with them and being in their company and doing nothing else. That model went out the window quite a few years ago. In the idea of the eclectic dancer who can do everything, the universities have a very important role in as far as the training.

mb There seems also to be a distinction between "I am the teacher and I will train you in this particular style" and class as more of a creative process. The role of the musician would vary depending on the emphasis.

ng Different choreographers come to this whole process with completely different feelings about where music is in their plan.

mb Have you ever felt superfluous?

ng Oh yes! Mostly with younger teachers who don't really know what they're doing as teachers but who draw dancers to study with them because they are up-and-coming as choreographers. They haven't really refined their teaching yet and it's not about the music. It's about the personality of the person teaching and what fun ideas they're exploring in terms of movement. There are no hard and fast rules about it. It really depends on the personalities of the two people in the classroom, the teacher and the musician, on chance, on a lot of things.

mb You had an example of another unusual approach to the music-movement interaction that seemed to be a hybrid of some of the types above.

ng Joe Alegado, who used to dance with the Limón Company and has been dancing internationally for a while, doesn't teach with a musician. My understanding is that he had recorded music for the entire class but that it was really set and well planned, not something he just grabbed on his way out the door. He taught two-week modules using the exact same music for *pliés,* another piece that stayed the same for the *tendu* combination, etc., through the entire class—six or eight different pieces of music that stayed the same for two weeks in a class as more of a repertory situation. The students, university dancers in this case, got to know the movement material and the music at the same time. He called on them to relate specifically to some nuances in the musical texture and he had a huge range of musical sound and style. He puts time into choreographing to the music, developing this whole package. So, it represented a very different kind of teaching situation. It seemed to be a very personal thing, but certainly one that might be fascinating to explore.

mb And it just shows that while there are all these experimentations going on, there is still the older tradition simultaneously happening, or variations like this particular variation.

ng His is certainly a variation even in a Graham class where you know exactly what's coming next, the musician doesn't play the same thing every day because usually he or she is improvising and probably trying not to!

mb You are also a teacher of music for dancers, getting them to think more about musical ideas, and I am wondering about the things that you feel are important for dancers to know now.

ng I'm a traditionalist in that I think that knowledge is power, so I think that you should know everything and then if you choose to throw something out that's your privilege. I really want dancers to be confident, to know what a steady rhythm is and to know what syncopation is and to know how to syncopate a phrase, to know what the form of the music is, or how to describe the form of the music. I want them to have a music vocabulary that will serve them in any situation. Another part of that is to be able to do rhythmic counterpoint, to find the pulse, and be able within that pulse to create your own rhythm visibly with your body, that stands against whatever rhythm is going on within that pulse. It's like being a member of the band. Actually, what's so interesting is that when we've done very general improvisations to music, we've noticed that the one thing that was missing when people improvised was that idea of a rhythmic contrapuntal phrase, because it has to be planned in a certain way. You have to really plan it so that it reads as a rhythmic phrase against another rhythm. It is always interesting to see that something like that can be totally missing in choreography. Same with syncopation. There are some people who would never, ever do it. They just don't move that way. And syncopation is a great spice to add into your choreography. We explore musical ideas like these that we hope will open doors, and I think that's a good way to do it.

joshua monten

5 something old, something new, something borrowed . . .

eclecticism in postmodern dance

Taking disparate movement styles and quoting from them directly, assembling dance spectacles eclectically, borrowing freely from various sources—these formal devices have become common in the choreography of the past thirty years. The supply of source material available to choreographers for this borrowing and quoting grows steadily larger. Generations of modern dancers have forged and left behind their personal choreographic styles; "new" dance styles like capoeira and butoh regularly arrive from abroad and are added to the melting pot of metropolitan dance-making; subcultural movement forms like break-dancing or square-dancing are periodically rediscovered and popularized; private dance studios, university dance programs, and dance festivals all pride themselves on the breadth of their offerings. Choreographers feel free to draw on all of these sources or scavenge for new materials in ever more varied locales, from sports and martial arts, to social dances, B-movies, animal documentaries, and the vernacular movements of everyday life.

What is of greatest interest for the purposes of this chapter, however, are the ways that choreographers have found to incorporate so many different dance languages into their own. I identify here three basic strategies. One I will call the *revue:* stringing together a series of discrete, contrasting dance episodes—often with a short pause for applause and costume changes—such as one might have seen in the Ziegfeld Follies or in an evening of works performed by Diaghilev's Ballets Russes. A second form of combining ingredients I term *fusion:* blending disparate dance elements together so thoroughly that they appear to fuse together into a new, hybrid dance form. Fusion seems to have been around for quite a while; one is reminded of Katherine Dunham's use of Caribbean elements in her *Cuban Suite,* or of the stylized ethnic dances used in the divertissements of classical nineteenth-century ballets such as *Swan Lake.* Although fusion's estimated value has seen a sharp rise in recent decades, I consider it to be a ubiquitous process in the history of European-American dance: it is the most typical manner by which influences are assimilated and reconciled.

A third strategy for combining ingredients—and the focus of my essay—I call *eclecticism.* In much recent choreography, combined dance elements don't always seem to be so clearly separated as in a revue or so smoothly fit together as in a fusion. A culinary analogy may be helpful. Rather than being presented with an array of platters, each filled with a different raw vegetable or, on the other hand, with a thoroughly cooked and puréed sauce, we encounter what French cooking calls a *compote*—a mixture of ingredients, with each maintaining some measure of its original color, texture, and flavor. It is more exactly this phenomenon—analogous to the *compote*—which I am labeling eclecticism, and which I believe to be a distinguishing feature of postmodern dance. Eclecticism in dance often takes the form of quoting, or "repeat[ing] or copy[ing] . . . , usually with an indication that one is borrowing another's words" (Oxford English Dictionary, hereafter OED). It is as if phantom quotation marks were hovering in the air above a dance performer's head, telling the audience that some of this material comes from somewhere else.

I'll give a concrete example. In the midst of an intricate, abstract *terre-à-terre* variation in Twyla Tharp's piece for American Ballet Theatre, *Push Comes to Shove* (1976), a ballerina arrives in a simple first-position stance—and then her torso suddenly topples forward and her hands flop to the floor. "I'm so pooped," her body seems to say, "I can hardly stand up!" A moment later she rolls back up, regains the exalted, impervious demeanor of an ABT soloist, and continues her strenuous variation. It is a jarring moment: the continuity of a geometrically precise phrase is unexpectedly interrupted by what seems like an alien way of being in one's body: a quotidian and unrefined toe-touch.

I find disjunctive moments like this intensely interesting. For students of other forms of postmodern culture, the rise of eclecticism and quotation (also known as *bricolage,* the French word for assembling objects from haphazardly found ingredients) is a well-recognized fact (see Jameson 1991; Jencks 1981; and Lyotard 1984). Common though these elements may be nowadays, I suggest that they represent a distinctive development in the field of concert dance in the United States. In the following pages, I sketch the historical spread of eclecticism and quoting, and then examine some of the effects they have had on the experience of training to become a dancer.

a brief historical sketch

In the great nineteenth-century classical ballets, such as *The Nutcracker* (Petipa/Ivanov, 1892), one of the principal attractions was the great number of *divertissements:* confectionery set-pieces that purported to represent exotic foreign cultures: Spanish, Arabian, Chinese, etc. These divertissements were connected to one another in the style of a revue: recall the Kingdom of the Sweets scene, for instance, and how the coterie of Spanish dancers finish up their spicy, ardent variation: with one last head-toss and wrist-flick, they pose for a final tableau; the music stops, the audience applauds, the dancers bow and run off-stage. Then the Chinese dancers prance their way on-stage, pointing their fingers and smiling, ready to begin their lighthearted variation. Toreador vests and flared skirts are replaced by silk jackets and pantaloons; the tight, Castilian sound of a syncopated trumpet is replaced by flute trills and *pizzicato* strings.

The sort of juxtaposition of dissimilar foreign cultures that we see in *The Nutcracker* has a certain formal safeness to it. In terms of technique and choreography, exotic peoples are represented by a few characteristic gestures embedded in the common medium of classical ballet style and choreographic structure (fusion). In terms of the *mise-en-scène,* we see that these exotic dioramas are separated by frames, as in a museum gallery, where two contrasting paintings could be hung a discreet distance from one another, separated by negative space and ornate wooden frames (revue).

What would juxtaposition look like if it were less measured, more dissonant? Enter the Denishawn Company, which in the early part of the twentieth century endeavored to present its own compendia of the world's dances. According to Elizabeth Kendall's third-hand account, a typical 1916 Denishawn concert proceeded as follows: "After the Nature idylls [Ted Shawn] placed the Indian, Egyptian, and Japanese, amplified by new additions of the Hawaiian and Javanese, and then the modern numbers, the Fokine and Nijinsky imitations . . . and the ballroom routines" (Kendall 1979, 120). Observers noticed certain "'incongruities that bewildered,'" such as the "'inexplicable *pirouettes* in the middle of Egyptian friezes'" (121). One wonders which of the juxtaposing effects were intentional and which were not, but in any case it would be fair to identify this unruly menagerie as a sort of postmodern eclecticism *avant la lettre.*

Kendall's account sketches a correlation between Denishawn's "impossible jumble" and the era of ragtime music, when "anything was likely to be juxtaposed with anything." If we cast our net of references a little wider, we would pick up on other varieties of modernism that were beginning to emphasize extreme juxtaposition: Picasso and Braque's cubist painting, Joyce's prose, Eliot's poetry, and Stravinsky's music. In the field of concert dance, however, Ted Shawn and Ruth St. Denis were rather ahead of their time. Few other dance makers during the next fifty years were quite so willing to embrace this "modernist" Ragtime style of putting dance programs and phrases together with such ragged sutures.

Instead, the next generation of choreographers seemed much more interested in fashioning their own unique personal idioms. For these modernist choreographers, "making stage work was inseparable from teaching an approach to dance" (Siegel 1979, 10). Through the dual practices of inventing choreography and devising systems of technical dance training, these modernist choreographers lived out idiosyncratic and yet highly systematic visions of what modern dance should be.

To clarify this point, I'd like now to examine the role of eclecticism (or the lack thereof) in a few examples of mid-century modern dance-making. In Alvin Ailey's *Revelations* (1962), we see a wide range of tableaux and styles, corresponding to the diversity of African American religious experiences. "Fix Me, Jesus" is a carefully paced duet full of reaching and turning away, and with a number of slow lifts reminiscent of the adagio from a classical *pas de deux.* "Sinner Man"—a trio for three men—is an up-tempo jazz dance number, sparkling with fast turns, giant leaps, and bravado rolls to the floor. Another section, "Wade in the Water," depicts a joyous baptism scene, whose celebrants dive into breathtaking *penché* arabesque turns and deep second-position *pliés,* while broad white streamers flutter across the stage.

Is this eclectic? Despite the broad range of scenes and the varied demands which this piece places upon its performers, I suggest that the answer is no. Each episode is safely ensconced in its frame: the music stops, the audience applauds, a new set of dancers enters. Each episode is also firmly grounded in Alvin Ailey's distinctive (and self-consistent) blend of Horton, Graham, jazz, and ballet techniques. The emphasis on strong, controlled movement, articulate pelvises and spines, and highly charged emotional intensity persists throughout the work. To the extent that certain nondancerly movements are imported into the choreography (for example, dancers praying, embracing, cooling themselves with fans), they are filtered through Ailey's blend of techniques and are performed in very close unison in a consistent company style: bit of a revue style, lots of blending and fusion, but not eclecticism.

Perhaps the clearest examples of modernist stylistic consistency—the very antithesis of eclecticism and yet the fodder for so much subsequent quotation—would be the work of Martha Graham and George Balanchine. Both created dozens of ensemble dances, each one of which bears the unmistakable imprint of its choreographer's idiosyncratic style. Both also developed long-term programs for training dancers to perform their choreographic styles. These well-known technical programs are so meticulous and have become so ingrained in students' bodies that the dancers thereby trained can be permanently branded with the badge of "Graham dancer" or "Balanchine dancer." This pedigree enables them to perform the master's work in what we would call the most proper manner; it can also seriously impede their ability to dance with another choreographer who may work under an alternate paradigm.[1]

Even when Balanchine or Graham *tries* to work in a different style, the result looks no less distinctively his or her own. For instance, take Balanchine's *Union Jack* (1976), a tribute to the sprightly music and dances of British sailors. Dressed in loose sailors' outfits, arms akimbo, clicking their heels together, and flashing bright smiles, the New York City Ballet *en travesti* looks no less like the New York City Ballet. Their nautical high-spiritedness notwithstanding, the dancers' musicality is just as emphatic, their formations on stage as precise, and their limbs have no less of the sparkling geometric precision than we'd expect to see in a more conventionally Balanchinean piece like *Agon* or *Diamonds*.

It is worth mentioning here the tendency of many modernist art forms to isolate themselves by wearing the mantle of "highbrow" art—to be clearly distinguished, on the one hand, from shoddy, mass-manufactured products, and, on the other hand, from equally unrefined popular "folkloric" traditions. The commitment to the idea of theatrical dance as a high art—held aloof from tawdry burlesques, ersatz toe dances, and vernacular dances—meant that modernist choreographers wouldn't allow themselves to reproduce materials from such sources outright. They had to be purified, refined, "cooked." In practical terms, this means that modernist choreographers generally handled quoted materials by fusing them into the medium of their own technique, thus enabling them to become more "enduring," "universal," and theatrically legible.

The bulwark of concert dance's respectability and claims to universality lasted from at least the 1930s to the 1960s but was finally breached by the members of the so-called Judson Church movement. The first dance-makers to be called "postmodern" (because they "saw as their task the purging and melioration of historical modern dance" [Banes 1987, xv]), the Judsonites made little use at first of quoting and bricolage. Nonetheless, they play an important part in the history of eclecticism.

As an illustration, take Yvonne Rainer's *Trio A*, or, *The Mind Is a Muscle, Part I* (1966), probably the most famous and widely performed of the Judson-era dances. Recalling the ballerina's toe-touch in *Push Comes to Shove*, *Trio A* is replete with quotidian gestures and activities. Abstractly geometric movements (the foot taps a semicircle on the floor, the arms and legs extend in straight lines in a variety of directions) alternate with activities taken more recognizably from daily life (walking, running, touching one's face). The dancer's apparent nonchalance notwithstanding, this was revolutionary material at the time, which "drastically" violated many of the "canons of classical theatrical training" (Banes 1987, 48). Rainer and her colleagues should be credited with championing the idea that dance could be made out of any movement, without any a priori limits, thus "making a historical shift in the subject of dance to pure movement" (54). This was a powerful blow to the modern dance "technocracy," and it opened the gates to a much broader understanding of what dance could encompass.

Still, *Trio A* is hardly eclectic. Despite Sally Banes's statement that "the achievement of *Trio A* is the resolute denial of style and expression" (54), there is in fact an exceedingly consistent and studied style to the piece. In Laban Movement Analysis Effort terminology, *Trio A* is marked by neutral Effort: moderately sustained movement, diminished flow changes, neither strong nor light use of weight. It is the very soul of uninflected blandness and homogeneity. When Banes remarks that "the homogeneity of the execution masks the utter disjunctiveness of the series" (46), she indicates precisely how Rainer's combination of common/pedestrian with nonreferential/abstract dance movement is the same sort of "dance fusion" encountered earlier.

Yvonne Rainer was also a member of the Grand Union improvisation group for the entirety of its existence (1970–76), together with other Judson choreographers such as Steve Paxton, Douglas Dunn, and Trisha Brown. However analytic and austere these participants' independent work may have been, when they began to improvise together, the invention and variety of their dancing knew no bounds. Following (or disobeying) the slightest of plans for the evening's show, the Grand Union performers would perform set choreography, improvise skits, quote stock characters and movement idioms, extemporaneously devise new characters, and comment meta-theatrically on these activities as they were happening. According to Banes, "a social as well as an aesthetic world invaded the stage":

> They jog around like football players between plays; they make boxing movements, kick backwards. . . . People are doing gymnasts' flying angels, or using each other's weight to lean, stand, and sit. . . . [The Grand Union]

> stretched the material and formal limits of their art by incorporating objects (and gestures) from everyday life, using imagery (including sounds) from popular culture, and making long, rambling words in a flexible format with a constantly changing stream of images and meanings. (205–9)

Few other choreographic experiments seem to have adhered so fully to the letter of architect Robert Venturi's prescription for postmodern vitality: "I like elements which are hybrid rather than 'pure,' . . . redundant rather than simple, vestigial as well as innovating, inconsistent and equivocal rather than direct and clear. I am for messy vitality over obvious unity" (Venturi 1996, 326).

The next chapter in my story belongs to Twyla Tharp. Choreographing set dances at the same time that the Grand Union was performing their improvisations, Tharp pioneered the technique of binding "messy vitality" into the flow of fixed choreography, attaching varied movement idioms while preserving their individual characters.

As an illustration of eclecticism, another episode from the second section of Tharp's *Push Comes to Shove* (1976) is noteworthy. Haydn's Symphony No. 82 in C strikes up and Mikhail Baryshnikov soon appears on stage, with derby hat, legwarmers, and velvet breeches. Baryshnikov performs an exuberant, mercurial solo that veers erratically between different movement styles. We see what looks like a mesmerist's hypnotic gestures; a sudden glare at the audience, as if to indicate, "You lookin' at me?!"; a few hand gestures resembling a baseball pitcher's coded signals and a New Yorker's obscene "up yours!" insult; classroom ballet exercises gone awry, like a *pirouette* that flings the dancer wildly off-kilter or an *entrechat-huit* jump that is "marked" without ever leaving the ground. Interspersed with this jumble of references are the occasional virtuoso steps, done "correctly" for a change: *cabrioles, grands jetés en attitude,* and a final six-turn *pirouette* ending in an astonishingly prolonged *relevé.*[2]

It seems as if Attention Deficit Disorder were the underlying aesthetic of this solo. Baryshnikov's character samples rather aimlessly from numerous movement idioms, only to be interrupted by fits of boredom or hyperactive energy. No dance better illustrates Sally Banes's thesis that "the key post-modern choreographic device is radical juxtaposition" (1987, xxiii). A real-life person might not switch between ways of moving quite so quickly—or so the choreography would suggest—but his or her movements would still end up as a tissue of various imitations, influences, and ever-changing impulses. At the same time that we see the jumbled detritus of past experience, however, we see an enactment of the practice of "making it new." Tharp casts her lead dancer as a movement investigator, a perspicacious innovator forever casting about for different ways of moving.

Push Comes to Shove was first performed in 1976, and seems to have caused a certain frisson of transgression for the balletomanes in the audience. Although the extent to which "characteristic moves from one tradition are intercalated into phrases from another" is relatively common to Tharp's work in the 1970s (Foster 1985, 49), I can only surmise that seeing a ballerina inelegantly stretching her hamstrings or seeing the premier danseur perform a razzmatazz soft-shoe tap number before launching into his more traditional multiple *pirouettes* and *grands jetés en manège* was a novel and disquieting experience for the work's first viewers. Twyla Tharp was a pioneer of using eclectic methods of dance composition, and this was one of her first pieces performed by a classical ballet company before an audience of thousands.[3] In contrast to many of her no-nonsense Judson colleagues, Tharp offered a distinctive interpretation of what up-to-date dance could be: highly kinetic and urbane, virtuosic, and eclectic. Taking movement ideas from a dozen sources, the most recherché oddities and crass banalities would be fused together into the most unlikely combinations. Few previous choreographers had traveled so far from home in their search for novelty.

In 1979, dance critic Marcia Siegel called this "raffish, ragpicker jumble of ideas . . . one element of a new style that is Tharp's alone" (352). A funny thing, however, about the dance-making community—and about the interconnected, ever-new era of postmodernism—is that certain innovations can spread like wildfire. Faster than you can say "intellectual property rights," the technical, compositional, and presentational innovations of last week are snatched up by the choreographers of today. For reasons that surely relate to Tharp's influence as well as to larger trends outside of the dance world, Tharp's "ragpicker jumble of ideas" didn't take long to become par for the course.

Nowadays, without the modus operandi of quoting and eclecticism, a dance work is liable to appear naive, predictable, or just quaintly old-fashioned. Numberless are the choreographers whose work is said to draw upon an eclectic, quirky range of movement, or create a fusion of disparate elements; legion are the dance teachers whose technique classes offer their own idiosyncratic, culled-from-many-sources movement sequences. Besides Tharp, other well-known choreographers and ensembles who employ bricolage are Mark Dendy, Rennie Harris, Bill T. Jones, Meredith Monk, Mark Morris, Tere O'Connor, and Jawole Willa Jo Zollar; as well as Inbal Pinto in Israel, Dairakudakan in Japan, De La Guarda in Argentina, Pina Bausch in Germany, Matthew Bourne and DV8 in England, Les Ballets C. de la B. and Jan Fabre in Belgium, Maguy Marin and Philippe Decoufflé in France, and so on.

A complete list would include a good half of today's professional and nonprofessional choreographers from around the world: student choreographers, ballet choreographers, Broadway and *Tanztheater* choreographers, independents as well as directors of major dance companies. Two surprising late-hour additions to the list would be modernist stalwarts Martha Graham and Hanya Holm, whose work in the 1980s (such as *Maple Leaf Rag* and *Jocose,* respectively) lightheartedly poached material from earlier, more serious phases of their careers.

And this is still quite an incomplete list, for if we move away from the more exclusive end of the high-art/low-art continuum,[4] we note that quoting and eclecticism have become the *sine quibus non* of contemporary movement composition, that which allows choreography to interface and crossbreed more fluidly with contemporary music, visual art, film, video, and Web production. Carnival parades in Rio de Janeiro, break dancing demonstrations in Union Square, MTV videos, aerobics classes in Bordeaux, cheerleading competitions in Dallas, videogames on the Sony PlayStation: as likely as not, moves will be swapped between these different locales with few reservations or logistical difficulties.

eclecticism and the dance performer

What difficulties *do* exist in the contemporary climate of rampant eclecticism are felt acutely by dance performers. Eclectic choreography places very specific demands on dancers. In one sense, the imperative to be highly skilled in different dance techniques means that the aspiring performer must learn to negotiate physical imperatives that often seem mutually exclusive. Here I would like to cite some of my own experiences as a graduate student in the Department of Dance at The Ohio State University (OSU).

Over the course of two years, I studied and practiced a typically broad range of dance styles: classical ballet, Cunningham- and Limón-based techniques, release technique, West African dance, Contact Improvisation, yoga, and capoeira. Although the cumulative effect of these varied subjects was a general, slowly increasing physical proficiency, interferences and confusion did occur along the way. In capoeira class, for instance, I was training to develop a constant—almost instinctual—low, crouching stance combined with a sense of solidity in the upper body. These habits played almost no part in—and often contradicted—the lightness, verticality, and lengthening that I was daily trying to develop in ballet class. This was not just a theoretical problem; specific instances of interference did occur. Practicing capoeira's multiunit spinning technique (picture the whole upper body acting like the crank on a wind-up toy) had only a pernicious effect on my ballet *pirouettes;* at the same time, my capoeira kicks and spins had an inappropriate (but indelible) lightness to them, and a recurrent classical tendency to elongate my spine earned me the depreciative capoeira nickname "Girafa" (Giraffe).[5]

During the course of a typical week's training, other difficulties appear. The practitioner of Contact Improvisation learns how to improvise a dance in dialogue with his partner, as in capoeira, but he cultivates an instinctive tendency to lean into his partner and to rely on his sense of touch much more than his eyes—tendencies that can be disastrously inappropriate in the context of high-speed capoeira play. Going to a Cunningham-style technique class the next day, he works to shape his limbs with a precisely bound flow into forms and motions of geometric clarity, thereby tightening up some of the release he had found in his Contact activities the night before. And the Cunningham class can cause some interference with the earlier-mentioned ballet studies, for despite a common technical base, ballet's sense of lightness and sequentiality in the upper body does not mesh entirely well with Cunningham's unified, simultaneous attack.

These examples are just the tip of the iceberg. Besides the subjects already mentioned, OSU offers training in Bharata Natyam, North and South American social dances, tap and jazz dancing, step dancing, and a few different styles of West African dance. Resources permitting, the curricula of many dance conservatories and university dance programs around the United States are similar in breadth. As students go from class to class, the range of their experiences increases, but so does the possibility of interference. Not for nothing did Graham and Balanchine jealously guard their company dancers from studying with outside teachers, with whom they stood the risk of corrupting their technical pedigree (see Kirkland 1986; Taylor 1988; Cunningham 1985). Now that such protectionism has waned, learning how to negotiate conflicting technical demands has become an inevitable component of formal dance training in the twenty-first century. Forty years ago, Graham-centered modern dance programs trained for commitment and consistency; now, the key principle underlying many eclectic curricula has become versatility.

In the above discussion of interference between techniques, a reoccurring term was "instinctive." Considering the number of muscles, joints, dynamics, rhythms, and outside events that dancers need to coordinate, it is often a blessing to be able to bypass deliberation and rely on one's instincts. *Instincts:* one's "natural propensities to act, without conscious intention" (OED). To the extent that a dancer's technical training is about making choices, about developing versatility, a diversity of training techniques is surely a boon. But to the extent that technical training is about instilling *instincts*—patterns of movement so consistent that the body can respond correctly in an instant—having too many training techniques can be quite problematic.

Twyla Tharp, whose formative training was extremely varied, makes this point eloquently in her autobiography, *Push Comes to Shove* (1992). Arriving in New York City and taking ballet classes with Robert Thomas, Tharp can't help but compare herself to classmates who have received only strictly classical training. "The movement I struggled to make sense of . . . Toni [Lander] performed effortlessly. My movements were rational decisions, choices made among thousands; hers were so natural that they seemed like instincts" (48). Referring to her studies in tap, baton, jazz, violin, piano, Graham, Cunningham, Horton, and ballet, Tharp realized at Thomas's studio that "I was suffering from my eclectic training. . . . I had been given too many options. . . . To fly straight into an arabesque with no hesitation or to hold the body serenely in balance for eight *pirouettes* demands a solid, unquestioned technique" (48–49). (The phrase "I had been given too many options" is a useful gloss on Tharp's choreography; as we saw earlier, her work thematicizes this very situation of a body with too many choices.)

Are these difficulties insurmountable? Only partly. Tharp writes that she never reached the level of seamless, integrated classical dancing that she was aiming for. But she found something equally valuable. "I was coming to understand that each of these demands could work together to combine, ultimately, into something more than a patois of isolated techniques, become a new language, capable of saying new things—or old things in new ways. I was beginning to imagine a special niche for myself, a place in this swirling kaleidoscope of choices" (54).

This "new language" coalescing amidst a "kaleidoscope of choices" became the province of what Tharp describes as the "crossover dancer," supposed to be "capable of any technique" (54). Susan Foster, writing on the same topic, describes the "hired dancer"—"competent at many styles"—as the dancer of choice for many independent, postmodern choreographers. "The new multitalented body resulting from this training melds together features from all of the techniques discussed above: it possesses the strength and flexibility found in ballet necessary to lift the leg high in all directions; it can perform any movement neutrally and pragmatically, as in Cunningham's technique; it has mastered the athleticism of contact improvisation . . . it articulates the torso as a Graham dancer does" (Foster 1997, 254–55).

The appearance on stage and screen of a multitude of "hired bodies" in the 1980s was a hotly debated topic among dance critics. Watching with an eagle eye from her perch atop the masthead of the *New Yorker,* Arlene Croce once bemoaned the fading of "those technical and stylistic distinctions among companies which used to be the glory of American modern dance" (Croce 1982, 366). Other dance critics were pleased to note the progressive features of the "hired body." Elizabeth Dempster, for one, celebrated its anti-ideological, "deconstructive" features as follows:

> The development of what might be termed the postmodern body is in some senses a deconstructive process, involving a period of detraining of

> the dancer's habitual structures and patterns of movement.... The postmodern body is not a fixed, immutable entity, but a living structure which continually adapts and transforms itself. It is a body available to the play of many discourses. Postmodern dance directs attention away from any specific image of the body and towards the process of constructing all bodies. (1988, 48)

But the "postmodern body" which Dempster celebrates does have its drawbacks. Although it may "continually adapt and transform itself," its eclectic training may also send it heading towards a bland least common denominator. Susan Foster describes the distinct visual impression made by many a "postmodern" or "hired" dancer: instead of displaying "its skills as a collage of discrete styles," the "hired body" often "homogenizes all styles and vocabularies beneath a sleek, impenetrable surface... a rubbery flexibility coated with impervious glossiness" (1997, 255). This isn't entirely as bad as it seems: sleekness and glossiness may actually be required by certain choreographers (one thinks of work in the 1990s by Stephen Petronio and Donald Byrd). In distinctly eclectic choreography, however, a "collage of discrete styles" is what is called for, and achieving this is no easy feat.

Again, I will provide an example from my own experience. In *Three Bird Songs,* a piece that I composed and performed in my graduate concert in February of 2001, I choreographed a sequence that required me (a) to spring from a low, crouched capoeira-style *rolê* turn with my hands on the floor, immediately into (b) a sudden and brilliant classical *pirouette en attitude,* which would just as suddenly collapse with an extra turn to leave me (c) standing knock-kneed, facing the audience, already beginning a flowing sequence of hand gestures. The technical challenge—not uncommon in an age of eclecticism, but a challenge nonetheless—was to make the transitions into and out of (a), (b), and (c) as abrupt and distinct as possible.

I used a video camera to coach myself. I noticed that during the *rolê* turn I would straighten my posture and prepare for the *attitude* turn too soon, thus making the previous *rolê* less distinctive than it needed to be. And it was hard to stay in the *attitude* position for the full amount of time necessary: my back leg would drift down, preemptively preparing for the knock-kneed turn which was to follow. After working to correct these problems, others would appear. Perhaps it would be harder to release my head from its extended line in the attitude pose in time for the gestural material that followed; perhaps, too, the low, bent standing leg of the *rolê* turn began to linger too long into the *attitude* turn. The phrase improved with practice, of course, although I suspect that each of the three elements was still missing a bit of its flavor by virtue of being so very close to the others.

The moral of this story was anticipated in Foster's cautionary words about the "hired body": "It does not display its skills as a collage of discrete styles but, rather, homogenizes all styles and vocabularies" (1997, 255). Another way to say this is that dancers struggle mightily to present the sort of sharp juxtapositions that filmmakers can achieve with the simplest of splices or cross-fades, or computer graphics designers with a few cut-and-paste keystrokes. These technologies of reproduction have no real equivalent in the field of dance, however choreographers may try to mimic them.[6] When a dancer sets out to reproduce a style accurately, one is rather reminded of the elaborate technique of Jorge Luis Borges's fictional, twentieth-century Frenchman, Pierre Menard, who chose to copy Cervantes's *Don Quixote* with an inordinately rigorous and impractical method. Instead of simply reading the book and transcribing it, he decided "to know Spanish well, to re-embrace the Catholic faith, to fight against Moors and Turks, to forget European history between 1602 and 1918, and to *be* Miguel de Cervantes," so that the words of the book would just naturally flow out of him (Borges 1962, 49).

Learning another dance technique well often requires the same sort of imaginative labor that a Belle Epoque French writer would need to recreate a seventeenth-century Spanish text without actually looking at it. Imitating movements and shapes is usually just the first step; it must be accompanied by studying and internalizing elaborate anatomical, functional, and expressive metaphorical systems that give color and meaning to that movement. Again, Foster's work is informative.

> With repetition, the images used to describe the body and its action *become* the body. Metaphors that are inapplicable or incomprehensible when first presented take on a concrete reality over time, through their persistent association with a given movement. . . . Each dance technique constructs a specialized and specific body, one that represents a given choreographer's or tradition's aesthetic vision of dance. . . . Training not only constructs a body but also helps to fashion an expressive self that, in its relation with the body, performs the dance. (1997, 239, 241)

When described this way, dance study can be understood as more than just training for strength, flexibility, and coordination. Any given technique will also carry with it a subtext, an ideology, a philosophy, a somatic paradigm. Recall Martha Graham's famous words: the inner "law" that governs the outer aspects of the dancer's life is that "[m]ovement never lies. It is a barometer telling the state of the soul's weather to all who can read it" (Graham 1991, 4).

As a final point to consider, I would like to draw the reader's attention to the echo that Graham's (and Foster's) words strike with those of the philosopher-historian Michel Foucault in his book, *Discipline and Punish.* Many of the dozens of strategies and practices that Foucault delineates in his history of discipline have been incorporated into dance training. One could even consider classical ballet training to be the example par excellence of a body of disciplinary techniques. As it was developed in the seventeenth, eighteenth, and nineteenth centuries, the question in ballet training (just as in military training, medical care, or criminal justice) was "not of treating the body, *en masse,* 'wholesale,' as if it were an indissociable unity, but of working it 'retail,' individually" (Foucault 1979, 137). The toes, the ankles, the knees, the hips, the different layers of muscles, the bones, the eyes, the fingertips: each receives individual attention, and each is subject to correction and improvement. Not all of classical ballet training's many hybrid offspring and relatives (i.e.: many of the dance techniques mentioned in this essay) work in exactly the same ways, but all inevitably seem to share the axiomatic feature that "although they involved obedience to others, [they have] as their principal aim an increase of the mastery of each individual over his own body" (137).

If we return our attention to the phenomenon of eclectic dance training, we may speculate as to what new inflections it may have wrought on disciplinary practices and effects. In most cases, one would expect to see an intensification of disciplinary effects, as dancers learn to master the use of their bodies and minds in an ever-broader range of occasions and ways. A possibility that sparks my interest, however, is the extent to which disciplinary techniques might also be lessened (or short-circuited) when they are juxtaposed in a single body and mind. Recall Twyla Tharp's complaint that her training left her with "too many choices."

Foucault's implication is that, no matter how apparently benign the context, discipline should be understood as being intimately connected with larger projects of fostering political docility and economic utility. Engaging in a regimen of dance training, however, is for most people a relatively voluntary choice, which often places one against the grain of many social and economic imperatives. In such a situation, one generally wants this voluntary sort of discipline to *work,* and gets frustrated with obstacles in one's body and mind, interference, and other mute forms of resistance. In the context of Foucault's book, on the other hand, these rare appearances of obstacles to the constant encroachment of disciplinary subjection are highly desirable. The question we are left with—an issue that will be inflected on each dancer's mind and body in different ways—is whether experiencing the challenge and confusion of eclectic training may provide us with any recyclable tools suitable for resisting Foucauldian discipline in other realms of our lives. At the moment, resistance to discipline has become the Holy Grail of a number of lines of academic inquiry, especially in cultural studies, and it is fascinating to detect this elusive phenomenon in the context of contemporary dance training.

notes

1. Could a dancer from Graham's company, deeply molded by her technique, ever have performed with Balanchine's New York City Ballet? To my knowledge, only one—Paul Taylor—was ever given the opportunity. He felt he "was drowning at sea" and only performed one role in *Episodes,* the historic concert that Balanchine shared with Graham in 1959 (Taylor 1988, 90, 95). Could a dancer trained by Balanchine's School of American Ballet migrate over to Graham's company? Erick Hawkins was the first to make the switch. Four more were given a temporary opportunity for the *Episodes* concert. One imagines that only with an extensive period of debriefing and reprogramming would a more permanent crossover have been possible (89).

   Since her death, Graham's company—like those of Paul Taylor and Merce Cunningham—has gradually grown more receptive to the idea of ballet dancers in the company, and of ballet companies performing the choreographer's works.
2. My account of this ballet is based on the 1984 video recording, *Baryshnikov Dances Tharp,* which includes a revised version of *Push Comes to Shove* (originally choreographed in 1976).
3. Another crossover "modern ballet" was Tharp's landmark *Deuce Coupe,* choreographed for the Joffrey Ballet in 1973.
4. The high-art/low-art distinction, by the way, has been nearly inundated by the flood of bricolaged dance and media. Where could we possibly place Twyla Tharp's choreography for the popular movie musical *Hair,* or the trash-talking, T-shirted dancers in Tere O'Connor's *Hi Everybody!* or the modern dance-trained go-go dancers who stand on the podiums at nightclubs in Columbus, Ohio, and demonstrate the refinements of release- and African-based dance technique to the grinding audiences below? See John Seabrook's recent *Nobrow* (2000) and Jameson's *Postmodernism* (1991, 2–3).
5. Besides these different interferences, harmonies can develop as well. I spent the summer of 2000 studying capoeira at an academy in Salvador da Bahia, Brazil. Although it does have a stable technical base, capoeira is a constantly evolving, syncretic form, and after I was observed furtively practicing some ballet-style *barre* stretches between classes, I noticed that the teacher had incorporated them into his capoeira class the next day.
6. Choreographer Tere O'Connor can be quite deliberate about this mimicry, often asking his dancers to generate certain cinematographic effects. As an example, I'll paraphrase some of the instructions O'Connor gave during an audition in New York in June 2001: "This movement should look like when a film projector stutters, and an inch of film gets played again and again." "You start to fall in this direction, and then suddenly your arms pull you in another direction and you're twisted like this—just like a badly-edited film, where there's no continuity between cuts."

works cited

Banes, Sally. 1987. *Terpsichore in Sneakers: Post-Modern Dance.* 2nd ed. Hanover, N.H.: Wesleyan University Press.

Borges, Jorge Luis. 1962. *Ficciones* [1956]. Trans. Anthony Kerrigan. New York: Grove.

Croce, Arlene. 1982. *Going to the Dance.* New York: Alfred A. Knopf.

Cunningham, Merce. 1985. *The Dancer and the Dance.* New York: Marion Boyars.
Dempster, Elizabeth. 1988. "Women Writing the Body: Let's Watch a Little How She Dances." In Susan Sheridan, ed., *Grafts: Feminist Cultural Criticism.* London: Verso.
Foster, Susan Leigh. 1985. "The Signifying Body: Reaction and Resistance in Postmodern Dance." *Theatre Journal* 37, no. 1.
———. 1997. "Dancing Bodies" [1992]. In Jane C. Desmond, ed., *Meaning in Motion: New Cultural Studies of Dance.* Durham, N.C.: Duke University Press.
Foucault, Michel. 1979. *Discipline and Punish: The Birth of the Prison* [1975]. Trans. Alan Sheridan. New York: Vintage/Random House.
Graham, Martha. 1991. *Blood Memory.* New York: Doubleday.
Jameson, Frederic. 1991. *Postmodernism, or, The Cultural Logic of Late Capitalism.* Durham, N.C.: Duke University Press.
Jencks, Charles A. 1981. *The Language of Post-Modern Architecture.* 3rd ed. New York: Rizzoli.
Kendall, Elizabeth. 1979. *Where She Danced.* New York: Alfred A. Knopf.
Kirkland, Gelsey, with Greg Lawrence. 1986. *Dancing on My Grave.* Garden City, N.Y.: Doubleday.
Lyotard, Jean-François. 1984. *The Postmodern Condition: A Report on Knowledge* [1979]. Trans. Geoff Bennington and Brian Massumi. Minneapolis: University of Minnesota Press.
Seabrook, John. 2000. *Nobrow: The Culture of Marketing, the Marketing of Culture.* New York: Vintage.
Siegel, Marcia. 1979. *The Shapes of Change: Images of American Dance.* Boston: Houghton Mifflin.
Taylor, Paul. 1988. *Private Domain: An Autobiography.* San Francisco: North Point Press.
Tharp, Twyla. 1992. *Push Comes to Shove.* New York: Bantam.
Venturi, Robert. 1996. "Complexity and Contradiction in Modern Architecture" [1966]. In Lawrence Cahoone, ed., *From Modernism to Postmodernism: An Anthology.* Oxford: Blackwell.

melanie bales

6 ballet for the post-judson dancer

evil stepsister or fairy godmother?

Examining the role of ballet in the training of the post-Judson dancer produces fascinating and paradoxical phenomena. Often, its role changes over time as a dancer considers and reconsiders if and why to take ballet, as can be seen in the interviews in this book. Some dancers don't take ballet anymore because they don't take anything. A recent conversation with former Trisha Brown dancer Carolyn Lucas revealed that she and other company members routinely studied their bodies through somatic techniques rather than any dance style.

I have personally heard many New York dancers lament that the only classes you can take are ballet classes, so that is what you take. Certainly the economic realities in that city have forced many a change as studios are lost and companies go abroad to survive. Still other dancers continue to firmly reject taking ballet for now, or forever, while others take it without really questioning why they take it at all. If a dancer or choreographer has been educated in the university, which grows more common every day as living in New York has become economically forbidding and universities hire professionals, he/she will at least have had ballet as part of the curriculum.

Ballet might be seen now as a common denominator during a time when training practices define the term eclectic or as one of many components along with yoga, Alexander Technique, so-and-so's modern class (see Chapter 1). It may be embraced as practical and effective as a class practice, yet simultaneously shunned as elitist, sexist, racist, and repressive as an art form. In a way, the post-Judson interface with ballet is a litmus test. If the early moderns defined the split between ballet and their new dance forms, the work of Merce Cunningham made that split less essential,[1] and during the Judson era ballet became more part of a blended family than a hated relative.

In her article "Sibling Rivalry: The New York City Ballet and Modern Dance," Sally Banes agrees that the tango between the two genres has been both intimate and distant since modern dance emerged, with certain "shifting points" occurring through history where the two forms seemed to be especially close to one another within a particular dance or a certain choreographer's work (1999, 75). Whether ballet has absorbed what it needed from modern, or modern has capitulated to ballet, the "question" of ballet is still being asked by nonballet dancers on many levels: artistic, cultural, political, sexual, individual.

In this article, I examine more closely some of these questions and present the thoughts of other writers who have considered adjacent issues or arguments. Finally, I offer some ideas drawn from Laban Movement Analysis (LMA), not so much to simplify or to solve, but rather to suggest additional dimensions of meaning.

fairy godmother

In his 1986 article "The Objective Temperament: Post-Modern Dance and The Rediscovery of Ballet," Roger Copeland cites recent work of choreographers David Gordon, Twyla Tharp, Lucinda Childs, and Laura Dean as having moved "from the realm of the technically vernacular to the technically spectacular." He goes on to say that "the apparent rediscovery of ballet by erstwhile minimalists and Judson-era celebrants of the pedestrian may turn out to be the most important choreographic realignment of the 1980s" (1986, 6). Significantly, he argues that it is not that these and other choreographers suddenly changed their stripes in working with ballet dancers, but that they, unlike their modern dance predecessors, actually share certain aspects or sensibilities with ballet and always did so.

Qualifying this, Copeland names the aspects that postmodernists and ballet enthusiasts share: impersonality, lightness, verticality, theatrical legibility, and finally and more recently (as of the 1980s), the classical vocabulary itself.[2]

I find the basic premise of the article interesting and persuasive for several reasons. First, making a dance from a vocabulary that already exists does somehow more closely approximate the process of using found, borrowed, or improvised movement as the mode of creativity. This is not to say that early moderns did not find, borrow, or improvise, but that the emphasis was shifted in the direction of a specific kind of personal expressiveness with modernist originality, rather than on a more open-ended acceptance of what would emerge or follow along from a process of collaging and crafting. The experimentalists of Judson didn't set out to create a new dance language (though I think at least one, Trisha Brown, did) unlike foremothers Martha Graham and Doris Humphrey.

Second, I agree with the idea that lightness and verticality figure more prominently in both the ballet vocabulary and work post-Judson, especially in the choreographers Copeland cites (1986). I would extend the term lightness to include both the illusion of bodily lightness (light Effort quality in the Laban vocabulary) and expressive values of lightness such as whimsy, wit, absurdity, hyperbole, and irony. These are generalizations and it would be no trouble to find counter-examples: *Giselle* isn't very funny and the work of Charles Weidman was. But I do find that there is a shared sensibility on several levels between the ballet world and postmodern dance, which Copeland sums up as the Objective Temperament (1986; see also Banes 1987, 15).

As for verticality, that is something that extends into the classroom very directly. The classical *barre* and center floor exercises reflect most directly the classical repertoire. In both, developing verticality is of the essence: how to get the upper body over the lower, how to "get on your leg," how to balance and appear as if suspended from above. However, it is getting harder to find a trained ballet dancer who hasn't had some experience with floor work. Some ballet academies offer Graham Technique, which would seem to fly in the face of Copeland's point that ballet and Graham are like oil and water (1986, 7). I think it is appealing to ballet schools because it is a highly codified, well-known style and, like ballet, can be approached in a bound, shape-oriented way, although that limits both. There is also something anachronistically heroic about the two styles and the fact that classical ballets illustrate fairytales, while some of Graham's works drew from myth.

Back to the notion of verticality figuring more prominently in the ballet and postmodern vocabularies: post-Judson classes are generally "standing" classes, even though there may be parts of class where you lie on the floor doing Bartenieff Fundamentals or go to and from the floor in a combination. Perhaps the turn toward pedestrian movement (walking, running, skipping) during Judson precipitated a turn in focus on locomotion, and shifted the emphasis away from the sitting sequences essential to the classes of Graham, and her descendants like Hawkins. Many of the Judson choreographers came from Cunningham's school or company and certainly the Cunningham class is a "standing" one. Yet, because of the freedom inherent in post-Judson class design, other kinds of classes coexist alongside lower-body centered ones. So-called upside-down classes, prevalent on the West Coast but also a good descriptor of New Yorker David Dorfman's teaching, work on rolling, falling, handstands, etc., and reflect influences like Aikido, gymnastics, Contact Improvisation, and circus techniques.

There are important distinctions between the two genres in terms of how the training interacts with the choreography. Ballet, as a form that has developed over many years, changing and adapting as it goes, has established a very direct relationship between the training and the repertoire. Theoretically, all you need to take is ballet class to become a ballet dancer, although this is becoming less true as companies engage nonballet choreographers while the world waits around for the next George Balanchine. Ballet, as a classical form, has generally been more accepting of innovation in choreography (Nijinsky, Fokine, Robbins, and Tharp, for example) than in *immediately* absorbing new vocabulary into the lexicon. In the much less organized world of dance post-Judson, where training is mostly self-styled, and choreographic material can (again, theoretically) come from anywhere, there is no such direct link between training and repertoire. Lucinda Childs's comment in *Democracy's Body* about taking class with Mia Slavenska while starting to work with other Judson artists is telling: "Everybody seemed to be going to Slavenska, so I went, too. You had to keep your body together, even though there was a dichotomy between the discipline of that technique and the actual activity you were involved in" (Banes 1993, 99).

While Childs was referring to events in the 1960s, the fact still persists that, despite the possibility of a shared sensibility between ballet and post-Judson dance, the role of training in each was and is very different. While many dancers then, as now, take ballet and establish a bodily and aesthetic relationship with that technique, it is not synonymous or even very directly related to what they will be performing or choreographing. Even if, as dancers, they work with a choreographer who uses the ballet vocabulary in a dance, it is not the same as dancing in a ballet.

There is no doubt that styles are mingling differently now than in other times—David Gordon setting a work on ABT (1970s) was as boundary-crossing then as Mikhail Baryshnikov dancing in a Yvonne Rainer work (PastForward Project) is now. It is becoming more difficult to draw lines that once separated one style from another—or are there just more dancers who can cross those boundaries? If the post-Judson dancer takes ballet class, albeit for different reasons and purposes than the ballet dancer, even given the idea of a shared sensibility à la Copeland, what might some of those reasons be?

Although *Swan Lake* or *Sleeping Beauty,* or even the *Four Temperaments,* may seem light years away from a given dancer's personal aesthetic, he/she may find reasons to train in ballet that have to do with things like alignment, strength, speed, endurance, efficiency, suppleness, articulation. Any really strenuous activity can build strength, speed, and endurance and many dancers build exactly what they need through the repetition of rehearsal. Ballet class offers a concentrated, well-ordered, relatively predictable, and logical workout, but also a chance to develop "leg dexterity," one of the essential features of the form. Through the convention of the *barre* work, the dancer can explore both the separation and interaction of standing leg and working leg (stability and mobility), practice subtle shifts in sensing balance and tension while maintaining verticality and outward rotation of the legs, and work on the heel-sit bone connection. A typical statement of "why ballet" is expressed in a paper written by Anna Leo, who danced in New York in the 1980s with Bebe Miller, among others: "The manner in which a ballet class is structured is ideal for establishing alignment and finding efficient ways of using the muscles" (1990).

Over my twenty-something years of teaching ballet to aspiring modern/postmodern/post-Judson dance students (we still call it modern in my department), attitudes to taking ballet class cover a wide area. There seems to be some notion that being versed in the vocabulary makes one more marketable—never mind that a marketable dancer is an oxymoron—or at least bumps one up a few technical notches. Along with this goes the idea that ballet will make you more versatile, which has some truth to it, not so much because they will be called upon to do actual ballet steps but because the training is so thorough. Also, dancers in the professional world and university students often appreciate that ballet class can be recuperative, or a complement to what they are rehearsing at the time.

Donald Blumenfeld-Jones's article "Form, Knowledge and Liberation in Dance: a Philosophical Inquiry" examines dancers who reject formalized vocabularies of movement because they believe that "[s]tudying forms made by others and attempting to become perfected in the other's forms is to submerge and negate oneself" (1987, 21). He then argues that embracing such knowledge (i.e., a major modern technique or ballet) does not have to squelch the self, but "requires a self which encounters, not a self which disappears, and the experience can become a dialogue" (21). Such a dialogue has an added benefit because "[f]orms contain the memory of their origination and when we enter a form we have a chance to revive that memory and, in some measure, come to know the maker" (22). So, if dancers can accept the challenges of studying a style that may seem to run counter to the freedom of more contemporary styles, they may benefit from the study as a kind of historical inquiry through the body.

Some students take it like medicine, or have high hopes for ballet curing what ails them, and I sometimes hear it recommended, or rather prescribed, as a cure for bad feet, tight hamstrings, sway back, lack of flow, no sense of line, and so on. (Conversely, ballet study is blamed for some of the same things and more: stiffness, inability to sense weight, held thoracic spine, stubborn mannerisms, and so on. As for ballet's dark side, more will be said later.)

Up to now, for the sake of argument, I have been referring to ballet class monolithically, which of course is not accurate. Even beyond the distinctions created by national identities or teachers (as in Cecchetti, Vagonova, Royal Academy, Balanchine), there are really as many classes as there are teachers, unless you give exactly what your teacher gave, and even then, your comments will be your own. A particular type of class has emerged over the last thirty years or so that identifies itself as ballet for modern dancers or is known as such by dancers via word of mouth. I studied intensively with Nadine Revene for a year or so in the mid-1970s in a class of "mixed" population: aspiring ballet dancers, recreational students, modern dancers (during my time, members of Dan Wagoner's company). As a bona fide "bun-head" at the time, I found it interesting standing next to a modern dance body at the *barre.* To me, they had a solid intelligence about their movement and their bodies seemed "realistic"—more like an athlete's than what I categorized as a dancer. They struggled with different parts of the material (extension, *épaulement, port de bras,* and fast footwork), and excelled in other parts where many of us struggled (*grand allegro,* transitions). They appreciated the class in a different way than I did, it seemed, but I wasn't sure exactly how.

Since that time, I have found myself in the roles of both modern dancer taking ballet class with professional ballet dancers and, more often, teacher of ballet for aspiring professional modern dancers. Over the years, what I perceived as somewhat of a novelty in the 1970s has become ingrained in the training of contemporary dancers of all stripes. I am quite sure Nadine Revene did not set out to be a resource for modern dancers, post-Judson or otherwise, but they found her. To us in the ballet world, she was simply an inspiring and intelligent teacher with a gentle, lovely presence. Other teachers who have been, or continue to be, important to self-identified nonballet dancers include Jacqueline Villamil, Marjorie Mussman, Ernie Pagnano, Janet Panetta, and Jocelyn Lorenz, to name a few.

These teachers in New York and other large urban areas became popular because they were accessible, teaching in studios where anyone could come in for a class—versus braving a class at a ballet school, if that were even possible.

Through word of mouth, people often enjoy studying where other people they know go; taking class with peers is less intimidating and enables networking. Ballet teachers popular with moderns make it possible for a dancer not all that well versed in the ballet vocabulary to take something away and make it "apply" to whatever creative work he/she is doing.

I believe particularly successful teachers are able to reveal movement principles embedded in the form and to make them emerge in a way that dancers versed in other forms can follow. Once a dancer visits or revisits ballet class, especially with a particularly "legible" teacher, a complex process unfolds where it becomes difficult to say how or when that knowledge will influence his/her work. What once seemed foreign may not seem so strange anymore. Translations are made, gaps are filled, questions are asked and answered, techniques expand.

A negative side to looking for something universal is trying to frame ballet as the *Esperanto* of dance; I have been shocked to hear my students on occasion describe it as "technique," rather than *a* technique. Also, a class can veer off the ballet path entirely; often a lack of musical sensitivity is revealing. If the music selections are too similar in tempo or qualitative/dynamic range, the individual character inherent in each exercise or step cannot be revealed or practiced. A *frappé* is short and strong; *fondues* have *rubato; adagio* develops mastery of *legato* movement. When the rhythms and musicality are flat and metronomic, the experience edges towards workout furniture with a ballet veneer. No good teacher of ballet in any context will neglect music and phrasing—it is built into the lexicon and is part of what does the teaching. I am standing briefly on the soapbox here in reference to the idea of ballet as "technique" because I feel it is important to remember that if the ballet class is flattened into a series of exercise units for defining this or that muscle group, an essential part of the whole has been removed. No matter how students and teachers "sanitize" ballet, or think they are doing so, ballet technique cannot be separated from the style, and that is what makes it beautiful. Therein also lie The Problems.

the evil stepsister

Is something dark and ominous lurking behind the orderly and upbeat exercises of the *barre* and center floor? It is no wonder that both teachers and students can become complicit in an attempt to ignore the context that comes along with the style. Anthropologist Joann Kealiinohomoku's important 1970 article reminded us that not only does ballet reflect the cultural heritage and customs of its origins in Renaissance Europe, but that the aesthetic values "are shown in the long line of lifted, extended bodies, in the total revealing of legs, of small heads and tiny feet for women, in slender bodies of both sexes, and in the coveted airy quality . . ." (Kealiinohomoku 1983, 545). Just as the form arose from the soil of its origins, as the Blumenfeld-Jones article also points out, and the development of the technique followed the dictates of the form, we must conclude that studying the technique generates some inextricable relationship with the form itself. If a dancer has decided to embrace the engagement, she is confronted, depending on her stance, with a codified classical lexicon of movement choices, or ballet baggage. In any case, it forces an inquiry upon the dancer.

Ballet has been "problemitized" in several different circles of thought. And indeed, there are disturbing aspects of the training and of life in a ballet company (see Gordon 1983). I will, however, provide comments on a few articles that shed light on some of the paradoxes surrounding this issue.

Susan Foster's fascinating article "The Ballerina's Phallic Pointe" covers quite a bit of ground in the guise of a cautionary tale or call to arms, ostensibly to the next generation: "those seven-year-old girls . . . as they draw their hair back in to a bun, pull on their pink tights, and head downtown in Hong Kong, Havana, New York, Buenos Aires, Sydney . . . for their weekly class" (Foster 1996, 17). The identity of contemporary ballet ("harder edged bodies, the abstract geometries, the athleticism") and how it grew out of, yet distinguishes itself from, earlier chapters in ballet history is problemitized as promising "a homogenizing medium for the expression of cultural difference" and providing a "seemingly neutral *techne*" (2). Hence, her warning to ballet girls in other countries where ballet, the dance version of pernicious colonialism, has taken hold. Although the ballerina-as-phallus is just too Freudian for my Jungian sympathies, the mention of ballet as universal language is well taken in the context of this article. Though Foster's *bête noire* is, like other feminist writers', the codified gender roles in the ballet repertoire, I appreciate her linking the training to the form: "[T]he prevalence of ballet technique as a form of physical training, regardless of the aesthetics of the choreographic tradition—modern dance, jazz, experimental or ethnic—mandate a consideration of all these gendered identities" (3), and her recognition of the changing persona of ballet over historical eras.

Foster focuses on the global visibility of ballet as a reason to consider the gendered identities inherent in the form. What about the post-Judson dancer taking the daily ballet class? Is he/she somehow exempt from such considerations? Perhaps she is less likely to end up mirroring "the leggy, anorexic, hyper-extended ballerina" (Foster 1996, 16) or participate in the sexism[3] than the aspiring ballet dancer would be. Still, any ballet student confronts a vocabulary that once had two quite distinct lexicons for males and females. I am always amused when my female students insist on doing the men's *grand allegro* along with the slower tempo. I see no reason why they shouldn't—in our context, bucking that tradition makes sense.

Before returning to the class itself, let us look at some of the other Problems. Two fairly recent articles about the role of Africanist elements in Balanchine's work bring forward some of the delicately complex interplay of race and style. Both authors, Sally Banes and Brenda Dixon Gottschild, argue persuasively that part of Balanchine's transformation of ballet stemmed from his contact and engagement with African American dance of a rather wide spectrum. Banes puts the emphasis on Balanchine's artistic process as it impacted the times and his tastes and preferences. By incorporating Africanist elements including jazz into his work, "he imagined the academic ballet genre expanded, enlivened and enriched by references to the popular dancing of the culture he and his dancers inhabited" (Banes 1994, 68). Far from being "just a passing fancy for Americana; he incorporated his deep and abiding love for African American dancing into the very heart of his technique and choreography" (69). In her notes, Banes refers to a similar (earlier?) article by Brenda Dixon Gottschild that expounds a malicious appropriation stance. In "Stripping the Emperor: The Africanist Presence in American Concert Dance," Gottschild's stance seems to have shifted towards creolization as an organizing principle. She does state, however, "It simply will not suffice to say that jazz dance influenced his work. That term, jazz, has become another way to misname and silence the Africanist legacy; systematic exclusion of African Americans from American ballet has done the same. Buried under layers of deceit, that legacy in ballet has been overlooked" (Gottschild 1995, 118).

And then there is the title—can Gottschild really be implying Balanchine had "no clothes"? I believe that his ability to create a new style within the ballet lexicon is precisely part of what made him so great. Her list of Africanisms (culled from other writers) is a welcome effort to describe movement in more detail and to connect movement with meaning and context. I find Banes's article more balanced and less polemic than Gottschild's by viewing Balanchine from a more well rounded, less defensive perspective.

This brief review reveals at least two important elements germane to the topic at hand. First, in our era of concern for authenticity, the question of "whose ballet is it?" looms: ballet is ethnic in the sense that it originated in a certain time with certain people. It is also a steadily adapting form, where an individual, drawing on sources outside ballet, can bring about major shifts as Balanchine did. As Joan Acocella said in a recent *New Yorker* article about Twyla Tharp: "Ballet combined with 'lower' form? Big deal. That's what Marius Petipa did in *Swan Lake,* combining ballet with folk dance. It's also what Balanchine did, crossing ballet with jazz dance. Like other great forms, ballet has good digestion: you can feed it almost anything" (Acocella 2001, 106).

But being adaptable is not the same as being universal or acultural. Today, rooted in our own times, we find the cultural vestiges that come along with the form are anachronistic, or racist, sexist, and so forth. Ann Daly, who wrote some of the most widely read applications of feminist theory to consideration of ballet and criticized postmodern choreographers for borrowing the ballet vocabulary with its offending ideology, has seen fit to reconsider her earlier writings (see Daly 1987, 1991, 1997). In a thoughtful contribution to the 2000 *Dance Research Journal,* Daly reflects on the fact that no theory (i.e., the male gaze) can remain eternally relevant. In "Using Lexicons for Performance Research: Three Duets," Marcia Siegel rebuts Daly's earlier article with a close reading of the movement in a duet from Balanchine's "Four Temperaments." Siegel shows how the Balanchine woman is as much or more active than the male, not at all a manipulated puppet (Siegel 1997, 214–15).

Ballet's idealization of form also opposes our contemporary notion of individual freedom and creative expression. Blumenfeld-Jones's assertion that dancers often equate structured knowledge (form) with limiting personal freedom comes to mind (1987, 21). Ballet does prefer a certain body type (limber, long-limbed, flexible feet) although nature and nurture play roles in the training of a professional ballet dancer through the combination of "natural selection" and the creating of the body through the training itself. This is surely in opposition to the postmodern or post-Judson everybody. Yet, despite these things that plague us, that prompt our resentment and resistance, ballet marches on, embracing more dancers in its fold than ever before.

conclusion

In the more recent Daly article, a particular sentence stood out: "Of course, the overlooked methodology in 'Hummingbirds' is movement analysis" (2000, 40). Movement analysis can enlighten in many contexts. In terms of style, and in our case of ballet, some essential elements seem to be consistent and form what Laban analyst Billie Lepczyk has called "the baseline of movement values."[4] Copeland's article outlined the emphasis on lightness and verticality (1986). From Lepczyk's dissertation contrasting three movement styles including ballet using the Laban perspective: "Although uprightness is fundamental proper alignment, it has expressive value in ballet" (1981, 57).

Similarly, Kealiinohomoku states: "The notion of tension through the etymology of European words for dance does reveal something about the Western aesthetic of dance which is apparent from the Western dance ideals of pull-up, body lift and bodily extensions" (1983, 542).[5] Theatrical legibility is in part "responsible" for the outward rotation of the legs (turn-out), another hallmark of the ballet style, and is connected to the expressive values of extroversion, presentation, and grandeur as explored by writers such as André Levinson and Lincoln Kirstein.

Some of these "movement values" will share elements with other styles, some will not. For instance, ballet presents a qualitative dualism in terms of the upper and lower body: the upper half (head, arms, shoulders) most often exemplifies the qualities of light (Weight), indirect (Space), and free (Flow), while the lower body is strong, direct, and bound. Naturally there are choreographic moments when this "rule" does not apply, but by and large, in the class, it does. Other dance styles may have upper body gestures that are predominately strong and bound, or relatively neutral. Another example: comparing a Tharp dance to a ballet (not including passages or dances where she borrows the ballet vocabulary directly), the use of passive weight or "weightiness" in her style contrasts to the more active lightness in ballet. How she works with ballet will differ from dance to dance, but the fact that we can still make observations about two different styles is significant, and points to the fact that a particular style represents a collection of movement values.

How does this relate to the post-Judson dancer standing at the *barre?* As dance styles merge, collide, collage, hybridize, layer, and otherwise mix it up, it becomes essential for the choreographer and dancer, not only the scholar, to recognize the cultural or individual contexts behind movement values. Some styles will die out, while others will prevail. Do we really want any form of dance, or any kind of training that is "style-free"? What would that train for, and what would it really give the dancer as an artist? The best teachers of ballet for any dancer would be those who not only make the "ballet-ness" of ballet the most discernible, legible, and useful, but also the most intriguing, challenging, and rewarding. They may accomplish it in many ways in infinite variations, even incorporating nonballet elements or systems (Pilates, Alexander Technique, etc.), but when the class is unrecognizable as ballet, surely it has missed the mark.

In addition to the historical and cultural legacy (or baggage to some) that comes along with ballet, the dancer experiences the technique on a highly personal level, a bodily or somatic one. For nearly every human, studying the technique is challenging and rigorous. For the professional ballet dancer, the artificiality of the style becomes ingrained, as the "effortless of expertise" develops. Each body will experience the particular shapes, steps, and rhythms of the ballet vocabulary in accordance with his or her physical makeup, training background, and even psychological relationship to the material. I recently listened to a dancer refer to a period where she "broke up with ballet," an apt expression of the dangers and complications of passionate, and possibly overextended engagement.

The post-Judson dancer may have to contend with the particular rigors of a form that offers challenges: keeping the back extended going down into *grand plié,* pointing the foot every time it leaves the floor, struggling for balance and aplomb, and so forth. Why should these experiences be nullified or avoided? With that kinesthetic experience, and an understanding of the style, the dancer or choreographer can engage in comparative analysis. One might ask: "How is this different from what I perform? How is it similar? How can I use what I experience here in *my* dances? What am I choosing *not* to use from this vocabulary?"

The post-Judson dancer may ask: "Why adopt, even for an hour and a half, an aristocratic *hauteur* from an undemocratic and strictly gendered time? Why not just concentrate on the more utilitarian side of things: working on vertical alignment, speed, strength, leg/pelvis interaction, and so on?" Feeling silly or false in a style that is unfamiliar (or too familiar) and reinforces gender stereotypes (whether you are the princess or the prince) cannot be underestimated. However, embracing the style may actually help to make the *épaulement* and the turn-out functional, and to grow stronger, faster, more articulate.

The early Judson experimentalists shied away from the cult of the personality and at the same time both freely adopted alternate personae with irony and wit, and revealed parts of themselves that were not glamorous, theatrical, or presentational. Dancers and choreographers who descend from that legacy, and in doing so are trying to find ways of moving that feel right and authentic should indeed ask themselves: why ballet? I believe the deeper engagement in the style will not only facilitate the technique, but also demonstrate how the two are linked and give more meaning to the class. Moving beyond the strictly utilitarian approach to the class may give the dancer more than he or she bargained for.

notes

1. See the new introduction in the Wesleyan edition of Sally Banes's *Terpsichore in Sneakers*: "In a sense, Cunningham moved away from modern dance by synthesizing it with certain aspects of ballet. Those who came after him rejected synthesis altogether" (1987, xvi).
2. Refer again to Banes's introduction: "gravity, dissonance, and a potent horizontality of the body . . . oppositional qualities applied to moderns" (1987, xiii).
3. "*Her* body flames with the charge wanting of so many eyes, yet like a flame it has no substance. *She* is . . . the phallus, and *he* embodies the forces that pursue, guide and manipulate it" (Foster 1996, 3).

4. "A Contrastive Study in Movement Style through the Laban Perspective" (Lepczyk, 1981) investigates the "core movement values" of ballet and the work of two modern dance choreographers, Graham and Tharp.
5. For further comments on the quality of lightness in ballet, see Melanie Bales, "Ballet Class and LMA: Style as a Resource for Comparative Learning" in the 1996 Congress on Research in Dance (CORD) proceedings.

works cited

Acocella, Joan. 2001. "Boogie and Beyond." *The New Yorker,* March 12.

Banes, Sally. 1987. *Terpsichore in Sneakers.* Hanover, N.H.: Wesleyan University Press.

———. 1993. *Democracy's Body: Judson Dance Theater, 1962–1964.* Durham, N.C.: Duke University Press.

———. 1994. *Writing Dancing in the Age of Postmodernism.* Hanover, N.H. and London: Wesleyan University Press.

———. 1999. "Sibling Rivalry: The New York City Ballet and Modern Dance." In Lynne Garafola, ed., with Eric Foner, *Dance for a City: Fifty Years of the New York City Ballet.* New York: Columbia University Press.

Blumenfeld-Jones, Donald S. 1987. "Form, Knowledge and Liberation in Dance: A Philosophical Inquiry," in CORD annual conference Proceedings, 1987.

Copeland, Roger. 1986. "The Objective Temperament: Post-Modern Dance and the Rediscovery of Ballet." *Dance Theatre Journal* 4, no. 3 (Autumn).

Daly, Ann. 1987. "The Balanchine Woman: Of Hummingbirds and Channel Swimmers." *The Drama Review,* vol. 31, no. 1 (Spring): 8-21.

———. 1991. "Unlimited Partnership: Dance and Feminist Analysis." *Dance Research Journal,* vol. 23, no. 1 (Spring): 2–5.

———. 1997. "Classical Ballet: A Discourse of Difference." In Jane C. Desmond, ed., *Meaning in Motion: New Cultural Studies of Dance.* Durham, N.C.: Duke University Press.

———. 2000. "Feminist Theory Across the Millennial Divide." *Dance Research Journal,* vol. 32, no. 1 (Summer).

Foster, Susan L. 1996. "The Ballerina's Phallic Pointe." In Susan Leigh Foster, ed., *Corporealities: Dancing, Knowledge, Culture, and Power.* New York: Routledge.

Gordon, Suzanne. 1983. *Off Balance: The Real World of Ballet.* New York: Pantheon.

Gottschild, Brenda Dixon. 1995. "Stripping the Emperor: The Africanist Presence in American Concert Dance." In David Gere, ed., with Lewis Segal, Patrice Koelsch, and Elizabeth Zimmer, *Looking Out: Perspectives on Dance and Criticism in a Multicultural World.* New York: Schirmer.

Kealiinohomoku, Joann. 1983. "An Anthropologist Looks at Dance." In Marshall Cohen and Roger Copeland, eds., *What Is Dance? Readings in Theory and Criticism.* New York: Oxford University Press.

Leo, Anna. 1990. "In Defense of Ballet, or, Some New Ideas about an Old Technique." Ohio State University. Unpublished manuscript. Used by permission of author.

Lepczyk, Billie Frances. 1981. "A Contrastive Study of Movement Style in Dance through the Laban Perspective." Ph.D. diss., Teachers College, Columbia University.

Siegel, Marcia B. 1997. "Using Lexicons for Performance Research: Three Duets." *New Approaches to Theatre Studies and Performance Analysis.* Papers presented at the Colston Symposium, Bristol. Tübingen: Max Niemeyer Verlag.

part ii

deconstruction

The contributions in Part II present discussions on the facet of dance training we have designated with the term, "deconstruction," as outlined in the Introduction. Referring to training as a deconstructive process, Elizabeth Dempster describes the dancer's body as "a living structure which continually adapts and transforms itself. It is a body available to the play of many discourses" (1995, 32). Indeed, the last twenty-five years have seen a burgeoning of practices within the dance training arena that offer methods for repatterning, finding movement efficiency, or ridding the body of unwanted habits of movement. These practices fall under the umbrella term *somatics* and include such practices as Bartenieff Fundamentals, Alexander Technique, Feldenkrais Awareness Through Movement, Ideokinesis, and Body-Mind Centering, among others.

When one considers current dance writing, or peruses the curriculum of most dance departments and contemporary dance studios such as Movement Research or Dance New Amsterdam in New York City, it is evident that somatics has become an integral part of the dance scene. When Martha Myers began offering the body therapies at the American Dance Festival beginning in 1969 dancers studied practices such as the Alexander Technique or Bartenieff Fundamentals in tandem with their dance classes. "Nobody was integrating," according to Myers, "It wasn't there" (see Chapter 7, page 91). The following generation, however, attempted to integrate dance and somatic practices. Others have begun to question the viability of traditional dance techniques altogether. Jane Hawley, a colleague teaching at Luther College in Iowa has devised a new curriculum for the dance students, where they are no longer offered courses in traditional techniques such as modern, jazz, and ballet. Instead, their course of study includes Movement Fundamentals I, II, and III: Practices of Alignment and Function, Range and Efficiency, and Vocabulary and Intention, respectively. Contact Improvisation is also a key component in the training sequence.

This begs a key distinction between definitions of training: learning existing vocabularies and deriving technical skills from the study, whether or not a dancer performs in that style, or focusing on the skills themselves through alternative practices. Other questions surrounding the issue of nondance movement practices (of which somatic practices are a subset) in dance training arise, such as:

— Are there aesthetic values embedded in bodywork systems, and if so, are dancers and teachers aware of this?
— Are dance and somatics really at cross-purposes?
— If dancers use movement practices outside traditional modern dance classes in part to "debrief" their bodies of unwanted patterns or tension they may have acquired in technique class, what does that say about the dance training itself?
— Are technique teachers utilizing somatics in an effort to develop a "style-free" technique?
— Will a teaching style based on somatics also become gradually codified, as in modern styles such as Graham, Cunningham, and Limón?

These and other related questions are illuminated in the chapters in Part II.

Included in the following chapters are a variety of styles and perspectives from the dance science and somatics fields. First is an interview with Martha Myers (Chapter 7), a pioneer in the field who was instrumental in bringing the somatic work into the dance arena, beginning in 1969, via the American Dance Festival (ADF) and through her seminal 1983 article "Body Therapies and the Modern Dancer: The New Science in Dance Training." In this interview, Myers describes the early period in the development of somatics in dance at ADF, discussing the influence of these practices on choreography and issues comprising style.

Chapter 8, "First It Was Dancing: Reflections on Teaching Dance and Alexander Technique" describes a dance and Alexander Technique teacher's journey through the process of integrating two seemingly incongruous approaches to teaching. The author's questions and points for discussion are enlightened by comments from six other professional dancers whose work has been influenced by the Alexander Technique. The issues raised in the chapter are applicable to the intersection of any of the somatic practices and dance technique teaching.

In Chapter 9, "Re-Locating Technique," Wendell Beavers updates and comments upon his 1993 article for *Movement Research Performance Journal.* He discusses the usage of the word "technique," the revolution and evolution of "new technique," springing first from Mabel Todd, who published *The Thinking Body* in 1937. An influential teacher, Beavers is still active in downtown dance circles and shares some thoughts on what in dance has meaning and significance for him.

Dance educator and physical therapist Glenna Batson exposes two different theories of human posture and movement, and discusses the paradoxes that exist between the objective and experiential points of view in Chapter 10,

"Teaching Alignment: From a Mechanical Model to a Dynamic Systems One." Melanie Bales draws on Lakoff and Johnson's *Metaphors We Live By* and Laban Movement Analysis in Chapter 11, "Falling, Releasing, and Post-Judson Dance," where she links ideas on dance since the Judson era to notions about falling and gravity, meaning and metaphor.

The following readings, along with the bibliographies from the articles, are recommended for further information on some of the somatic practices referred to throughout Part II.

—Rebecca Nettl-Fiol

works cited

Dempster, Elizabeth. 1995. "Women Writing the Body: Let's Watch a Little How She Dances." In Ellen W. Goellner & Jacqueline Shea Murphy, eds. *Bodies of the Text* (New Brunswick, N.J.: Rutgers University Press, 1995).

suggested reading

Alexander, F. Matthias. *The Use of the Self.* New York: E. P. Dutton and Co., 1932. Reprinted by Long Beach, Calif.: Centerline Press, 1985.

Allison, Nancy, ed. *The Illustrated Encyclopedia of Body-Mind Disciplines.* New York: The Rosen Publishing Group, Inc., 1999.

Bainbridge Cohen, Bonnie. *Sensing, Feeling, and Action: The Experimental Anatomy of Body-Mind Centering.* Northampton, Mass.: Contact Editions, 1983.

Bales, Melanie. "Body, Effort, and Space: A Framework for Use in Teaching." *Journal of Dance Education* 6, no. 3 (2006): 72–77.

Barr, Sherrie. "Fundamentals and Dancing: Students Weaving the Link." *Impulse,* October 1996.

Bartenieff, Irmgard, and Dori Lewis. *Body Movement: Coping with the Environment.* New York: Gordon and Breach, 1980.

Batson, Glenna. "Dancing Fully, Safely, and Expressively—The Role of the Body Therapies in Dance Training." *Journal of Physical Education, Recreation, and Dance* 61, no. 9 (November–December 1990): 28–31.

———. "Stretching Technique: A Somatic Learning Model. Part 1: Training Sensory Responsivity; Part II: Training Purposivity through Sweigard Ideokinesis. *Impulse,* October 1993 and January 1994.

Brodie, Julie, and Elin Lobel. "Integrating Fundamental Principles Underlying Somatic Practices into the Dance Technique Class." *Journal of Dance Education* 4, no. 3 (2004): 80–87.

DeAlcantara, Pedro. *The Alexander Technique, A Skill for Life.* Ramsbury, Marlborough, Wiltshire, England: Crowood Press, 1999.

Dimon, Theodore, Jr. *A Brief History of Mind-Body Techniques.* Boston: Daystreet Press, 1998.

Dowd, Irene. *Taking Root to Fly.* Manchester, N.H.: Cummings Printing Co., 1981.

Eddy, Martha. "The Practical Application of Body-Mind Centering in Dance Pedagogy." *Journal of Dance Education* 6, no. 3 (2006): 86–91.

Feldenkrais, Moshe. *Awareness through Movement.* New York: Harper and Row, 1972.

Fortin, Sylvie. "Somatics: A Tool for Empowering Modern Dance Teachers." In Sherry B. Shapiro, ed., *Dance, Power, and Difference: Critical and Feminist Perspectives on Dance Education.* Champaign, Ill.: Human Kinetics, 1998.

———. "When Dance Science and Somatics Enter the Dance Technique Class." *Kinesiology and Medicine for Dance* 15, no. 3 (Spring/Summer 1993): 88–107.

———, and D. Siedentop. "The Interplay of Knowledge and Practice in Dance Teaching: What We Can Learn from a Non-Traditional Dance Teacher." *Dance Research Journal* 27, no. 2 (Fall 1995): 3–15.

Franklin, Eric. *Dance Imagery for Technique and Performance.* Champaign, Ill.: Human Kinetics, 1996.

———. *Dynamic Alignment through Imagery.* Champaign, Ill.: Human Kinetics, 1996.

Gelb, Michael J. *Body Learning,* 2nd edition. New York: Henry Holt and Co., 1994.

Green, Jill, ed. *Somatics in Dance Education.* Special edition. *Journal of Dance Education,* 2, no. 4 (2002).

Hackney, Peggy. *Making Connections: Total Body Integration through Bartenieff Fundamentals.* New York: Gordon and Breach, 1998.

Jones, Frank Pierce. *Freedom to Change: The Development and Science of the Alexander Technique.* London: Mouritz, Ltd., 1997.

Knaster, Mirka. *Discovering the Body's Wisdom.* New York: Bantam Books, 1996.

Myers, Martha. "Body Therapies and the Modern Dancer: The New 'Science' in Dance Training." *Dance Magazine,* February 1983.

———. "Dance Science and Somatics: A Perspective." *Kinesiology and Medicine for Dance* (Fall–Winter 1991–92).

Nettl-Fiol, Rebecca. "Alexander Technique and Dance Technique: Applications in the Studio." *Journal of Dance Education* 6, no. 3 (2006): 78–85.

Olsen, Andrea. *BodyStories, A Guide to Experiential Anatomy.* Barrytown, N.Y.: Station Hill Press, 1991.

Richmond, Phyllis. "The Alexander Technique and Dance Training." *Impulse,* January 1994.

Rolf, Ida P. *Rolfing: The Integration of Human Structures.* Harper and Row, 1977.

Sweigard, Lulu. *Human Movement Potential: Its Ideokinetic Facilitation.* New York: Dodd, Mead, 1974.

Todd, Mabel Elsworth. *The Thinking Body.* New York: Princeton Book Co., 1937.

rebecca nettl-fiol

7 somatics: a current moving the river of contemporary dance

an interview with martha myers

The following interview was conducted by Rebecca Nettl-Fiol with Martha Myers on August 2002, with a follow-up interview in November 2003.

rnf You have been instrumental in bringing the somatic work to the dance world through your foresight in hiring somatic practitioners at the American Dance Festival as early as 1969. Could you describe how you became interested in the field, and say a little about the term "somatics"?

mm The somatic systems are a gold mine, as vast a resource of information and insight for creating dances as they are for improving technical study and performance. The applications are vast, extending across disciplines from rehabilitation of the body to psychotherapy, nonverbal communication [understanding human interactions], anthropology, and beyond. While I have been interested in many of these areas, bringing multiple practitioners to the American Dance Festival

School (ADF), and Connecticut College, my own work has been in application to dance technique, coaching, choreography, and performance. This interest in finding new ways to move, and to escape expressive as well as motor habits drove my study and personal exploration of somatics, from the late fifties. When I became Dean of the Festival in 1969 I had a venue to help open this work to a broader audience in the dance world. It is entwined now with many other influences but still remains a base from which I still work in my Choreolab, occasional classes at ADF in Durham, North Carolina, in New York, and occasional residencies.

The term somatics covers many individual systems, each branch offering a particular point of view and practice to the whole. Over the past quarter century or so of growth, the field has developed a solid theoretical base. But its power rests on experiential work, "hands-on" between practitioner and pupil singly or in groups. Verbal explanation is an inadequate substitute at best. Like a dance concert, the work begs for live experience and examples. This is in part because it explores beneath the level of gross muscle action, to deal with subtleties of individual movement, deepening awareness—the critical ability to sense and respond to micro-movement of the soma. The aim is through this to "unravel"—as one somaticist has described it—old habitual neuromuscular patterns, and replace them with new, more efficient ones.

rnf Describe the early period of the development of somatics at ADF.

mm Yes, let's see. Charles [Reinhart] and I began in 1969, bringing in folks for the first time. At first, none of the faculty went to these classes, other than dear Thelma Hill. She was wonderful, and after she'd been to a couple of classes she came back to my office and said, "Oh wow! I don't know that I can ever teach again. This is incredible; how can I keep my students from knowing what I don't know?" And of course, therein lies the crux of the problem.

Other people walked out because they were scared to death. We all have that vulnerable place, that "God deliver me from ever revealing what I don't know." But we continued with anatomy and kinesiology, and each year I kept introducing a new body therapy. Now part of this, I must confess, came from selfish motivations. I was stuck in New London, Connecticut, and I was determined to learn something. That's been a tremendous motivation. I felt the kind of things I needed to know had to do with my teaching, and I presumed many teachers needed it. Since we had a number of people returning every year to ADF it seemed like a logical thing to do. We offered Feldenkrais, Alexander, we didn't have BMC [Body Mind Centering] until we moved to North Carolina; at that time BMC was still developing. And those classes gradually grew until there were waiting lists for them in North Carolina. But that was quite far along; in the beginning, it depended upon the teacher as to how popular those classes were.

rnf Did you usually offer the somatics separately? For instance, did people take a Feldenkrais class and then dance technique, or did you try to get someone that integrated that work into their technique class?

mm Honey, nobody was integrating. It wasn't there.

rnf I'm an Alexander technique teacher, so I am interested to know if other dance teachers who also practice Alexander try integrating any of it into dance technique class, or whether they feel it's more effective not to. Or do they use it as their own knowledge base, without making a conscious effort to try to synthesize the material?

mm One of the things that Donna Krasnow [Department of Dance, Centre of Fine Arts, Toronto] says they have discovered in research on imaging, was that people who only did imaging didn't improve. Because it was too hard, from the feedback the subjects got, for them to be thinking about that at the same time they were trying to learn a complicated movement.

rnf Right—it's the transfer to training issue that's really interesting.

mm I know when I tried to teach it at Conn [University of Connecticut], we made it a requirement. If we hadn't I'm not sure anybody would have come.

rnf What was the requirement?

mm Something that I called Body in Motion. But it wasn't so much motion; it was lying on the floor, doing a combination of these things that I had integrated from Laban [Bartenieff Fundamentals]. It was offered right before a technique class, so they would sort of stagger in to technique after that, having worked internally for an hour and a half, having to suddenly switch their gears. Finally it occurred to me that that might not be ideal, and eventually we shifted things. Those are the kinds of things we were learning then.

rnf So you didn't feel it was good to have this experience right before technique class?

mm No. The students said it didn't work for them. It seems to me that it is interesting for it to be a separate class someplace, but then some of it has to be at least referred to in a technique class, so that there is some kind of follow-up integration.

rnf I feel we have a nice situation here at the University of Illinois [Dance Department] because I teach an Alexander for Dance class, which is an elective class. And we have several other teachers who are also Alexander teachers and can use the vocabulary in the right situation, especially if the students have already had some Alexander lessons. Unless there is some familiarity though, I find the students can resent having that material brought into technique class.

mm I think you're right. Or even if they don't resent it, it just goes over their heads.

rnf Or they think they know something that they don't know. But when you can make the right formula for them, it can really be exciting.

mm And what it does provide, which we don't in dance—and this has always perplexed me—is that we are the only art form that has no individual instruction. Nada. So the body therapies are one way to go with this. Although everything that we brought to ADF had to be taught in groups. The Laban work, particularly the Fundamentals, can be done in small groups. So the somatics teachers who came were often learning to work with groups as they taught; June Ekman has taught Alexander for groups.

rnf A lot of people try. We do the best we can with that.

mm It is tricky, but it offers dance students an opportunity to get hands-on work, which can make for significant improvement.

rnf Could you discuss your use of somatics in the teaching of choreography?

mm The value of the various somatic systems was evident to me in teaching dance technique back in the seventies. Even earlier I had read Laban, and Alexander, but didn't integrate these into my thoughts and practice of choreography until later than that. Perhaps my body had to absorb it before it could function for me creatively. But for the past twenty-five years those ideas have been of equal importance to the explorations I direct in Choreolab. I don't claim to teach choreography—at least not directly. But I am interested in what happens when we begin to examine some of the "givens" of inventing movement: gestures, posture, organization of steps, initiation of movement, use of body parts: thorax, pelvis, legs/feet, head, facial expression. The "how" of the body-in-motion is the "what" of the images we see in performance. Taking all of the above apart, scrambling syntax, syllables, combining and recombining them as in strands of DNA to see "what happens," can be greatly aided by somatic referents. Many times, out of this cauldron a germ of material will emerge, ferment, and produce the beginnings of a piece.

The somatic work opens doors for me, incredibly, in terms of what I see, so then I can help the students open doors. I'm of the school that 99 percent of the choreography is performance. I don't mean that as a denigration of formal tools, which I deeply believe in. But the flick of a wrist makes all the difference in the world in terms of the quality of movement. How that flick is done, and what it is. We all know that.

I recall observing a student performing several long phrases from a work-in-progress. Her torso remained virtually unchanged (held in vertical tension) with no visible change of shape or shaping in her upper body as she breathed. Thus there was no fluctuation in the intensity of her involvement in the movement other than in disassociated gesture. Participants gave their responses, one describing the performance as static—a blanket term. I try to tease out what's under the blanket. What you have is a further collection of words, more descriptive; but beneath those are even more difficult psychogenic factors that contribute to this picture. Suggestions from several somatic practices suggest themselves, such as noting the performer's use of her weight (back on her heels); exploring movement from different quadrants of her torso (upper/lower, right/left, diagonally right/left), sensing her spine widening and lengthening, the head riding freely on top. These made a small but visible change—the movement became softer, yet projected more energy than before, and a new liveliness infused her face. The circumstances of a choreography session necessarily limit the deep personal work needed to bring about more permanent changes. But often, I have found, insight will occur as explorations of new ways of moving give a performer glimmers of new ways of sensing his or her self. It has led to some "aha" responses—which can be the catalyst for a fruitful journey.

I have wondered if the changes I see in a participant's performance in Lab, after such simple experiments in the dynamics of movement, might not be a delusion, a conjuring job rather than something evident, "out there," as a skeptical friend suggested. Most often, however, others in class recognize the change also. This is different from asking if others see what I see, or insinuating that they ought—a definite no-no! Anyway, be assured they won't—certainly not always. But, in fact this is the kind of discussion that is the crux of our sessions. I have found the vocabulary of Laban Movement Analysis (LMA), particularly helpful addressing the vast and often elusive components of body expression and behavior. It has been tested by its practitioners to verify agreement among trained observers watching a movement sequence, and has been consistently high in observer consistency and accuracy. I am an educated layman in my use of the LMA language; but I have been astonished at how profoundly the concepts can affect a performer's qualities of movement, and extend a choreographer's range of expression. This is, of course, only a part of the choreographic process.

rnf What you are talking about here is coaching?

mm Yes, but it can give a whole other meaning to the choreography. And you put that together with what they've done formally, and you try to work the front and the back against the middle. I think if you have experienced in your own body a variety of qualities of movement, and have the—I want to say mind-body training because technical training is not only the body—then you have the means to expand your range of qualities. For instance, I am a light mover and I had to learn to connect with my pelvis . . . If anybody heard us talking, by the way, they would say we were both mad! "What do you mean, connect with your pelvis?" But sensing the weight, in other words: to be able to manipulate degrees of weight, or degrees of lightness, any of these things, to not become stuck or stale. And have no idea that you are stuck. Which makes all your choreography look exactly alike! And even if you can't get it out of yourself, for heaven's sake, if you know about it and understand it, perhaps as a choreographer you can recognize it when you're picking people for your company, and then help them grow.

To summarize, my experience with somatic information has deepened my understanding of choreographic processes as manifest in the body. It has helped to integrate the more abstract of these—space and time—and to organize it all into some apprehendable whole. It is an essential part of my ongoing experience with "making things"—things that I, and the participants in Choreolab, believe will offer others moments of experiencing the world freshly, insightfully. It has helped me to "see" more accurately, and to respond on more levels (even if I invent them myself) to the work I view, to go beyond a simplistic visual registry and to explicate something beyond a "gut" response.

rnf Do you see the influence of somatics in choreography in the field in general?

mm New techniques (which became also forms of performance) entering the mainstream of dance in the past fifteen or twenty years, such as "release" and "contact," were directly influenced by somatic techniques. They are also an amalgam of principles and practices from other sources—especially Eastern systems of bodily training, and psychogenic practices that became popular through the Esalen Center in California. As technique inevitably repatterns and shapes the body, it also deeply affects choreography emerging from it. So these systems of neuromuscular repatterning have spawned new visual and contextual styles, altering how the messages are received, and how they "mean." All movement techniques send their special signals, signs, and cognates; they stimulate us nonverbally, and elicit from us new body-mind responses, both as audience and practitioners.

Somatics has also affected basic elements of technique, such as alignment, offering new models for teaching it. Each system gives new information: from BMC, a consideration of how the organs affect stance, or Alexander's emphasis on release of the spine—widening and lengthening. Quite different from those days I remember at the *barre,* with a teacher who tapped us on the back, or back of the leg to urge us to "stand up straight." Posture is not just a question of aesthetic taste (although it is still that to a degree), it is the base from which we create qualities of movement, and from these define character. Thus for better or worse, technique is not separate from choreography.

rnf Do you see any inherent conflict between somatic practices and choreographic or aesthetic choices? You talked about it a little bit in your 1991 article, "Dance Science and Somatics: A Perspective," from *Kinesiology and Medicine for Dance,* about "good" versus "bad" movement; people getting ideas that maybe certain kinds of movements are acceptable or good movements, and other movements aren't.

mm The more I notice about alignment, and become aware of all aspects of movement—the anatomical, the qualitative, the emotional—things stand out like "roots sticking up," and that will drive me crazy sometimes. For example, when a dancer has an extreme lumbar lordosis [concave, contracted lower spine], or even a moderate version, I find it aesthetically unpleasant. Not only does it allow the viscera and organs to protrude forward of the pelvic bowl, but also it bothers me because it is the stance of a very young child. Or, conversely, a chronically forward-riding head and shuffling feet will conjure up the gait of the elderly. Alignment is our emotional and physical history written on our bones. What is learned in the studio, if learned mechanically, reads as the same mindlessness on stage. But a "mind-in-motion" creates poetry within flexion and extension, or finding just the right tone in a tilt versus a turn of the head, sensing the energy extending beyond the borders of the limbs, the full dimensionality of the body. It brings a range of movement options within the dancer's control. Any deviation from a posture as close to "neutral" as possible compromises access to one or another or all of the subtle variations needed to participate in and fulfill the choreographer's vision. In dance one works to become as clear a vessel as possible, but this doesn't mean mechanical. The neuromuscular patterns and body attitude learned in the studio walks onto the stage unchanged. If this smacks of retro-values in a "celebrity culture," perhaps it's not too forbidden to consider alternatives to the "going thing" as a creative artist?

rnf You are talking about these issues as a viewer of choreography.

mm Yes, but that's really what our goal is. What worries me is that not everyone sitting in the audience has a background in this material, and they may not know what's wrong anatomically, but the emotional overtones, the psychological implications of what's happening on stage comes through. We are all adept at reading movement.

rnf Right, that's true. Again, I was reading in your article about how some of the professional dancers really rejected the whole idea of somatics; it was a newer idea then, now it seems everybody knows about it. Do you feel the professional world still rejects the field of somatics, or is it more accepted?

mm Without any question, there's more tolerance, if not actual embracing.

rnf And do you see some choreography as influenced by it?

mm The Trisha Brown company technique is one that has been based on somatics for years, as has that of [Erick] Hawkins. It has given those companies the basic qualities that comprise their "style." The practices of "release" and "contact" forms and performance also derive in part from somatics. That is evident in younger choreographers such as David Dorfman, Jeremy Nelson, Mark Jarecki, Stephen Petronio, Ron Brown, Claire Porter, and Wendell Beavers when he was still actively performing. The next generation has added new sources—such as hip-hop and club styles to the lexicon.

rnf How do you both teach students to make safe and intelligent choices in their dancing and at the same time challenge them to push their limits?

mm That's always a question. And I think at the beginning with somatics, everybody was oohing and ahhing . . . saying, "No no no, can't do this, shouldn't do that." I think a lot of that has softened. I think anybody in his right mind comes around to the conclusion that if you run a racecar, you might be running the risk of hitting the wall. Dancing is a dangerous profession. I'm being hyperbolic, but it is. And what's sneaky about that, for students, is that it may not be immediately apparent. Having lived this long, I have students in their fifties and sixties, so I have seen quite a bit, and part of it has to do with bodily structure. Just the other day, a professional dancer who is well known had an MRI done and was told that he had no cartilage left in his knee. He started dance late, and he pushed, as we all do—I'm sure that's why I have had two hip replacements. I started dancing seriously relatively late, and I pushed, taking many, many ballet classes with limited turnout. When you start in your early twenties or even late teens and you push too hard, it's not good. Too many deep *pliés* are a no-no. And they don't do any good anyway. I was writing about that twenty-five or thirty years ago, and now the research is finally proving me right!

rnf And now what I'm observing is that everyone is doing yoga.

mm Yes, and yoga's marvelous. But another thing that Donna's [Krasnow] research showed is that training for alignment in stillness and alignment in motion are two different things. Then there is another thing. My husband is a big baseball fan: I was talking to him this morning, and he said that in baseball, you see people with the craziest swings; they break every rule in the book. And yet they hit homers, you know, season after season after season. And look at Baryshnikov, who really doesn't have the greatest turnout, and manages to spring up to heaven.

rnf What's that telling us?

mm One of the things I really truly believe in is the value of getting tested for muscular balance. For trying to know what their limits are, which leg is more turned out than the other, what their real turnout is like, how they can increase that safely. I compare it to psychotherapy: begin to know yourself, know your structure, and have some sense of what you can do. And by the way, we don't know our limits. The orthopedist might say that you have only so much range of motion at your joint, but that doesn't necessarily limit you technically, or limit the illusions that you can create. That's really what Gerry [Gerald Myers] was talking about this morning. You can be taught the right way and all the right rules. But there is always someone who comes along and defies the rules. What you do in performance, in motion when you're dancing, may be quite different from what you can do by focusing on alignment.

rnf It makes you wonder, do we need to spend all that time?

mm I really wonder if we need to spend all that time doing technique. What we suffer from most in terms of injury is repetition. So if one could cut down on the amount of repetition, in *barre* work, for instance—but then you have all that repetition in rehearsal. But at least you don't have both of them.

rnf It seems that some of the most active performing dancers in New York don't take technique classes.

mm No, they don't. And maybe that's good.

rnf They're the ones that are doing the somatic work, or the conditioning work, or . . .

mm . . . yoga or Pilates. It's good on one level, but again, it may not be stretching them qualitatively. Something that the body therapies do well is micro-level muscular action. Ballet dancers are still taking daily classes. It's the modern dancers, partly because they don't have any well-defined technical standards to fulfill. You know what I mean by that? Each choreographer's technique is totally different: what David Dorfman is demanding of them, Trish Brown isn't. There aren't any absolute standards of performance. What they are asked to do often has no name, it doesn't have three hundred years of perfection that has to be met. If you look back to [Martha] Graham or Merce [Cunningham] or Trisha [Brown], the really top folks have invented their own techniques. Including [Paul] Taylor, who took Martha's and twitched a little this way and a little that way . . .

rnf Although Trisha has never really developed a technique class. She just expects her dancers to be warmed up for rehearsal.

mm . . . and ready to go. Then she brings the people to her studio who can make the kind of dancer she wants to see.

rnf And then there was always the idea of the generic technique class.

mm Oh, well, that's a myth, that's a total myth.

rnf For a while I read about that, but not so much lately. I think people have rejected that idea.

mm They haven't rejected it; they've given up on it! But the other thing that humbles us deeply in dance, is that maybe the whole damn thing is genetic. In other words, maybe these fabulous dancers came out of the tube that way! But I do think the bottom line is that somatics work has made a big difference, and I think gradually more and more people will be aware of it and integrate it into their classes. I hope so. One more thing, however: I'm worried about Pilates. I think Pilates is wonderful, and one of the best at strengthening. I used to object a little bit to the fact that it was so vertical and two-dimensional, but they have gotten machines now that work you in other dimensions, and that's marvelous, and very important because our muscles don't grow up and down, they go around. Pilates has been on the dance scene for maybe a decade, but lately it has gotten so much play from Hollywood. It is all over the place. I think that should worry dancers. If it is the latest fad, it will also be the latest lost fad. The waiting list for Pilates at ADF this summer was two pages long. And again, it's a form of conditioning; it doesn't do anything for quality. However, it might allow dancers to extend their qualitative range of movement as they extend control.

rnf Here at the University, we used to think the students needed two classes a day: ballet and modern. Now there is a need to offer them other things such as somatic work, but there are only so many hours in the day; it gets complicated considering it all.

mm It's very complicated. And we struggle with this at ADF; we've struggled with this at school too.

rnf Maybe they only need one class a day, but make the class two hours, so some time can be devoted to somatic work.

mm Yeah!

rnf Then maybe we can fit all of it in. I am looking at what people are doing in the professional world to see how it relates to how we design our training component of the curriculum at the university; we are the ones preparing the dancers to go out into the profession. Here is where they are getting their technical training, their foundation. And when they get to New York, they don't or can't take class regularly.

mm That's right, and they don't have time for it, because they're working, rehearsing.

rnf What trends are you seeing in training currently, and where do you see it going in the future?

mm Walk into a dance studio in almost any part of this country, and you will see students warming up with floor movement that is derived from Irmgard Bartenieff's Fundamentals, often without any knowledge of their source. Watch the beginning of class and you'll hear as well, directions, injunctions that remind you of Ideokinesis, Body-Mind Centering, Alexander, or the Trager System. Somatics has become a current moving the river of a majority of contemporary dance performers today. It is taught in various guises in colleges and universities across the U.S. and has migrated to Europe, where some of the systems originated.

Does somatic work risk falling into history as so many training techniques in the past have? Possibly . . . but more likely, it will be absorbed into the mainstream of the culture, as so many innovative ideas and practices are. On the other hand, influences from mainstream sources such as medicine and rehab can be seen in somatics, as its practitioners incorporate personal educational backgrounds into their work. An evident model is that of modern dance and ballet, which innovative young choreographers use interchangeably in their works. Within a world of ever more rapid transformations, "purity" goes.

A number of young artists in New York today don't study dance technique at all—certainly not as it was known before the eighties. They have made their own fresh compounds from principles and materials of the various somatic systems. One of the tenets of early modern dance was that each work must have its own newly minted vocabulary. Truth is, there are only so many movements or movement modules—units of movement—to get you from here to there. But there are an infinite number of combinations, and a universe of qualitative resources with which to invent fresh material from these. Somatic study offers dancers and actors an especially rich data bank from which to draw. The primary systems have evolved over a quarter century, some far beyond that, developing principles of safe and efficient neuromuscular patterning. Understood and practiced properly, any one of them, or a combination, can help dancers move with more ease, extend their range of qualities, and survive careers in dance that make ever increasing demands on the body.

rebecca nettl-fiol

8 first it was dancing

reflections on teaching and alexander technique

before zen, a mountain is a mountain.
during zen, a mountain is no longer a mountain.
after zen, a mountain is once again a mountain.
—zen proverb

When I was about halfway through my Alexander Technique training some fifteen years ago, people began asking me, "How is this study affecting your dance teaching?" "Good question," I would respond. How were these recent discoveries, these extraordinary insights that were so profoundly affecting my own use, influencing the way I taught dance technique? Wouldn't the answer be obvious? Wasn't I already an expert in matters of the mechanics of the body, having taught dance technique and kinesiology for many years already? Wouldn't it simply be a matter of incorporating this information into my knowledge base, and then imparting this new understanding to my students through my dance technique teaching?

But wait, not so fast! Much of what I was learning in the Alexander Technique was to stop, to notice, to say no to my established habits, and replace them with new directions. Through hands-on work with a skilled teacher, I was learning about deeply ingrained habits that had persistently interfered with the most optimal use of my body. Through daily practice in the technique, I had begun to experience an ease, a lightness, a sense of freedom in my movement, not to mention a dramatic reduction in a chronic knee injury. What teacher doesn't wish to pass these kinds of revelations on to her students? However, I was also realizing during this time that as much as I wanted to share this extraordinary information, the learning process did not fall within the traditional dance technique format. In dance, we are in the business of *doing,* and Alexander Technique is rooted in the idea of *non-doing.* How could I reconcile this? How could I continue to ask groups of students to perform dance exercises and combinations when I could see even more clearly now the things they were doing wrong? My dance teacher's "eye" had improved significantly; at the same time, I had gained the understanding that what I had once thought were good "corrections" were simply ways of fixing symptoms, rather than getting at the root of the situation from a holistic or systemic perspective.

My whole system of teaching came into question. Can I make any kinds of significant changes for students within a technique class? How can we alter patterns that have taken years to develop? Do I continue giving corrections to students, or will that practice do more harm than good? How can I teach my newly-gained knowledge, normally learned in a quiet setting, taught one-on-one, while keeping a class moving and maintaining an appropriate energy level? If I begin to espouse Alexander principles, will I alienate the students? But if I don't share my expertise in Alexander Technique, won't I be guilty of withholding valuable information, tools that have the potential to enhance their dancing, reduce injuries, and change their perspectives on life? Have my responsibilities as a dance teacher changed now that I have a new area of expertise? I was in turmoil, unsure how to proceed in a field where I had once felt confident.

In the many years since I received my Alexander certification these questions continue to morph and evolve, but remain in some form or another. With the recent influx of the somatic practices into dance training, I recognize that these kinds of questions have arisen in relation to other practices such as Feldenkrais, Bartenieff Fundamentals, and Body-Mind Centering, among others. While discussing these matters from my perspective as an Alexander teacher, my aim is to elucidate points that relate to a greater picture—the intersection of somatics practices and dance training.

In my quest for deepening my own understanding, I decided to conduct interviews of other dance professionals whose work had been influenced by their study of Alexander Technique. I chose six dancers whose work I admire; three who are certified Alexander teachers, and three who have studied the technique extensively and though not certified in the technique, consciously use the principles in their teaching. The certified teachers include Anne Bluethenthal, a choreographer and dancer working in San Francisco, who completed her Alexander training in 1985; Shelley Senter, former dancer with the Trisha Brown Company, who received her certification from the American Center for Alexander Technique in 1994; and Luc Vanier, former dancer with Ohio Ballet, currently an Assistant Professor at the University of Wisconsin in Milwaukee, who trained at the Urbana Center for Alexander Technique 1998–2001. The other three interviewees are Chris Aiken, contact improvisation specialist who has engaged in a number of somatic practices, including a year on an Alexander training course; Kathleen Fisher, former Trisha Brown dancer, now dancing with Bebe Miller and Jane Comfort, who has studied Alexander for over twelve years; and Wil Swanson, also former Trisha Brown dancer, who studied Alexander and incorporates it into his dance technique teaching. (See Appendix B for short biographies of the interviewees.) The interviews took place over a two-year span, giving me food for thought, clarifying my own viewpoints, and providing insights into many of the questions embedded in the dance technique and somatics discussion.

the alexander technique

The Alexander Technique has become well recognized in the dance world—many dancers have had at least a taste of this work sometime in their training. But a brief explanation of the key principles will be useful in contextualizing the remainder of this essay. Clearly though, it is difficult to convey the experience one gets through private Alexander lessons. The metaphor often used is that it is like trying to explain what swimming is like without actually getting wet. I refer the reader to the Suggested Readings at the end of the chapter for more in-depth discussion of the origins and principles of the Alexander Technique, and to Appendix A for definitions of terms.

The Technique was developed by Frederick Matthias Alexander (1869–1955), an Australian actor and reciter who had suffered persistent vocal problems during his early career. Unable to get satisfactory treatment from the medical profession, he resorted to rigorous self-observation over a period of nine years, eventually discovering the patterns of misuse that had led him to his vocal troubles. In his case, the habits he found included the tendency to pull his head back and down, depressing his larynx, causing him to gasp for air. Discovery of the habit was not as profound as finding a method for interfering with this deeply ingrained pattern of misuse. Alexander observed that the specific habit could not be addressed without looking at the functioning of the whole organism, referred to as the *Self,* and when he was able to change the way he coordinated himself as a whole, his specific habits improved consequentially. In fact,

Alexander's vocal problems eventually disappeared, and he saw improvements in his health overall.

I can relate Alexander's story directly to my own experience, which I daresay is a typical scenario for many dancers. In my early twenties, I began to experience knee pain for seemingly no reason other than the increased activity during graduate school. I saw doctors, physical therapists, and specialists, all of whom had various remedies for me including ice, ibuprofen, rest, limiting range of motion (no *grands pliés*), weight lifting, and donning large rubber braces designed to support the kneecap. Each remedy worked for a short period of time, but the knee problems continued to plague me intermittently for several years. I began studying the Alexander Technique out of curiosity and interest in self-improvement overall, but was amazed when I noticed after only a few months that my knee pain had gradually disappeared altogether! My teacher never focused specifically on my knees during lessons but, rather, had gradually given me a new awareness of the habits and patterns of movement that had created the conditions for my knee problems. I had learned to redirect my thinking, and thus, my habitual patterns of holding and bracing myself gave way to a more efficient and better coordinated use.

Key concepts of the Alexander Technique include the following:

- The *self* is a *psychophysical unity;* a person acts as a whole, the body and mind cannot be separated. It follows that specific habits cannot be separated from the use of the whole self.
- The way you use yourself affects the quality of your *functioning.* To improve your *functioning* then, requires a change in the way you use yourself.
- One cannot rely on the sense of feeling to change habits. What we think we are doing is often not what we are actually doing. Alexander called this discrepancy *unreliable sensory appreciation.*
- Our tendency to achieve an immediate goal, or *end-gaining,* rather than paying attention to the process of getting there, leads to misuse.
- The dynamic relationship of the head to the neck, and of both the head and neck in relation to the back is central to one's coordination, balance, and functioning. This ever-changing relationship is termed *Primary Control.*
- In order to initiate change, it is necessary to *inhibit,* or prevent our automatic way of responding to a stimulus.
- After inhibiting the habitual response, the next step is *direction,* which involves a process of thinking with intention in preparation for movement. "It is not the degree of willing or trying but the way in which the energy is

directed, that is going to make the willing or trying effective." (Alexander, *The Use of the Self* [London: Mouritz, 2004], 57)

One of the greatest differences between dance training and learning the Alexander Technique is the focused individual attention one gets during private lessons. The teacher uses her hands, along with verbal instructions, to elicit changes in the student's fundamental movement patterns. In contrast to the vast majority of dance training which occurs in class situations, this one-on-one training offers the opportunity to receive specific feedback from a highly skilled instructor about patterns of movement and ingrained habits that one might be unaware of. The teacher provides supportive, nonjudgmental feedback, facilitating change and improvements in the student's overall use.

In my experience, dancers who study the Alexander Technique (myself included) go through the following steps (not necessarily always in this order). First, one becomes aware of a habit, or a pattern of misuse, either by self-observation or through a teacher or peer. Second, one learns to stop the initial response to the stimulus (Alexander referred to this as *inhibition*). This step is probably the most difficult one for dancers, because inherent in our training is the stimulus to "do" or even "overdo," rather than "not to do." Non-doing allows the space for something different to occur. A series of directions: "Allow the neck to be free, so that the head may go forward and up, and the back may lengthen and widen" is then applied, eliciting one's primary control, eventually giving one a feeling of expansion and ease in movement. For dancers, discovering the natural, dynamic force of the body's design can be both exhilarating and confusing. As one learns to let go of holding patterns that once felt "normal," it is common to go through stages of feeling lost, of not knowing, of perceiving that one is not working hard enough. Indeed, students often experience periods of frustration during the process of undoing and relearning; however gradually, over time, the gains can be quite profound and long-lasting.

the questions

What follows are the various questions that had been on my mind for years, with comments from the interviewees along with my own reflections on the topics. In our discussions, other significant questions arose, such as "What *is* dance technique," or "How do we look at training now versus twenty or thirty years ago?" Clearly, these are topics for exploration in other research; however, it is interesting to note the paradigm shift in training that spawns the interest in the incorporation of somatic practices within dance training situations. In early modern dance training, dancers sought to embody the technique, the style, and the ideals of a specific choreographer. More recently, dancers typically take technique class to empower themselves. The goal is to elicit the dancer's individuality within the movement. Contemporary choreographers tend to be interested in distinct dancers that have a keen understanding of themselves as artists, as well as being technically proficient.

Although the discussions that follow are based on the Alexander Technique specifically, I believe in most cases, they encompass a greater range within the field of somatics, and can be applied to other body-mind fields as well.

question 1 *Can the Alexander Technique be successfully incorporated into a dance technique class? Is this something we should strive for?*

This was my first overriding question. Is it possible, is it desirable, to mesh the Alexander Technique into a dance class? Or would it be best to leave the two forms separate in training dancers, maintaining the integrity of each? Anne Bluethenthal comments:

ab *I make a distinction between, "Can you teach Alexander principles?" and "Can you teach the Alexander Technique?" Because the answer is, you absolutely can't teach the Alexander Technique in a group of people. The real meat of the Alexander Technique happens one on one. Period. But can you teach principles? Absolutely, 100 percent. When you break down all the elements, everything is accessible, to anybody. There's nothing special, except they're all in a certain package. That's the Alexander Technique. Nowhere are you going to get that whole package except for in an Alexander lesson. You're not going to get the understanding of* primary control, *and you're not going to teach them* primary control *in a class. But you can make a lot of progress towards the other aspects of the Technique and awareness in general.*

Most teachers agreed that the Technique itself must be taught one-on-one, but that there were principles that could be explored in the context of a technique class. Several teachers described using improvisation as a tool to research some of the Alexander principles. Shelley Senter discusses her approach to integrating these principles into dance class:

ss *How the teacher directs the students' attention will affect how they learn to approach movement, whether "set" or improvised. I do this directly by saying the Alexander* directions *while students are moving, so that the directions can be included consciously while attending to the movement, or indirectly by distracting students* *from the movement itself, altering the* means whereby *they attend to it. I feel including a multi-directional awareness from the get-go is worth striving for, whether one is teaching a traditional technique class or an alternative kind of class.*

question 2 *Does the Alexander Technique influence the choices you make in designing the movement material for your classes?*

The Alexander Technique does not contain specific exercises or movement vocabulary from which to draw, as does, for example, Bartenieff Fundamentals, which is commonly utilized by dance teachers, including myself, in the development of technique class material. But because the Alexander Technique itself does not provide a series of movements, I was curious whether other teachers found impetus for movement invention, or felt they could use the movement choices they made as a vehicle for teaching Alexander concepts within a dance setting.

Anne Bluethenthal described a process of taking Erick Hawkins's exercises and redefining them for herself from an Alexander point of view.

ab *I still do the floor work and a lot of the vocabulary is similar, and the big part of what he works with is the center, the pelvis being the center of movement. It doesn't deal at all with the neck and head. But it's all very centrally initiated. So I don't stick to what he did, I really explicitly put in the Alexander words.*

Luc Vanier also works in a codified vocabulary, ballet. He describes one of the criteria he uses when making his choices of vocabulary:

lv *When I am choosing something within the ballet vocabulary, I'll choose something, first of all, that demands that the spine go from primary to secondary curves* [see Appendix A] *fairly quickly, and with a lot of fluidity. So I will resist giving an exercise that would ask students to be in primary or secondary curve for a long time. For example, to keep the arm in second position for a long period of time, I believe, is criminal for beginning students. It's much more beneficial for them to just keep taking the arm from first to second position, for example, as they're doing a* tendu *exercise, as opposed to holding it in second. If the arm is held too long, it's encouraging the back to stay in one or the other of the curves, depending on the student's habit. That can be problematic because it reduces the back's ability to adapt to the positions of the legs, the positions of the arms, and general coordination.*

Luc has designed an opening exercise for class that comes from his exploration of developmental movement through the Dart Procedures (see Appendix A):

lv *Informed by my exploration with developmental movement, my first exercise is my response, my own medicine if you will, to the rigidities that are sometimes present in ballet. So it's meant to be a very small antidote, so that if you do it gently over a period of time, you get to know your own personal patterns in regards to ballet. But the ballet class itself, the material comes from my tradition and from the teachers whom I most admired.*

Shelley Senter looks to the Alexander Technique for principles for movement invention:

ss *Some of the principles I draw upon for movement material include byproducts of my experience with the Alexander thinking: simplicity, specificity (specific thought—i.e., knowing what is the "head" vs. what is the "neck"), overlap and interruption of gesture (multi-directional thinking,* inhibition*), coordination (of thought and action). I have also been influenced by Trisha Brown's use of space. Some of her early pieces (*Locus, Set and Reset*) have taught me how to "see" space and use it as a support. Internal direction continues out into space, and the body (parts and whole) can follow it.*

Anne Bluethenthal also talks about finding exercises that are like *"positions of mechanical advantage—more advantageous for freeing up and getting some of the Alexander principles across. Then later, you can just throw yourself into a grande allegro (for example). At that point you say, 'Just dance and enjoy yourself. You don't worry about it.'"*

A consensus seems to be that the Technique is often used to inform the choices that are made, but it less frequently inspires the movement invention itself. Teachers, like Kathleen Fisher and Anne Bluethenthal, also noted that they approached the creative process less consciously the longer they had been teaching Alexander.

kf *I don't know if I'm designing the class material so consciously that way. But I feel like the work that I've done with it [Alexander Technique] is going to be in it. And the developmental forms are there in the way that I warm up. But the Technique has been a big influence on what movements I would do or not do, or the way I would put things together, or the time I would take with things.*

ab *What happens after awhile is that it's so much a part of me, that of course it informs everything I make up. Sometimes it's conscious and sometimes not. I think in the beginning, you just go make a bunch of stuff and then you look at what you've done and you break every minute down to see where you are getting "set," and if you can compromise a little bit less. And that was the beginning. But at this stage, it's* *more there for me in the moment. It's much less contrived than it was at the beginning, it's more organic now.*

In my own experience with movement invention for technique class, I strive to create movement that will give the students the easiest inroad into good coordination. This can best be described, I believe, as movement phrases that are musical in their inception, involve a recognition of the weights of the body, make use of momentum where appropriate, and encourage expansiveness of the whole system (body-mind). I aim to invent movement phrases that ask dancers to find efficiency and clarity, to "get out of their own way," so to speak, so that they have a chance to experience the sense of lightness, expansiveness, and freedom that is so often described by students after an Alexander lesson. My aim is to get at this through the way I build the movement material.

question 3 *Is there movement vocabulary that you avoid?*

This question emerged after I attended a workshop given by an Alexander/dance teacher where she identified particular dance movements that she no longer believed in. We all make choices about movement vocabulary for dance class based on our values, aesthetic preferences, and what we believe is most beneficial for training at any particular stage in the technical growth of the students. I was interested in knowing whether teachers with Alexander training made conscious decisions *not* to give certain dance movements or exercises.

Shelley Senter did not feel that she consciously avoided any movement vocabulary. Anne Bluethenthal, on the other hand, had made choices about certain movements of the spine that are typically taught in modern dance:

ss *Many modern dance classes begin with the roll down—no I don't do that. And I never do plough posture. That's one that I put in the category of "Why ever do it?" I avoid any of that joint rolling stuff. I don't think these things are necessarily damaging—I think the neck rolling is probably a little damaging—but I'm sure it's possible to do the rolling down without damaging yourself. I just don't find it a useful thing to do, for me. I think a lot of dance classes have elements that people just do because it feels good; because they've been doing it for so many years, and they just think it's necessity, they just really think that rolling through the whole thoracic spine is good because it feels good. While actually, what that area needs most is just to be left alone. It's so overused and so congested in most dancers, why not give it a break, and if anything, start thinking about the lower spine, because that tends to be more rigid.*

Luc Vanier has become more interested in how an exercise is introduced than what the components of the exercise are:

lv *I'm more interested in taking any movement and finding out, "So how does this work?" as opposed to saying "We're not going to do this because this is bad for you." For example, if I say, "In this exercise we're going to stand on* demi-pointe *the whole time," people are likely to prep themselves by doing something like squaring their jaw. If I can insert* demi-pointe *throughout so that people don't even notice it, then the student can find that they're warm, the strength is there, and if a double* pirouette *works, then they'll gain confidence, and after a while they won't be so afraid when it comes time to be there a little longer. To me it's about dealing with the perception of people, so much more than what the exercise is.*

question 4 *Does the Alexander Technique affect your manner of correcting students?*

It seems obvious that a skilled Alexander teacher would bring his or her expertise, especially in the use of the hands, to the dance technique class during corrections. There are obstacles to this, however. One is the time factor. How can we keep a class moving and take the time to stop and work quietly with individuals? Another potential problem that I have experienced is that, now that I have gained this understanding of parts versus the whole, correcting a specific area on a dancer will likely set up another set of compensations—how can I continue to give corrections in class at all? Should I stop correcting in class altogether, and just ask students to stay after class for a more in-depth exploration? These were all on my mind as I asked others this question.

Shelley Senter discusses her view on the relationship between dance class corrections and an Alexander approach:

ss *I try to talk about being specific rather than correct. And just as in an Alexander lesson, I try to tend to myself first. I will often point out the gap between what one thinks one is doing and what one is actually doing. It is great to stop a group when it is collectively relying on faulty sensory information—like having the arm up in vertical behind the torso, a situation where one cannot see the arm unless one turns the head to look—and point out that most arms are not in vertical. They get to see for themselves how off they are from their own intention to be vertical, and yet the blow is softened by the fact that it is a collective phenomenon.*

When I asked whether she uses her hands-on skills in class, Senter answered:

ss *Yes, very definitely. And I usually do a lot of partnering work, which also may involve students putting their hands on each other.*

However, Luc Vanier responded quite differently:

lv *Well, it's changed a lot over the years. Before Alexander training, I used a lot more hands-on than I do now. I don't even put my hands on to "listen" that much anymore. I've backed away from that, because I am trying for students not to have the perception of this as a different class than anything else. And I'm looking to become invisible as an Alexander teacher when I'm teaching ballet.*

In terms of general corrections, Anne Bluethenthal notes,

ab *I think everything I say to them is informed either by purely Alexander feedback, or purely about the passion of movement, of dance. Hardly any "get on your leg" kinds of corrections. I don't even know what it means to get on your leg anymore. Like what is "pulling up"? Mostly it's about directing their thought, their attention in constructive ways.*

Similarly, Luc Vanier talked about resisting giving students the answers all of the time.

lv *The main benefit of not always explaining everything is that it counters the students' attitude that the teacher knows, and they don't.*

In my own practice, giving corrections is an area where the Alexander work has greatly influenced my teaching. As Vanier points out, it is sometimes best to resist giving all the answers. If the student feels she is doing something "incorrectly," she will immediately go about trying to "fix" the problem, or do what she thinks is right. In Alexander, we learn to suspend our disbelief long enough to allow a teacher to interfere with our preconceived notions of how something should look or feel. In dance, we have to fight against the tendency to correct immediately and, rather, to encourage investigation. Putting this into practice can be daunting however, when faced with a roomful of eager students looking for right answers.

I have found that the hands-on skills I have learned from years of Alexander work enhance both my ability to learn more about a student's movement and holding patterns, and to effect change. Prior to Alexander training, I only used my eyes for observation; now an entire new world has opened up to me as a teacher. My knowledge of a student is amplified when I put a hand on her. I can sense such things as muscle tone, tendencies of the body to pull into directions, misdirected tensions, or holding patterns. The information I receive guides me in the amount and the nature of the suggestions I choose to give to the student. I also use hands-on to communicate specific directions to the student, not by pushing or pulling her, but by *directing* myself as I have a hand on her. I have begun to feel that it is possible in the context of class to give students an experience that they might be able to learn from kinesthetically, and perhaps, if I am lucky, to remember.

question 5 *Are you able to teach Alexander's concept of inhibition? How does this influence your teaching?*

The word *inhibition,* as used in the context of Alexander Technique, means to stop when you notice yourself responding to a stimulus in your habitual way. This moment of stopping opens the door to new possibilities. Rather than replacing an unwanted action with another action, instead, we stop the unwanted action, and wait. This is a key concept in the Alexander Technique, and one that many struggle to understand for quite some time during the learning process. It often goes against our tendencies to "do." Especially in dance, where we work hard at "doing," at "correcting," and "doing more," it is difficult to insert the idea of non-doing. Shelley Senter facilitates the students' understanding of *inhibition* by illustrating their tendencies toward "setting themselves" before beginning a movement sequence:

ss *One of the most obvious devices I use is to stop students right after the words "Ready, AND," or "Ready, SET," and point out how we all tend to set, or tighten up in response to those words in preparation for moving. I remember writing in my journal once that I must "Apply the principles to the principles in order to teach the principles." I often want to get in and give all this information to students and I have to say to myself, "Wait a second, just wait a second. Inhibit the impulse to tell them and see what they find on their own." This often points out* inhibition *in a bigger picture. I'd like to think that I try not to teach, but let them learn.*

Inhibition, or learning to pause and think for a split second prior to making a decision to move, allows for choice over habit. For the teacher, the concept of *inhibition* can also apply to the process of giving corrections to students. I find that it is useful to inhibit the tendency to point out everything that one notices is going wrong when a student performs a movement combination, in favor of a more investigative approach. Observing a student in a variety of contexts to see if I can notice patterns of movement, and then making suggestions that address the initiation of the movement pattern has been an effective teaching strategy.

question 6 *How does the technique influence your class format?*

I was curious to discover whether the Alexander study had affected the teachers' overall views of structuring a technique class. Had anyone considered an overhaul of their entire way of organizing a class?

ss *For lots of reasons, the format of my classes tends to be nontraditional. I do not do a linear warm-up, for example, and may not even do a warm-up at all, but have people dancing right away to get warm for more dancing. Since the body is always moving, on a certain level, warming-up to move is rather moot. What is important to me is giving time and repetition to practice coordinating thought, coordinating conscious* direction *with any given movement or physical idea. I almost always give a little bit of "set" material that I can show the students, as I depend quite a bit on my ability to embody what I'm trying to impart. In a workshop format, I am experimenting with having the first class or two be introducing and working with the principles and hands-on work; then have the following days be movement classes.*

Wil Swanson has let go of some of his class exercises and instead, has incorporated improvisation into his class format, giving students the Alexander directions as they improvise. He is interested in finding ways to teach the students to let go of holding patterns once they have to perform a choreographed sequence, and uses improvisation as a tool.

Luc Vanier basically sticks to the traditional ballet class format, with the exception of the opening exercise discussed earlier, but finds that studying the Alexander Technique has freed him from feeling that he has to adhere strictly to the ballet class structure.

lv *I would say the Technique has encouraged me to think for myself. Sometimes if I don't do a* frappé, *I don't do a* frappé. . . . *I don't stick to the agenda so squarely. And I would say that's what I had seen good teachers do. They would adapt and change according to what was happening in the classroom at the moment. So I'm encouraged to be a little freer within the ballet structure.*

question 7 *How does the Technique influence the environment you set up in class?*

When I think back to my Alexander training, one of the things that had the greatest impact on my ability to make changes, to delve into unfamiliar territory, was the nonjudgmental atmosphere that was created in the classroom and in private lessons by my teachers. This is one of the overarching concepts that I have taken into my own teaching. I strive to create an atmosphere in the classroom that promotes exploration, play, allows for mistakes without degradation, and supports the desires of the students to progress and learn. I believe that if students can focus on learning with curiosity and interest, as opposed to fixing or trying to be "correct," they will maintain a joyful approach to their work. This will manifest in a better overall use of the body-mind. A teacher is instrumental in establishing an atmosphere that promotes this. Anne Bluethenthal echoes this sentiment:

ab *I consider how to create an environment that has the least amount of fear possible in it, because that's the big problem in the dance class, is they're (the dancers) all scared to death. Maybe they're not anxious, like "I'm having performance anxiety," but still the environment is of fear and competition, and so how do I [as a teacher] soften that as much as possible, A), and then B), create material that's mechanically advantageous, material that enhances freeing. And so everything is expressive of that desire: the way I speak to them, the way I touch them, the way I organize the class, the choices of materials, so it isn't all about "free your neck, free your neck, free your neck," but what's the bigger part of that for me? Because when it comes right down to it, it isn't freeing my neck by itself that's that interesting.*

question 8 *Do Alexander teachers have certain movement preferences or aesthetic values? Are aesthetic values embedded in the Technique?*

This question, in one form or another, is often brought up by students in my Alexander for Dancers course. In our class discussions, students sometimes express a fear that studying the Technique might limit them to a smaller range in terms of style. Will practicing the Alexander Technique prohibit a dancer from wanting to engage in movement that is strong, muscular, wild, uncontrolled? Are we training dancers for the qualities of lightness, free flow, and ease to the exclusion of movement that requires more effort, and do we dare even say it, tension?

Most of the teachers I spoke with felt the Alexander Technique was a tool, not a style.

ss *If, as Alexander teachers, we are truly concerned with freedom, then all styles, choices, and aesthetics are permissible.*

ab *My assumption would be no, because there are as many different Alexander Technique teachers as there are humans, so I hope not. I hope that we're just like* *everybody else. But I think it's fair to say there would be a leaning toward. . . . If you're really devoting your life to non-doing in a way that you are when you're in the Alexander Technique, then I would say, if there were one hundred Alexander teachers more of them would be leaning towards the [Erick] Hawkins, Trisha Brown type of aesthetic. Which by the way, are really different. But yet you can see in both those groups of dancers something similar—something with a softer edge.*

But sometimes in the Alexander world, I feel that there's a tendency to be so controlled in that environment and I recoil at it. It almost can create the opposite of what it's intended to create. So that's why it seems counter to the ideas that a particular aesthetic would evolve from it. I would think it would make every aesthetic just more beautiful instead of creating an aesthetic of its own.

My own point of view, and the way I answer my students, is that the Alexander Technique empowers the dancer to choose, rather than relying on habitual patterns of movement which may be inappropriate to the demands of the choreography. The goal is not to be limited to one aesthetic or style, but rather, to perform the movement wholeheartedly, yet with awareness of what one is doing, and whether the amount of effort being exerted is appropriate to the intent of the movement.

Another question for the teachers was whether they thought Alexander work lent itself better to one style than another. Since several of my interviewees had danced with Trisha Brown, I questioned them about whether they thought Alexander Technique was instrumental in their success in Trisha's work. These questions sparked interesting discussions.

SS *I certainly feel that Alexander Technique lends itself to Trisha's work. As for my own experience, my understanding of both is nearly parallel. In Trisha's work I am concerned with spatial reference and direction, a sense of parts to whole, and allowing—the "getting out of one's own way" that lets the work be seen and speak.*

WS *Well, it certainly applies to Trisha's work and to my work, really, it's very suitable. It's a little harder to apply in some other situations. But I try to encourage dancers to improvise with the ideas, and try not to force it. In terms of work that can be very harsh, I've seen dancers take a lot of extra tension and effort out of what they're doing.*

If you soften your neck, can you move quicker? You can always move quicker when you do that. I'm forty-four and most of the dancers in my company are in their twenties, and I'm always quicker. And I wasn't a quick dancer before either. When there's less obstruction, and less in the way, it frees you to flight.

Kathleen Fisher discussed using the Technique to find ease and efficiency in movement, to give her body a chance to unlock, and for her body's natural instincts to work. I asked whether she thought Trisha Brown would value the ability to find an ease and efficiency within the movement that she choreographed:

kf *I think she would value it. It's more manifest, I think, in that the work is not over-performed, as in over-done, over-wrought. Because it's not that she doesn't like a big effort, or terse movement, or even a movement that's very muscular or tight. But then you drop it, you want to go in and out of it, so if you do have that quality, it's a decision, and it's an expressive effect or a visual effect, and it's not just a habit that everything is over-wrought. So I think she appreciates it in terms of more of a performance aesthetic, of not over-performing. You want it to be a choice. And you want to drop out of it when you need to; you want to have the ability.*

frustrations, pitfalls that we encounter

In my conversations with the six interviewees, examples of cases of misunderstandings that occur in the process of teaching the Technique to dancers came up. One of the early frustrations that occurs is that with the new information they are receiving, dancers often feel that they can no longer perform the technical skills that they had previously been able to do. As Luc pointed out, "The dancer feels she is going backwards. She used to be able to do three *pirouettes* and now she can't do anything."

When a student is placed in a different postural configuration, he invariably will feel "incorrect," as he is making judgments based on his idea of "normal." Alexander referred to this misconception of normal as *debauched kinesthesia.* It is often difficult for a dancer to trust that his long-established feeling of placement may not be the best or most efficient alignment.

ss *The challenge is letting students see and experience for themselves what they are doing (to themselves). When a student is willing to suspend their own sensation and kinesthetic experience as the criteria for judging what is happening, they must trust the feedback of the teacher, the mirror, or their peers, and so one must be trustworthy. As a dancer, I am frustrated with the limitations of the words "posture" or "efficiency" or "ease." I am pursuing freedom.*

I remember teaching a student with extreme holding patterns and pain in the lower back. She had been compensating by engaging in constant contraction of her abdominals. When I was successful in getting her to release some of the tension in her lower back muscles, her pelvis fell into place, and her whole alignment was able to lengthen and free up. The student noticed a greater ease in her back right away, but she had the sensation that she could not stand on her legs. She had lost her established way of holding, and had not yet found a new system of support. This transition period can be scary for a dancer, but is a necessary step toward overall improvement.

Another pitfall that I encounter is the tendency for dancers to mistakenly feel that if they get the "choreography" or the form, that they have mastered the concept. In the Alexander Technique, achieving the position is not the end, but a means to discovering one's habits or patterns that have been established over time. So getting the position "right" is not what we are after. This is a fixed idea, and does not allow for fluidity or freedom of movement.

In relation to this, many of the teachers pointed out the danger of becoming stiff in an effort to be correct within the forms that are practiced in Alexander lessons. An example might be the position referred to as *monkey,* which is used in lessons in the process of getting into or out of a chair. The tendency of a dancer is often to attempt to place his body in the position, thinking that he's "got it," when achieving the form is not the goal at all. Wil Swanson points out, "Anything can become a holding pattern. You know, some of my Alexander teachers have been the stiffest people I know! (laughs)"

Chris Aiken noticed this as well:

ca *My experience with watching the students who were training [in Alexander] and a number of Alexander teachers, is that there was an attempt to hold on to their poise and balance, so they became stiff. That's the total opposite of what they're after.*

It is important to convey to dancers that the Technique is not about being "correct." In fact, we must counter this urge to be right with a desire for discovery. Shelley Senter stated it beautifully to a group of students: "Give up knowing. Embrace finding out."

Student perception of the work is one of the keys toward success or failure in offering the Alexander Technique through a dance technique class. If students feel they are getting less rigor in their technical training by having a teacher with Alexander expertise, they can be resentful rather than embracing the concepts being presented in class. Misconceptions can certainly happen in this situation—they may feel they are not getting the "real thing," for example, in a ballet class where a teacher integrates Alexander Technique concepts within the class. If a teacher can give the students confidence that what they will gain by embracing Alexander concepts is an enhancement of their expressive abilities, rather than a stripping away of what makes them unique, they will certainly be more likely to delve into the work with enthusiasm.

habit—the crux of the work

It becomes obvious that one of the key issues we are addressing in this work is habit. We need to become aware of habits that may be interfering with the optimal use of our whole selves—body, mind, and spirit. Habits of thought, habits of relying on physical sensations that may not be accurate, physical habits, habits of the ways we go about doing what we do.

ca *Working with you [Rebecca Nettl-Fiol] and Joan Murray [Alexander teacher] has reawakened my love of the work, and made me see how one's thinking influences who one is on a somatic level—your posture, your movement patterns, your holding patterns, how you hold the tension, and how you express yourself. One of the things that seems so important to me from doing Alexander work is to understand the relationship between habit and posture and use of yourself. I've done a lot of studying about the mind in recent years, and I've come to understand that the mind is very prone to habits. That's the way it operates, so to counteract that habit-forming tendency of the mind, it's important to be conscious. And the reason for that is that we live in a culture that actually tends to guide you towards dysfunctional habits. We live in a society where there is a lot of stress, and having to be in a high alert state, but often, it never gets dissipated. How you deal with constant stress creates certain habits that are often holding habits in the body. And as they develop and continue, they actually increase in their dysfunctional effects on your body and your posture, so you create lots and lots of tension. In my work with the Alexander Technique, by having a teacher guide me back into my sense of poise, I am reminded of a more natural way of organizing myself in relation to gravity that's not emotionally-oriented or habitually-oriented.*

Discussing habits of sensation, Shelley Senter points out,

ss *As a group, dancers tend to be addicted to lots of sensation in the elbows, knees, and lower back. These sensations tell us that our arms are straight, our legs are straight, our feet are pointed, and that we are "creasing" in the hip joint. Of course what is really happening is that the tightening and holding that gives so much sensation is interfering with the freedom of the arm joints, leg joints, and pelvis. I would say that clarifying the sensation—or absence of sensation—of the torso away from the leg and the leg away from the torso can be one of the most revolutionary bits of information a dancer can have.*

I have seen the following scenario countless times, both in my own technical training and in teaching others: A dancer is used to doing a certain movement with a specific amount of effort. If she tries to do the same movement with less effort, it feels to her like she is not really performing the movement, since she doesn't experience the feedback of the sensation that she is used to receiving. The conscious mind, then, needs to engage in the process of relearning the movement.

Chris Aiken also discusses habits of thought:

ca *Being fluid in how you perceive means you have to be fluid in how you think. Alexander was right on that. He really understood how easy it is to become habitual in the way that you think, and how that can create patterns of using yourself that are not conscious and are very dysfunctional. And that over time, particular things pull you off your alignment, and create excess tension in the body, wearing out the joints and fatiguing you. So Alexander work is central to that work in my mind because his whole notion of* directions, of neck free to allow the head to go forward and up. . . . *to me that's a way of consciously patterning the self, as a way to counteract dysfunctional habits. It's like taking mental vitamins.*

Fluidity in thinking and performing, the ability to choose *how* you want to perform a task, to be articulate with the body, these are values that I embrace as an Alexander/dance teacher. It is not what movement or sequence you choose to do, but how you perform it that is important. It is not about holding on, trying to be perfect, but the ability to find a sense of poise after engaging in something that is stressful or taxing—that is invaluable.

ca *Joan Murray [Alexander teacher] often says to me, in terms of poise, "It's not about holding on to it, it's about getting back to it when you fall off of it." It's the capacity to realize "Oh, I'm off," and gently bringing yourself back to a sense of more poise and balance. To me, that is a metaphor for life, really, because any kind of holding onto a way of being in a world that's constantly changing is doomed to failure. And it will wear out your psyche and your physiology. In other words, if you're constantly holding yourself in a certain way to relate to the world, even if that worked for a little while, over time, you just wear yourself out. I find that it works much better for me to have a multitude of coping strategies for stress and living.*

movement efficiency vs. artistic expression—what are we after?

In training dancers in the Alexander Technique, I have found it critical to continue to question my objectives, my point of view in teaching this work.

What is the ultimate goal? What are we striving for? Yes, I would like the dancers I work with to find the most efficient use, to free themselves of unnecessary tension, to discover potentially harmful habits, to understand the idea of "neutral." But at the same time, I want them to stretch their range of possibilities, to move to their fullest capacity, to engage in that exquisite tension between being safe and going beyond your limitations.

Interestingly, this idea of efficiency versus expression came up in several of our conversations, unsolicited by me. Chris Aiken discusses this in relation to the somatics field in general:

ca *I read* The Thinking Body *[Mabel Ellsworth Todd], and I thought a lot about what she was saying. And what I hadn't realized before was that spending years working on movement efficiency and postural efficiency and working with function was important, but that it was not an expressive training. If you're always focusing on efficiency and function, you're not learning how to be expressive. To think of it simply in functional terms is a denial of who we are as human beings. We're not functional; we're not like scientific animals, trying to get to some perfect poise, and using all the systems well. It isn't about proper and efficient use; it's about expressive and poetic use in my mind.*

Anne Bluethenthal shares this perspective:

ab *It's not so much about the neck and the head and the back, it's about opening the heart, it's about living in a freer way, it's about being awake.*

the evolution of a teacher—first it was a mountain . . .

My questions about the incorporation of Alexander Technique into dance training have changed over the years, and I discovered this was the case with the teachers I spoke with as well. We have each progressed through similar stages, and I imagine this evolution may be comparable in dance teachers who have become certified in other somatic practices as well. In the beginning, there is a naive kind of zeal that comes with learning something that has had such a profound impact. We want to share all we know with our students. But we find it impossible to make the two worlds interface. There are many ways to see how they relate, but there are seeming contradictions also. We search for a balance. We over-do or under-do. But eventually, we begin to integrate.

ss *In the beginning, I completely deconstructed the whole technique class format, and really tried to give as much information as I could in a straightforward way.*

And then that eventually evolved into a more woven thing, still sort of maddeningly nonlinear. So we might go down to the floor in the middle of the class or the end of the class or in between every time. This was also just a device to scramble people's brains and expectations a little bit. But now I'm going to try this format of having days where they don't expect to be moving and warming up, so they can really just deal with the sensory information of hands-on, and intellectual information, and then have a dance class.

ab *After being so saturated with the Alexander Technique and then going to the studio, I felt that there was no way to teach class.* No way. *I understood why all these dancers leave dance when they do the Alexander Technique, because the whole thing from beginning to end is a humongo compromise. We are in the realm of hard-core doing, and I just left the realm of hard-core non-doing. And what can I do?*

I went through a lot of agony trying to edit and trying to create the perfect thing that wouldn't compromise my Alexander principles, and after awhile I just said, "You know what? You just teach dance because you love dance, and you love movement. And the students are there to move, and you'll work it out. It is a compromise, but so is life." I mean what are you going to do, sit around and lie on your back all day, or are you going to walk out into the world and live? You do what you do, and stay as aware as you can. That was a huge evolution for me.

ss *There are developmental phases that everybody goes through. And I think at first, just that lightness of being—you just want to explore quiet movement, or delicate movement, or you just don't feel like [demonstrates movement that is wild, uncontrolled] in the beginning. And then as it matures into your dancerly personality and self and desires and curiosities, then dancing is dancing again. You know the Zen saying:* Before a person studies Zen, mountains are mountains and waters are waters; after a first glimpse into Zen, mountains are no longer mountains and waters are not waters; after Enlightenment, mountains are once again mountains and waters once again waters. *First dancing is dancing, and then it becomes not dancing and all these other things, and then it just becomes dancing again.*

conclusion

The Zen saying eloquently sums up my experience in the evolution of integrating Alexander Technique into my dance teaching. It is an ongoing investigation, and one that I continue to be engaged in on a daily basis. Learning the Alexander Technique has provided a philosophical and practical base, underlying the choices that I make as I create movement, present material, and interact with students during class. I am able to fluidly move from consciously using the principles to inform my work, to allowing the Technique to filter through my work more intuitively. For me, dancing has become dancing again.

appendix a

glossary of terms

dart procedures A series of movements developed by Alexander teachers Joan and Alexander Murray in collaboration with anatomist/anthropologist Raymond A. Dart, sequentially retracing the path of development and evolution.

direction Giving oneself the following thoughts: "Let the neck be free, to allow the head to go forward and up, and the back to lengthen and widen." These directions facilitate the functioning of the primary control, and help in the process of learning to use ourselves better in activity.

end-gaining Going after a goal, paying little attention to the means, or process by which the goal is attained.

inhibition Stopping; consciously giving up the habitual response to a stimulus.

means-whereby Paying attention to the process, as opposed to the product, or end.

non-doing The opposite of doing. "Getting out of one's way" so that the right things can "do themselves."

primary control The dynamic relationship between the head, neck, and torso. The way the primary control is used directly affects our coordination and functioning.

primary and secondary curves of the spine Primary curves are those that the newborn baby is born with: the thoracic and sacral curves. The secondary curves are the cervical and lumbar curves in the spine.

self The whole organism: body, mind, and emotion.

unreliable sensory appreciation A distortion of kinesthesia; the discrepancy between what we think we are doing and what we are actually doing.

appendix b

biographies of interviewees

chris aiken is a leading international teacher and performer in the field of dance improvisation and Contact Improvisation. His movement experience also includes theater, Alexander Technique, yoga, release techniques, and athletic training. Aiken has performed and collaborated with many renowned dance artists including Steve Paxton, Kirstie Simson, Nancy Stark Smith, Peter Bingham, Andrew Harwood, and Angie Hauser. He has been presented at the Walker Art Center, Jacob's Pillow Dance Festival, Dance Theater Workshop, and Bates Dance Festival, among others. Aiken received his MFA degree in dance from the University of Illinois at Urbana-Champaign in May of 2003. He is an Assistant Professor at Ursinus College in Pennsylvania, where he codirects the dance program.

anne bluethenthal is founder and Artistic Director of ABD Productions. Winner of the SF Bay Guardian's 1996 Goldie Award for Dance, she has been choreographing, performing, and teaching in the Bay Area since she arrived in 1982. Bluethenthal established her company in 1984, having performed and choreographed throughout the country. She has collaborated extensively with Bay Area theater, dance, and music artists. She cofounded the SF Lesbian and Gay Dance Festival and recently created the Dancing the Mystery series. Bluethenthal has been teaching her unique approach to dance technique for over twenty years, is currently completing her MFA, and maintains a private practice in the Alexander Technique. She is certified by both the North American and London Societies for Teachers of the Alexander Technique and her writing on Dance and the Alexander Technique was published in Jerry Sontag's book, *Curiosity Recaptured.*

kathleen fisher is a performing artist, teacher, and body worker. She was a member of Trisha Brown Dance Company from 1992–2002, and subsequently performed in Bebe Miller Company and Jane Comfort and Company. She has appeared as actor or vocalist in several theatrical productions and short films. Her teaching is influenced by these varied performance and creation situations, exploration of improvisational forms, study of the Alexander Technique, investigations of breath and sound, and training in Trager work and Kripalu bodywork.

shelley senter has performed and taught throughout North America, South America, Europe, Asia, Australia, and Russia as an independent artist, director/advisor/collaborator and as a member of such companies as Bebe Miller and Company and the Trisha Brown Company. She continues to work with the Trisha Brown Company as a guest artist: teaching, performing, and helping to direct residencies. A certified teacher of the Alexander Technique, she teaches workshops and private lessons around the globe. Her work in the Alexander Technique has been written about in various dance and Alexander Technique publications and is known for its application and influence in the arts.

wil swanson is a native of Colorado with a background in music, visual art, and figure skating. He began his dance training at the University of Minnesota -Duluth, studying Cunningham, Graham, and ballet techniques. Swanson produced his own work with Wil Swanson and Dancers, and was a founding member and resident choreographer of Minneapolis New Dance Ensemble. He then enjoyed ten years of dancing and creating work with Trisha Brown. He currently directs Wil Swanson/Dance Works. Swanson was chosen as the 1999 Cowles Chair at the University of Minnesota-Minneapolis.

luc vanier, originally from Montreal, Quebec, first started to dance at L'Ecole Superieur du Quebec under Daniel Seillier. In 1998 he retired from Ohio Ballet as a lead dancer and one of the company's choreographers to train in Alexander and explore, through his graduate studies, its implications and connections with dance. He received his MFA from the University of Illinois and certified as an Alexander Teacher in May of 2001. He is currently an Assistant Professor at the University of Wisconsin, Milwaukee. His recent work explores the use of live motion-capture technology. Luc is also an active performer; his repertoire includes in part works from Anthony Tudor, Paul Taylor, Kurt Jooss, George Balanchine, and Sara Hook.

suggested readings

Alexander, F. Matthias. *Conscious Constructive Control of the Individual.* London: Mouritz, 2004 (reprint of 1946 original edition with additional materials).

———. *Man's Supreme Inheritance.* London: Mouritz, 1996 (reprint of original 1946 edition with additional material).

———. *The Universal Constant in Living.* London: Mouritz, 2000 (reprint of 1946 edition with additional material).

———. *The Use of the Self.* Long Beach, Calif.: Centerline Press, 1984 (reprint of 1939 edition).

Batson, Glenna. "Conscious Use of the Human Body in Movement: The Peripheral Neuroanatomic Basis of the Alexander Technique." *Medical Problems of Performing Artists,* March 1996, 3–11.

Bluethenthal, Anne. "Before You Leap." In J. Sontag, ed., *Curiosity Recaptured.* San Francisco, Calif.: Mornum Time Press, 1996.

Dart, Raymond A. *Skill and Poise.* London: STAT Books, 1996.

DeAlcantara, Pedro. *The Alexander Technique, A Skill for Life.* Ramsbury, Marlborough: Crowood Press Ltd., 1999.

———. *Indirect Procedures.* New York: Oxford University Press, 1997.

Gelb, Michael J. *Body Learning,* 2nd ed. New York: Henry Holt and Company, 1995.

Goldberg, Marian, ed. *Beginning from the Beginning: The Growth of Understanding and Skill.* McLean, Virginia. The Alexander Technique Center of Washington, D.C., 1996.

Harris, Christy. "The Influence of the Alexander Technique on Modern Dance Aesthetics." *Movement Research Performance Journal* 19 (Fall–Winter 1999): 18–19.

Jones, Frank Pierce. *Freedom to Change.* London: Mouritz, 1997.

Richmond, Phyllis G. "The Alexander Technique and Dance Training." *Impulse,* 1994, 2, 24–38.

———. "The Alexander Technique and the Dancer—Preventive Care During Activity." The British Association for Performing Arts Medicine's *Performing Arts Medicine News* 3, no. 2 (Summer) 1995.

Stevens, Chris. *Alexander Technique.* London: Macdonald & Co., 1987.

wendell beavers

9 re-locating technique

In 1993, I wrote an article for the *Movement Research Performance Journal*, volume 7, entitled "States of the Body," which appears below (see p. 127) with new commentary. Contributors were invited to consider, among other things, "the relationship of dance as a body-dependent art to a technological and mediatized society."

It is possible that, in its present manifestation, dance is both the last repository of the truth in human history and a place where we can continue our evolutionary journey. Conversely, not dancing could mean an evolutionary dead end. Dance is the place where we escape his story, her story, or time altogether. By dancing, we range freely through pre-history to the forward edge of the future. This is an activity where we could, and often do, transcend the industrial revolution and technological obscurations of mind and body, practice transformation of animal-god states, merge environment and self, exchange self for environment, environment for self, become water, fire, air, matter, decompose, recompose, de-evolve, evolve.

Dance's place in the technological world is a subversive one. It is radical by the corporeal nature of the activity. Dance is an ephemeral or nonmaterial art, it is said, because movement exists by definition only in the present. An action in time and space is done and it is gone. But, taking the larger view, nothing that appears is capable of disappearing and all things come from nothing at all. So, in fact, what is danced remains, affects, alters the landscape forever, actually fulfilling what the more material arts—like architecture—purport to do. Gesture, shape and energy, given form in space and time, rather than being the most abstract of activities is the most real, more real than building a house.

In my own experience, and in my observation of others dancing and teaching, "technique" arises from the necessity of knowing how to do something. It is increasingly clear to me that this necessity is directly attached to glimpsing one's own possibilities. In other words, discovering what is possible creates its own necessity, which gives rise to techniques or practices. So, in fact, there is always a technique behind the technique. This is what a lot of people are focused on now. This is a much subtler practice of making research based on sensing, and direct perception into "Well, what do we have here anyway?" "What is this body/mind?" "What is possible?" "What can this body/mind do?" "Just exactly how does it do it?" Some of us choose to bring back artifacts from this research and call it choreography; others focus on the process of moving and the phenomena of being, remaining in the realm of improvisation or "performance." This activity in which one applies many ur-techniques of sensing, being, and doing is the ground for creating new "dance techniques" or entering modern styles of the past. This research is often applied to building therapeutic systems and political systems as well.

Near the end of the twentieth century, increasingly, there is a personal search or journey that all movement artists are expected to make. One takes this journey by applying these techniques behind the technique. This is, at first and perhaps remains, always a process of uncovering, of undoing, and not of doing. Things do get a bit confusing because there is a usage of the word technique, left over from the nineteenth century as far as I can tell, and obviously reflecting our postindustrial state of body and mind, which usually means training muscle-bone-body-mind to conform to certain configurations or actions in a prescribed time and space. A useful skill, perhaps, but completely ludicrous as a description of what is really involved in practicing a physical art. This dysfunctional definition usually presupposes an architectural stage or theater as part of the time/space element. An interesting postmodern strategy to escape this was practicing (through contemporary American improvisation), the creation of a stage or theater on the spot, any spot, through intention or awareness of the performer.

A lot of Western twentieth-century technical theory, as it has related to dance, has been a response to the cutting off of whole areas of psychophysical function in

Western life and thought. Modern art has been a defensive action to bring back the possibilities of the individual organism to know, to understand, to be part of the whole. In order to keep this legacy alive, we clearly, inevitably, right now, are involved in the emergence of the technique behind the technique. This emergence is not out of the blue and our ability to engage in this activity is supported by clear antecedents.

A revisionist dance history of techniques starts with Mabel Todd and her book The Thinking Body, *published in 1937.*[1] *What Todd wrote was very much part of a whole flow of thought and art of her time. Basically, she patiently explained that a lot of what was being discovered about the nature of the phenomenal world applied directly to how we function. If form follows function, then how we walk, sit, run, think, how we do things, has everything to do with our postural structure and kinetic possibilities. Practically, she validated physical sensation, not visual form or lyrical conformity, as a prime mover and source of physical expression and form in the body. Her student, Lulu Sweigard, later extended this into what became known as Ideokinesis. Ideokinesis, as technical practice, translates as, the mind moves the body, the mind forms the body. Image, therefore, has an impact on structure. The nonmaterial activity of thought literally changes the material structure of body. This was a thoroughly non-Western view of mind's relationship to matter and the opposite end of the stick from the ballet/modern tradition of repetition of form to train muscle. Ideokinesis placed the mind's ability to posit imagery, and the body's possibility of responding fully to this imagery, at the core of technique.*

Refinement of muscle-bone technique through repetition of form has continued and certainly has its place. However, there has been a revolution in technique, if you can call a fifty-year layering of experience a revolution, whose main focus has been the body-mind relationship. New technique has taken its working principles from developmental, evolutionary theory, new physics, and Eastern discoveries of the nature of mind and phenomena. Previous Western definitions of dance and technique began, a long time ago, to look narrowly culture- and class-bound and the longing to break out of this has moved from quixotic impulse to the possibility of a complete aesthetic change gradually being supported by a technical base. The intense improvisational exploration of the past twenty-five years is part of this revolution, as are many new techniques, practices, processes or whatever you want to call them. They include Ideokinesis, Release Technique, Kinetic Awareness, the Experiential Anatomy, and developmental work of Body-Mind Centering™, Alexander Technique, Feldenkrais, Wayne Technique, Authentic Movement, Contact Improvisation, postmodern yoga, etc. All of this work includes learning to work with body feedback and self-observation on the subtle level of sensing, perceiving, and doing. The collective movement experience, which has come from this kind of activity, has generated many new forms and the possibility of physical virtuosity, and expanded qualities of movement. This physical virtuosity is divorced from traditional modern or classical techniques and pedagogical forms. All of this work is allowing a reinvestment in technique because it grounds technique in much deeper self-knowledge. Dance's most neurotic moments, historically and personally, have come when undigested technique dictates content. There is the possibility, through all of this self-knowledge of movement, to get on top of technique, to uncover many techniques that are used to support and extend discoveries of the artist/mover. One of the most exciting things about this time is that we could move beyond technique by understanding how and why it is made. The idea is not to do without technique but to reinvent it over and over again in whatever way the moment requires.

Technique is basically figuring out what works, remembering this, and not starting from zero the next time. There are, however, techniques about how to recognize and start at zero that are essential to figuring out what works, and it seems that these need to be mastered. Moving beyond the need to continually return to zero or square one is achieved by mastering some techniques. One way of accomplishing this is taking zero with you when you go, thereby going nowhere at all. This does correspond quite well to our actual situation and participating in this kind of journey without goal, allows us some synchronicity, technical mastery, or some would say, mind/body virtuosity, which is good dancing.

At this time, I am teaching what seems to be technique and I am watching a lot of people teaching technique in a nontraditional way. Technique used to mean we had to refer to certain vocabularies of movement based on certain principles. To be recognized as technique we had to conform to a certain teaching form like: some floor work, some standup work, some across the floor combinations, and out the door. I realized a while ago that many people were teaching technique in a whole new way, choosing not to call it technique to get out from under certain limitations.

In my own work I have been teaching vocabulary based on developmental/evolutionary principles. The technical goals have been whole body integration, differentiation, and synchronization. A fascinating by-product of new movement vocabulary—perhaps even a style—has emerged. My teaching focus has shifted from taking people through the process of generating new movement, based on these principles, to the opposite entrance of teaching particular movements or sequences that people follow. Through watching myself learn and teach, technique has come to mean "the principles of organization which underlie mind/body response." These principles are experiential and are measurable or able to be valued in terms of efficiency of response. The goal of this technique is achieving a variety of responses or "appropriate" response. In developmental language this is an integrated response. In physical terms, integration has come to mean a process of first being open to a very wide spectrum of information or possibilities, and then, allowing the information to organize or balance without narrow, cognitive, cortical override. Teaching has become leading people into a way of moving that begins to develop its own principles, rules, and values, which in turn opens out into more movement possibilities.

I find myself working more and more exclusively with the basic or primitive patterns that underlie bipedal, vertical locomotion. It seems to me that aspiring to a style of movement that emphasizes spirilic, contra lateral, extended movement requires a strong relationship to the patterns, reflexes and the basic organization of limbs and spine, center and periphery, which underlie such movement. I consider that the basis of technique is practicing de-evolution or repatterning as a means to develop further mind-body response or coordination, balanced flexion and extension and full integration of all six limbs (head, hands, feet, and tail), and equality of initiation and support through all surfaces of the body. These are some of the goals of such a technique.

This work relies on a direct experience of anatomy through sensing, and a direct experience of natural forces such as gravity, momentum, friction, and the physical laws of bodies in motion. The forms or container for this experience are developmental patterns. These locomotive patterns also serve as reminders of developmental/evolutionary memory and act as pathways to explore our personal and evolutionary movement history.

Funny things occur with this way of working; like our history is our future and the more things differentiate the more they integrate. This latter experience is proving very useful in this time of flying apart, of disunity, of multiplicity of techniques and views of dance. It seems important to keep letting things differentiate and consider that the difference between disintegrate and differentiate is only one of state of mind.[2]

Writing in 1993, I found I had lot of frustration around the subject of technique and some confusion about the enticing openness but parochial narrowness, which combines to create the flavor of dance in our culture. I had a lot of personal experience navigating as a dancer, choreographer, and teacher through the post revolutionary 1970s and 1980s in New York City. By 1993, my experience ran the gamut from perennial student and experimental choreographer, to director of a theater program at NYU, which, at least in my vision, was attempting to establish a synthesis between postmodern dance and European physical theater forms. As student, artist, and educator I had myself often struggled and thought about the rather vast and sometimes fraught territory of dance technique. I often felt as though I was fighting for my life in regards to technique and technological society, which perhaps was a good thing in that it brought a life-and-death quality to my work, including my teaching.

As a teacher and someone sometimes called upon to organize or create curriculum I apply my own experience of realizing, at some point, that I had to do it all myself. As a teacher, I try not to forget that each dancer will ultimately have to create his or her own technique. They will have to create their own lineage from their own selective view of history. Most essentially, they will have to reinvent dance. They will go through dance's evolutionary stages in their own developmental style. The sum of this experience will be who they are as artists.

As time has accumulated my aspirations for the sort of dance and contemporary training, which would prepare and liberate another generation to recreate the medium have come down to three areas of redirection:

question 1 *The Reintegration of Theater and Dance, Especially in the Arena of Training.*

Specifically, this means considering the sources of the actor and the dancer to be on a continuum. A foundation performance training would familiarize students with the complete pallet of the performer without reference to the technical lines traditionally drawn between acting and dancing. The sources of space, time, shape or line, kinesthesia, image and story worlds, and emotion would all be treated inherently as equal and available. This equality of sources should extend itself to an aesthetic equality of forms that would value emotional image work as equal to the geometries of space and the body. In this way, prospective dancers would be equally familiar with emotional and story/image sources of generating movement as they would be with line or kinesthetic sensation or abstract gesture. Conversely, the actor would be completely conversant with kinesthetic sensation and abstract movement generated by perception of spatial relationship and open timing as they are currently with image and storytelling strategies and sources. The fact that dancers are not required to rigorously investigate and map their psychological terrain or cultivate the tools to access and channel their rich psychophysical image worlds and energies is debilitating. There is no way they can go beyond twentieth-century modern dance ideas of representation of emotion, etc., without these tools.[3]

question 2 *Instituting Somatic-Based Curriculum.*

Somatic work provides the means for students to experientially thoroughly investigate the anatomical systems of the body, their roles in movement and generating forms. It is essential, at long last, to redress the muscle-bone bias of Western dance forms by opening up the whole body as a medium and generator of form. Developing the curricular means to go beyond "functional anatomy" and training through reiteration of styles into the worlds of "experiential" anatomy would be a breakthrough and would break down the boundaries between existing cultural forms. This kind of study would enable us to enter a new era of World Dance rather than always working from an American Modern Dance aesthetic bias. The foundation for this work does relate to the new somatics, experiential anatomy work, and the breakdown of human movement into developmental and evolutionary studies. Basically, the foundation for dance training should be physical investigation of the body as it is—our capacities and qualities, all possibilities of moving, emoting and creating forms in space and time. This possibility rests on techniques of sensing and perceiving. In this way one comes to understand and trust the process of being led by sensation and perception into nonconceptual worlds. This would allow students to fully give over to investigating space, time, visual form, and sensation, for example, while simultaneously recognizing and relating to emerging external forms.[4]

question 3 *Generally Encouraging the Lovely, Skeptical, Rebellious Anti-Establishment Counter Culture Critical Impulse.*

This means emphasizing postmodern forms of improvisation as the ground of creative process. It would be good to resurrect improvisation not only as a viable performance form but also as a technique, which lies at the core of composition. Improvisation should be placed also at the core of choreography. The postmodern generation bequeathed a very sophisticated set of forms and tools to disassemble both the dancer and the dance and created at least the possibility of a multiplicity of aesthetics. Contemporary dance curriculum must address the nature of forms, how they are generated as well as how they are inhabited. Postmodern improvisation as it was originally derived from the work of John Cage, Robert Dunn, and many others is a powerful and effective way to understand these things. Dance training lags well behind the pedagogies of music and the visual arts in its willingness to fundamentally explore and reinvent. This is primarily because our own postmodern tradition has been somewhat rejected or ignored.

Training dancers across the board as working in an emotional, psychophysically transformational medium, not only related to manipulation of physical forms and kinesthetic energy; training in experiential techniques with mindfulness/awareness techniques at their core allowing for a shift to somatic view; and articulating a more sophisticated relationship to creative process which is accompanied by a more inclusive aesthetic would go a long way to quelling my own angst, longing, and desire for dance to sustain a radical, radicalizing stance and presence.

Dance as an art, as it is reconceived by each of us daily in our creative work, can claim to be radical in its flexibility, responsiveness, and transparency. Dance, I think, is a radical, lonely road. It cannot be truthful in today's world and not be confrontational. To confront may be to bore, to defy expectations, or to counter. Dance should defy and be flexible in the sense that it would celebrate our oneness in a world bent on separation of each from each; or when the world celebrates conformity and the power of the group, dance would celebrate the nonconformist, individual aloneness, and difference of each. When the world only recognizes success, dance should celebrate failure. When the artistic currency is neurosis and a general sickness, dance should celebrate basic goodness. *Not to please* would be a good motto; but rather to *investigate* and *know* and *show the truth* even if one finds oneself dancing on an empty plane for only the stars; this would guarantee the continuation and relevance of dance.

notes

1. Mabel Elsworth Todd. *The Thinking Body: A Study of the Balancing Forces of Dynamic Man*. New York: Dance Horizons, 1937.
2. Wendell Beavers. "Locating Technique." *Movement Research Performance Journal #7: States of the Body*, September 1993, 4–5.
3. My experience of this as curriculum is primarily at the Experimental Theater Wing (ETW) at NYU. Mary Overlie's Viewpoint work has begun to have a profound influence on American Theater training as it does fully lay out sources and forms of performance as a field of six: space, time, shape, kinesthetics, story, and emotion. This work, derived from dance experiments of the 1960s, originally has been picked up and understood in its ramifications more fully by theater practitioners (particularly the director Anne Bogart) but it remains a means of advancing the frontier of contemporary dance work as well. Here, I am basically restating Ms. Overlie's theory and technique as an aspiration.
4. Bonnie Bainbridge Cohen's work with Experiential Anatomy and Developmental Movement has formed the basis for my own work in this area. It is through working with her and her Body-Mind Centering approach that I first encountered a somatic approach.

glenna batson

10 teaching alignment

from a mechanical model to a dynamic systems one

"aristotle correctly observed,
'matter will surely not move itself.'
a foundational dynamic animates living matter."
— mckeon r, ed.,
the basic works of aristotle

abstract

Dance educators historically have based their teaching of alignment on Cartesian mechanics. The mechanical model of posture, adopted by kinesiology and conventional Western medicine, dominated dance science and pedagogy throughout the twentieth century. This model promised efficiency and effectiveness in movement performance. To fully subscribe to the mechanical model meant employing conditioning methods of motor learning where repeated muscular effort was required to achieve the aesthetic. The move away from reductionistic theories in science toward dynamical systems theory (Sheets-Johnstone 2000, 323) has altered our view of human posture and movement. The concept of "the dancer's instrument"—a machine neatly obeying laws of mechanics and following the dictates of the will—has evolved to a more dynamic view of organizational behavior. Human movement is self-regulating, nonlinear behavior that is spontaneously assembled and environmentally embedded.[1]

In the last few decades, biology, psychology, neuroscience, and other branches of science impacting on the study of human movement have found their foundational principles altered by dynamical systems theory. The tradition of dance pedagogy also has been influenced by many forms of improvisation and somatic approaches reflective of systems thinking. Their use in alignment training, however, has been marginal or controversial (Simpson 1996, 1–5). In this chapter, the author discusses the historical transition of alignment training in dance from the Cartesian mechanical model to a dynamic systems (DS) one. The tenets of the DS model (resonant with dance improvisation and somatic approaches) can be incorporated into more holistic approaches to alignment training (Musil 2001, 148–53).

the paradox of dance teaching

Human organisms organize themselves through habitual patterns that, in part, help resolve the perplexing dualism that is at the foundation of their existence.[2] This dualism—an integral part of the history of Western science and philosophy—is that of the mind and body (Kelso 1982). We appear endowed with two bodies—an "objective" structure and a "relational" or functional process (Sheets-Johnstone 1992), two "minds," categorical and holistic (Tamboer 1988, 439–61), and two primary modes of existence, space and place (Tuan 1977). We are endowed with two vantage points: "third person" (the objective viewpoint of science) and "first person" (the experiential viewpoint of personal experience) (Hanna 1988, 341). The resolution of this paradox has been the thrust of many fields of knowledge, movement training (dance) among them. We exhibit a "structural dualism, linearity and non-linearity [that] . . . creates a corresponding dualism of function: that at the same time in the same mind we all have a propensity towards order *and* a propensity towards chaos" (De Spain 1994, 59).

This dualism also sets up a paradox in teaching dance. At once, dancers learn by being told, shown, positioned, and invited to imitate or mimic another person's movement, as if to conform to an ideal of structure. At the same time, dancers learn by being informed through their own personal experience of moving, a somatic experience that is autonomous, adaptive, and improvisational.

Teaching dance at once is simple because movement integrates body, mind, and spirit. Teaching *how* to move to achieve a particular end called "dancing," however, is extremely complex. This implies conveying the general spatio-temporal and interpretive constraints of the desired movement, while providing each individual student with the means of mastering the degrees of freedom inherent in each moment of execution (Bernstein 1967).

Dance, especially, unlike other art forms, "has no single universally accepted pedagogical or technical standard for instruction" (Ross 1994, 14). In no other form of education do so few "how to" rules exist. How can a dancer, with a potentially infinite number of neuromusculoskeletal combinations configure the right movement solution for a given technique command or choreographic problem? The teacher's role is to provide just enough direction to facilitate body-level problem solving but not too much as to impose his or her personal movement strategies on the dancer or suffocate the dancer's autonomous processes of self-organization.

Second, dance teachers are constantly embracing traditional aesthetic values in teaching basic vocabulary (*tendus*, roll-downs, for example) while pushing the pedagogical envelope. The moving body is a fertile resource of changing metaphors and insights. As artists, dance teachers forge new models of movement-learning that reflect the changing conceptions of the body coming from many sources—their own practice, science, philosophy, social concerns, and other art forms. As educators, dance teachers cannot teach the science of human movement *as science*, rather they teach the *art* of dance, while understanding the *principles* of human movement science (HMS). The informed dancer is one who knows the anatomy and kinesiology but who can transmute that knowledge into dance technique. Dance "students need the opportunity to feel the beauty of scientific truth and its place within the art" (Simpson 1996, 4). Sounds good, but *how* is this accomplished?

dynamical systems theory

Over the last several decades in HMS (in motor development, motor control, and motor learning, particularly) many researchers have attempted to bridge the gap between mechanical analysis of movement and movement experience (Port and van Gelder 1995; Winstein and Knecht 1991). This research has influenced dance and—most likely, though not well-documented—dance has also influenced the field of HMS. One main paradigm shift in HMS has been away from the mechanical concept of the body toward a systems view of biological complexity. Rather than the body-as-object (a physical machine, separated from the thinking mind), the body-mind-spirit is an integrated whole whose subject is self-organization (Heckler 1997, 11). Autonomous, self-regulation lies at the heart of DS theory and exploration and discovery form the "pump" (Ingber 2000, 1165). Dynamicists suggest that human organisms act in ways that are complex and nonlinear (Thelen and Smith 1993). Human movement is a total "brain-mind environment" (Gendlin 1986, ix), inseparable from its context as we sense and move. Perception and action are tightly coupled (Gibson 1966), with sensory feedback providing "online" information as our intentions guide our actions. Rather than speaking of the body *and* movement, the terms "body-and-mind-in-motion,"[3] "body-in-the-making" (Sheets-Johnstone 1992, 15), "body-as-movement-system" (Goldfarb 1989, 12), "the soma" (Hanna 1987–88, 56), or "the use of the self" (Alexander 1932) have evolved to help resolve the dichotomy of mind and body—at least at the level of language. These terms imply that that movement is a *process*—not a product—of the body-mind.

In many areas of science, researchers have applied the concept of self-regulation from dynamical systems theory to their own fields, altering their foundational tenets. In biology, for example, the work of Humberto Maturana and Francisco Varela (1979) coined the word, "autopoiesis" to illustrate the inherent, self-regulating intelligence of the cell. Again at the level of microstructure, biologist Donald Ingber has shown that cells at all levels of complexity maintain their structural integrity according to principles of "tensegrity" (1998, 48), that dynamic interaction of mechanics and energy popularized by engineer-architect-futurist Buckminster Fuller.

Coincidentally, over the last thirty years or so, dance has absorbed many scientific ideas through improvisation and somatics (Beavers 1993–94, 5). Since the late 1960s and early 1970s, the explosion in improvisation in postmodern dance and in the field of somatics spawned a multitude of body learning practices based on the concept of autonomous self-regulation (Juhan 1986). Somatic practices found an easy entre into dance because of their emphasis on heightened awareness of the organizing potential of proprioception and kinesthesia. The main thrust of the somatics movement includes the transformative learning that issues out of cultivating conscious awareness of how one senses and perceives *while moving.* Since "learning dance happens directly through the kinesthesia," as Erick Hawkins said, somatics provided dancers with a greater measure of autonomy utilizing an already well-rehearsed "tool" (Hawkins 1992, 2).

Many principles from DS theory form the core of HMS and also of somatics. Practitioners of the Feldenkrais Method, for example, find resonance in systems principles as formulated by Thelen, Kelso, and other dynamicists. Non–goal-oriented exploration of environment while consciously attending to proprioceptive feedback from movement is a hallmark of the Feldenkrais work that resonates with systems principles (Reese 1999–2000, 18–26). Practitioners of Rolfing, the Alexander Technique, and Energy Medicine have applauded biologist Donald Ingber's work in cellular tensegrity, which helped explain emergent structural changes in their work.[4] The internal microtubular skeletal structure of the cell is a tensegrity operation (Huang and Ingber 1999), organization that starts at the molecular level and proceeds all the way up through the complex tissues. Tensegrity structures appear throughout nature as dynamic icosahedrons (like viruses, for example), reminiscent of Laban's spatial harmony work.

While many branches of science have influenced dance and vice versa, teaching alignment has remained a stubborn area (Musil 2001, 148), clinging to traditional notions of rigid mechanics. Dance education could use a good theory of alignment training that accounts for the changing dynamics of movement. How does a body with multiple degrees of freedom in a rich, complex environment, solve a movement task—accurately, reliably, repetitively? How do dancers learn this skill? Or more precisely, *what* is the skill they are trying to learn? The skill, perhaps, can be called kinesthetic "dexterity" (Latash and Turvey 1996, 21), the ability to access one's movement potential, the potentially infinite combinations of movements, and to be able to demonstrate enough stability to repeat movements with great precision, while being able to shift instantaneously to meet new movement challenges.

Both the shifts in scientific paradigms and the immense body of improvisation and somatic exploration of these last thirty years have allowed dance to reinvest in a technique that does not dictate "content" (a set of hard-wired rules) but instead allows the dancer to uncover many strategies that can be used to support and extend discoveries in dancing (Beavers 1993–94, 4). A look back at the history of alignment provides a perspective of where we've come.

the cartesian aesthetic

Philosophers view the body as "substantial" and "relational" (Tamboer 1988, 441). The substantial body is Cartesian—a concrete substance with sharply distinguished boundaries between mind and body, inner and outer reality, that is mechanical, predictable, reducible. This is the body of conventional Western medicine, and of Western culture, as well.[5] The substantial body of philosophy is the dancer's "instrument," a well-oiled machine, predictable, obeying mechanical laws, transforming only at the hands of the hierarchical commands of its master, the mind. The relational body is vital, interrelated to self and world, and irreducible in its wholeness (Hanna 1987–88). In spite of the enormous exploration of the body's adaptive and transformational capabilities, however, the focus of alignment training in dance ironically has been largely on physical mastery of the body as object. Dancers know that the seeming immobility of the upright, standing body is, in many ways, a fiction. What we see as the physical body on the outside masks the interconnected, self-assembling matrix of flowing movement inside. Yet, alignment training still conjures up images of postural positioning and holding.

Solutions to maintaining upright posture and mechanical balance evolved more from visual constructs—problems of form, proportion, position, and aspect (Sheets-Johnstone 1992). The Cartesian body occupies space along a set of perpendicular spatial coordinates. The Cartesian intersection of the median sagittal and the median coronal planes defines the line of gravity, or weight line, the vertical plumb line around which our body segments are mechanically balanced. When standing upright, the ideal posture reflects a vertical axis that transects the body so that the three large units of the axial skeleton (head, ribcage, and pelvis) are balanced equally around the line. We pivot around cardinal axes: up-down (vertical), in-out (or side-side, that is, coronal or frontal), and front-back (sagittal). The weight of the body is ideally transferred through the major weight-bearing structures as close to the central line of gravity as possible (Norkin and Levangie 1999; Sweigard 1975).

Once space is defined and the body "located," classical kinesiology organizes the body into rigid (bony) segments—head-and-neck, trunk upper arm, forearm, hand, thigh, foreleg, and ankle-foot. This arrangement alone can have a profound effect on movement organization. Imagine, for example, if you were to limit the number of possible degrees of freedom in your body by eliminating your hip joint. You would align yourself in such a way that your "torso" actually included your thigh, and that your trunk "stood" on your tibia rather than balancing your pelvis on the thigh joint. New thoughts and movement opportunities, and spatial relationships and constraints (both internal and external), become immediately accessible. The concept of rigidly organized joint linkages not only can make movement predictable but also dull and even possibly injurious.

The body not only shares properties with basic geometric shapes such as cones, cubes, and lines, but also with fractals. Fractal geometry is not a science of man but of nature. It is not about linear space (a solid grid) but how a form can fill a space (dynamically enfolded). In fractalian perception no single center or viewpoint exists where the viewer must stand to see all the elements (Shearer 1992, 144). Regardless of the where of standing, the body is the reservoir of infinitely nesting spheres. The deeper one penetrates into any of the "nodes," the more the enfolded complexity unfolds. The new geometric model frees us from the restrictions of visual habit and gives us a new matrix in which to appreciate space and form (149).

This new vision of space is sensed, palpable, and full of emergent possibilities. The emergent body in space is already etched in the brain, as a fractal reiterated within itself. It is as if the movement already exists in the mind-body as a potential, or as a "subtly enfolded order" (Peat 1986, 214). The body includes the potential patterns of interaction in which new words, meanings, situations, and functions emerge without ever having been in the body's known repertoire. This new vocabulary may be illogical, and have nothing to do with the particular "structure" ordinarily related to it (Gendlin 1986, 146). Rather than creating a new reality when we are aligning, we simply are evoking a potential that is already present—implicit and enfolded in our soma (Peat 1986, 216).

Sounds like improvisation again, no? Dancer Kent De Spain alludes to a model of the improvising mind as a "fractal hierarchy" of changes over time (1994, 58). Dance educator Pam Musil writes of how the study of fractal systems informs dance "that the principle of freedom is key in the evolution and formation of fractal shapes . . . it is the randomness and freedom within the formula's progression, which creates the resulting pattern" (Musil 2001, 151). Conceived in this way, aligning is less about connecting separate body parts and more about sensing thresholds of unfinished and/or potential events (150).

More than an abstract, anatomical blueprint of bones and joints obeying a set of mechanical laws or mechanical coordinates linked to fixed points in space, alignment is emergent, a property of a biologically complex, dynamic system (Sheets-Johnstone 1992, 135). It emerges from an awareness of the confluence of moving relationships at any given moment—the shapes, feelings, and forces that are sensed, visualized, intuited, and the impact of the environment and task constraints (Thelen and Smith 1993). Dancers can become sensitive and responsive to momentary changes in their somatic attunements—its dynamic oppositional pulls, momentary balances. Alignment, then, can function as two coincident space-time frames, as a discipline of working with the background metamorphic rock of structural stability (that which is slowly changing over the life span) against the shifting foreground of moment-to-moment fluctuations in spatio-temporal relationships. These relationships are dynamic features of a complex system of attention and intention in which part-to-whole self and self-to-world revolve (Gold 1992–93, 34–41).

Moreover, upright postural alignment carries mutable psychophysical attitudes for living (Feldenkrais and Reese 1985). Good alignment ideally reflects the confluence of many different psycho-physical-environmental gestalts in which all irrelevant and hindering urges and motivations are resolved. Laban discovered this long ago (Laban 1975), echoed, too, in the work of somaticists. Rather than thinking of the body as oriented along fixed spatial coordinates, Hanna described the psychophysical dimensions of our "latitude, longitude, and profunditude," somatic coordinates that are attitudes for living (Hanna 1980, 17–124).

alignment: historical fact, fiction, and transformation

A specific vision of alignment lies at the heart of our western dance tradition. It is an aesthetic vision, a vision shaped by aesthetics as well as by science. It is an integral theme in every dance class, spoken or unspoken. It allegedly gives order, form, and coherence to physical performance. The word "performance" does not have anything to do with *form,* however, but comes from the Old French, meaning, "to carry out thoroughly." Performance implies action, not shape; dancers perform a complex series of movements that embody numerous, simultaneous complex processes, such as attending, sensing, initiating, sequencing, locomoting, reversing, and *aligning.*

Perhaps no other tool of dance training has been so fraught with outdated, confusing, chauvinistic, contradictory, and potentially injurious metaphors. Educator John Dewey said that any concept, theory, or idea is bound to be pulled into the "gravitational field of our automatic thought," and alignment is no exception (quoted in Maisel 1989, 119).

According to Webster's Dictionary, the verb, "to align" (from the French *aligner,* meaning "line") means to arrange in a straight line. Secondarily, one can align oneself with a group, party, or cause. The first definition suggests a linear arrangement of our bony architecture, in this case along a vertical axis. The secondary definition of alignment is closer to attunement and allegiance, suggesting a movement toward conformity with a shared idea, body of knowledge, principle, or philosophy. Simone Forti describes a lovely encounter with a grasshopper in her hand where a sympathetic "alignment" enabled them to "dance" for many minutes together (quoted in Steinman 1995, 7). Conforming to a shared idea is similar to the dance connotation, that is, bringing the body into conformity with alignment requirements. The word could also imply an act of thinking relationally, a dynamic act of corporeal acknowledgment. Alignment (a noun) might benefit by giving way to the more active "aligning."

Our conceptual foundation for teaching alignment has been strongly influenced by mechanics (the body *extracted from* its spontaneous, self-organizing capabilities). Our methods have been more about imitation than exploration and self-selection, more about adopting or imposing a posture than training adaptive capabilities. Part of this has come from the hierarchical tradition of authority in teaching, in which the dance teacher is the major repository of knowledge (Stinson 1994). As one fourteen-year-old talented (conservatory trained) ballet dancer I once taught in a workshop on new approaches to dance training remarked: "This stuff is really different; No one ever asked me what *I* thought about how to do the movement!"

cultural aesthetic

Associations with visual constructs of skeletal symmetry and placement reflect specific cultural biases. Our words for describing alignment reflect a range of cultural values. "Good" alignment conveys ease, simplicity, symmetry, grave, elegance, balance, with minimal displacement from the central axis of the body (at least in appearance). When alignment is good, it is perceived as light, open, receptive, "lifted by gravity, not dragged down by it" (Myers 1988, 16). Other adjectives for good alignment stress the underlying state of motor preparedness, a physical attitude that is "alert, but not tense, and ready for contingencies" (Pierce and Pierce 1989, 58). The state reflects spontaneous, effortless movement that is readily reversible, breath-supported, and devoid of conflicting impulses. "Bad" alignment (or to be out of alignment) is considered forced, rigid, injurious, slouched (59), stiff, fixed, held, imbalanced, or "out of place, gone awry" (Steinman 1995, 13).

Persistent adherence to the Cartesian model of upright mechanical balance is what one somatic educator calls "anatomical Platonism" (Johnson 1980, 4–7). Uprightness carries a heavy moral valence in our culture. Gravity pulls us downward, toward "the lower depths," "hell," "old age," "submission," and "death." Our bony architecture thrusts us upward toward heaven. The vertical rectitude of our skeleton enables us to be physically, morally, and spiritually upright. Up and forward connotes progress, heavenly destiny, mobility, achievement, mastery over nature's forces. Upright posture is conceived of as "an action in its own right, a persistent achievement, based on obtained, not imposed stimuli" (5).

If we look at the postures of other cultures, we can begin to see that there are as many ways of aligning the body as there are ways of moving and existing. The way the world's people orient themselves offers a potentially infinite number of corporeal arrangements. What should immediately impress us when we compare our posture to other world postures is the conformity of how vertical, forward-facing, right-handed, sagittally-going we are. While teaching in Japan, I was astounded to learn that the Japanese have no word for alignment as far as the body and movement are concerned. While their dictionary roughly translates it as all parts oriented around a central line, no one ever uses this word to convey the body's orientation in space. A Noh actor, for example, works to attain *kamae,* a poised presence that is the result of mastering a global consciousness on all aspects of the body. "Kamae is thus defined as a posture open to all eventualities, as virtual movement" (Amazaki 1996, 28).

Many Japanese theater manuals describe the feet as being the point of orientation for posture. Theater master Tadashi Suzuki says this orientation brings the body *away* from the vertical thrust and closer to the earth. Western dance manuals also describe alignment as beginning at the feet (Fitt 1982), but for different reasons: feet form the basis of locomotion (the springboard for the body's vertical thrust into space). Since feet form the "base of support," the end of the kinematic chain, foot alignment dictates how the weight is centered and reflects the body's potential to move. In the introduction to *Dance Kinesiology,* Dr. Fitt states, "This book will consistently follow the pattern of starting at the bottom and working up the body. The rationale for this pattern follows the pattern of all structural analysis: the foundation is of primary importance. If the foundation is faulty in a building, no amount of strengthening the upper stories can correct the essential instability. Many of the misalignments of the knee, hip, spine, and even shoulders can be traced to a chain reaction of compensations that began with a faulty foundation" (19).

mechanics or aesthetics?

Comparisons of alignment to visual constructs of skeletal symmetry and placement have influenced notions of training in very specific ways. For decades, traditional modes of teaching alignment have been through imitation, rigid relationships of agonist-antagonist muscle holding, and mechanical repetition. In both theory and practice, dance superimposed the biomechanical model on its own aesthetic. Standing alignment is a *visual* ideal of skeletal parts balanced around the imaginary line of gravity, aesthetically arranged with symmetrical bony landmarks and classical proportions (Watkins and Clarkson 1990). Molding a dancer's unique anatomical constraints to conform to mechanical ideals of anatomical symmetry has been a basic strategy of alignment pedagogy. Structural and functional malalignments—many dance authorities say (Sparger 1970)—might compromise freedom of movement, discolor expressive neutrality, and possibly precipitate or perpetuate injury.

When dancers prepare to move, either at the *barre* or in free space, they align their body in the upright standing position. From a mechanical point of view, the object of this alignment is first to keep the center of mass within the range of foot placement during most locomotor movements. Aligning through the joint centers makes sense mechanically. When the body is well aligned in the vertical dimension, the weight is transmitted through the joint centers in the direction of gravity. When weight is balanced around the mechanical axes of the bones, abnormal compression or traction forces on the joints is avoided through balanced muscle action. If the body is vertically aligned and centered, theory says, the muscles or ligaments will be less tense and taut (Grieg 1994). Efficient alignment enables dancers to work more with less fatigue and strain.

A thin membrane separates mechanics and aesthetics in dance. As one author of a classic text on ballet states: "Any departure from the balanced posture will strain muscles and ligaments and will cause undue friction in the joints. If one segment of the body is out of line, all others will be affected. The spine is an excellent example of this. Going out of balance, out of alignment, not only appears to jeopardize the dancer towards injury, but is basically unaesthetic" (Hammond 1993).

In classical dance (both ballet and modern), however, alignment also has been linked to Western aesthetic ideals of proportion. The ideal (ballet) dancer's body is ectomorphic, with a low percentage of body fat, well-balanced proportions, long, slender, straight limbs, narrow hips, and well-developed arches. Generally "unacceptable" (that is, unaesthetic) for dancing are combinations of long trunks with short legs, big buttocks, a swayback, protracted shoulders, deep spinal curves, short necks, and big heads (Hamilton 1982, 82). The homonculous that comes to mind in imagining this "unacceptable" dancer would be hilarious, if there wasn't a ring of truth to it. The body aesthetic satisfied, the dancer's total form at once should look "placed," but not static and mechanistic in appearance. The static body—one without any forces acting on it—must project multipotentiality and must easily resolve into movement.

In upright static standing, the center of mass of the body is located in front of the lumbosacral junction. Dancers talk of "centering" their bodies, a mysterious metaphor that reflects, from a mechanical standpoint, the attempt to balance the body's mass around the center of gravity in the pelvis within the context of the three planes of space. The center of gravity (or more correctly, center of *mass*), is an imaginary point formed by the intersection of these three median cardinal planes, and is located in the static, upright body roughly anterior to the level of the second sacral vertebra. Centering also implies bringing the spine into closer conformity with the line of gravity.

This centering process in dance is to establish the balanced, poised readiness to move into length width and depth (Heckler 1997, 10). It also reflects the Eastern philosophy of martial arts. Centering is "when one commits wholeheartedly to a path of awakening and is guided by a masterful teacher . . . becoming something much more fundamental and universal than a prelude for refining a technique" (12). When aligning the body in the upright position, the spine (the body's vertical axis) ideally conforms as closely as possible to the weight line of gravity (formed by the intersection of two median Cartesian planes). To enhance motion, the dancer "lifts" the center of mass along the vertical axis to "free" the legs. The spine is lifted and the curves "lengthened," an image common to dance pedagogy. The centers of gravity of the parts of the body as a whole ride higher when the spine is less deeply curved. Lengthening the spine allegedly means that the curves ideally are reduced or diminished, but not eliminated (Sparger 1970). These mechanics carry an aesthetic valence: "Imbalance always shortens a body; improving the vertical alignment lengthens it. . . . The three primary curves of the spine . . . are softened . . . as the pelvis, chest, and head align themselves vertically over the arches of the feet" (32).

If not structurally inclined to meet this aesthetic demand, dancers frequently compensate muscularly to mask the offending malalignment, even at the expense of joint range. Three common dance strategies I have seen over the years for eliminating excessive spinal curves include:

1. An abdominal-hamstring synergy (tucking the pelvis) to hold the lumbar spine in flexion to decrease a real or perceived excessive lumbar curve;
2. Hyperflexing the anterior cervicals (tucking the chin) to center the head, and
3. Adducting and depressing the scapulae (pulling the shoulders down).

In other words, dancers contract the opposing antagonists to "hold" the new position to counter the excessive pull of culprit agonists. (Tight swayback? Pull in the stomach.) Continued repetition of seeking position breeds familiarity. What feels "right" to the dancer might be a malaligned and injurious arrangement of bones (Juhan 1986, xxvi). It is not uncommon for dancers to cross the threshold from feeling a "released" spine (one that is balanced and free of excessive tension that unduly increases the lumbar curve), to adopting one that is flattened and fixed ironically *by trying to re-create the sensation of release.* More chronic muscle tightness, weakness, and ultimate injury probably may have resulted from reductionistic attempts to correct complex neuromuscular imbalances in the body. Here a conditioning model of excessively controlled agonist-antagonist relationships has replaced any autonomous discovery of true balance. Traditional methods of teaching alignment have reinforced this as well. Verbal cues in technique class to correct a hyperlordosis (swayback) often result in tucking the pelvis. While the hackneyed cue, "pinch a dime between your buttocks," has given way to more kinesiologically sound and aesthetically pleasing metaphors, the outcome remains the same: Dancers still can easily upset the neuromuscular balance of femoral rotation and pelvic support by adopting similar compensatory strategies. Muscles will not relax and lengthen by forceful methods, rather, they reflexively resist, and what resists, persists.

a paradigm shift

The introduction of "somatics" into dance training was pivotal in shifting concepts of alignment training. Somatics is a set of self-care body and movement practices that emphasize autonomous self-regulation and intentionality as the fulcrum of learning through the undivided body-mind. The somatic learning model emphasizes the embodied, processual nature of the soma, where self-guiding and transformational capabilities are realized through a sensed, bodily experience. Popular with dancers for decades, well over one hundred somatic techniques exist today (Knaster 1996). Somatic movement re-education aims not only to correct faulty postures and movements by re-embodiment but also to foster a process of kinesthetic inquiry that leads to self-discovery of movement habit and potential, improved movement efficiency and overall well-being.

F. M. Alexander was perhaps the first somatic educator to realize that posture and movement formed one continuum (Reed 1989, 4). He abolished all references to posture and instead employed the phrase "The Use of the Self" (Alexander 1932, title). Moshe Feldenkrais helped liberate body alignment from the place of planes to a *field* of action. He used the word "acture" rather than "posture" to describe the continuum of posture and movement (Feldenkrais and Reese 1985, 108). Acture implied the *way* an action is accomplished, not simply the position chosen to achieve the action. A person had "good" posture when he or she showed absence of effort and resistance, ease of reversibility, lack of compulsion and habit, and easy breathing. This would enable a person to perform any movement (or reverse it) quickly and easily, with no miscellaneous, superfluous, inefficient movements or compensations (82).

The laws of leverage act differently when we are talking about a fluid, dynamically self-organizing system (Levin 1982). From a systems perspective, alignment is a part of the process of moving, an attractor in the pool of sensorimotor activities, that time-space element that constrains our activity at the moment (Thelan and Smith 1993). Alignment should be ripe with potential for movement because it exists in the realm of "interaffecting possibilities" (Juhan 1986, 223). Rather than thinking of the body as organized into bones or "parts" buttressed against the forces of gravity and movement, a better metaphor might be a permeable lattice or scaffold of fluid interactions. The act of aligning could reflect the way impulses gather, swarm, and stream into one region of the body, coalesce in a bevy of tensional pulls as a moment of poised stability, and resolve into movement (De Spain 1994).

Rather than a static metaphor, there are many other moving strategies and possibilities (Musil 2001). A scientific concept that fits this model is tensegrity, the engineering design that builds on "continuous tension, discontinuous compression" (Levin 1982, 2). Tensegrity evolved from the merging of engineering (mechanics) and systems thinking, reflected in the work of sculptor Kenneth Snelson, Buckminster Fuller, and biologist Donald Ingber. Principles of tensegrity essentially state that our form is the result of the continuous interaction of tension members (soft tissue) as dynamic support for bones (not the other way around). Structural integration of the body comes through this dynamic organization of tension members suspending the more rigid compression members (bones) in space. "A rigid, axial-loading, gravitationally oriented support system cannot be utilized as a model for animated structures, including the human spine" (Levin 1982, 4).

Mabel Todd and Lulu Sweigard revolutionized the field of "kinesthetic anatomy"[6] throughout much of the second half of the twentieth century. The Todd/Sweigard/Dowd tradition actualized the mechanical model by making it a moving action system through Ideokinesis. Following the dictate (paraphrased), "There is no thought without a motor response" (Todd 1937), both Todd and Sweigard designed ideokinetic imagery to reprogram the neuromuscular system and permanently alter malalignments. Instead of contracting antagonists to obscure the offending action of agonists, Ideokinesis provided dancers with a self-generated experience of balanced action, that is, the kinesthetic *sensation* and visual image of releasing overactive muscles and engaging underactive ones. Todd/Sweigard/Dowd methods of ideokinetic education revolutionized alignment training by creating a method in which sensing and visualizing a *moving* image through the body—however mechanically conceived—changed the existing neuromuscular pattern. This experience of freedom of movement and core support helped dancers free themselves of patterns of fixation and holding.

Instead of placement, timely, appropriate neuromuscular control was essential in promoting efficient, effective dancing. Lulu Sweigard spoke of human movement potential as evolving from priming the *neuromuscular* system through ideokinetic imagery (Sweigard 1974). Sweigard readily saw that passive mechanical balance of the skeleton was impossible in the human body—that skillful neuromuscular counterbalancing kept the skeleton poised. Sweigard provided an excellent analysis of one major cause of malalignment: voluntary neuromuscular interference with structural (mechanical) laws. This produced neuromuscular imbalance, whose long-term sequelae of strain was muscular hypertrophy and bony degeneration. "The two conditions most commonly found with persistent deviations from efficient skeletal alignment are (1) disproportionate development (hypertonicity) of those muscles which are most frequently and continuously engaged in maintaining equilibrium in the upright position, and (2) deformation (mechanical strain) in bones and cartilage resulting from the harmful stresses which occur with persistent and similar unevenness of the pressure of weight. These two conditions can lead to decreased ease and range of movement, and to increased wear and tear on the skeletal framework" (184).

Somatic approaches, such as Ideokinesis, originally were viewed more as "adjuncts"[7] to technique—recuperative tools to alleviate the strains of intensive, mechanistic conditioning, and the sheer occupational hazard of repetition and overuse. More recently, however, somatic approaches have been integrated into technique as fundamental strategies for organizing technical movements (Fortin 1993). Irene Dowd has extended this tradition way beyond its mechanical origins to include a greater understanding of the integration of perception and action (Dowd 1981, 1992) and Dr. Sylvie Fortin has written extensively of the implications of integrating somatic learning into the dance classroom.[8] Yet somatic practices have been met with controversy in the dance world in terms of their efficacy of training and carryover into dance technique and performance (Simpson 1996, 6).

summary

It is not that our concepts of alignment are so incorrect as that they are incomplete, emphasizing rigid body mechanics and hierarchical control of the nervous system. Systems theory has taught us that proper execution of movement emerges from many complex factors—mechanical, neuromuscular, psychosomatic, stylistic (individual variability), environmental—each factor perhaps taking more of a front seat role at any given time. Alignment, then, is always in a state of becoming, not a fixed achievement. Perhaps the old-fashioned word "poise" says it best. Poise is a balanced instantaneous center around which movement orients itself, a moment of anatomical stillness hovering before resolution. As one philosopher of aesthetics states: "Poise is a balanced concentration immediately prior to action. It is the a priori of a self-aware act. Poise itself is an action, but one of a wholly different kind. It differs from ordinary undertakings in point of origination, intention, quality of attention, rhythm, and reason. Poise is the response of awareness to the call of a situation. . . . In its continually renewed sensitivity, it is unlike its apparent siblings—control, steadiness, and firmness of intent. Poise has flexibility. It stretches, bends, adapts, and accommodates while the others remain fixed. Thus, poise is friable. It does not break or shatter in the face of a rapidly evolving confrontation. Poise is fluidity of response. . . . Before poise can reveal itself, a tension that is the psychophysical milieu of accomplishment must ease. Tension obscures poise and banishes it to the ideational realm, where it becomes the idea of relaxation or relief" (Applebaum 1995, 14–15).

While DS theory has helped dancers eliminate perceived contradictions between position and action, dance educators are still left with more questions than answers. What is the best method or approach for teaching alignment? How do teachers nurture flexible strategic problem solving in movement? What control is needed and how much? A summary of systems-based elements that can aid dance teachers in reconceptualizing their teaching of alignment might include:

1. Shifting from thinking of position to action;
2. Emphasizing autonomy and self-regulation in organizing movement;
3. Highlighting the inherent organization that lies within proprioceptive and kinesthetic awareness through movement;
4. Utilizing exploration and discovery as a means of improving neuromuscular control;
5. Conceiving of alignment as a function of creative problem solving, not repetition; and
6. Recognizing the role played by the environmental context.

In the end, is alignment training as we know it really necessary? As this next century evolves, dancers will find the answers to these questions as much in their own "laboratories"—their studios—as they will in those of science.

notes

1. The theoretical roots of the dynamical systems approach to human movement coordination have come from the mathematical modeling of rhythmic limb movements. See Chris Button, Simon Bennett, Keith Davids, "Grasping a Better Understanding of the Intrinsic Dynamics of Rhythmical and Discrete Prehension," *Journal of Motor Behavior* 33 (2001): 27–26. A definition for *dynamic* or *dynamical systems theory* can be found at http://www.artsci.wustl.edu/~philos/MindDict/dynamicsystems.html.
2. These concepts are elaborated among many investigators in the embodied cognition movement as well as those subscribing to dynamical systems theory. A good overview is found in F. Varela, E. Thompson, and E. Rosch, *The Embodied Mind: Cognitive Science and Human Experience* (Cambridge, Mass.: MIT Press, 1991).
3. This term comes from a course title in the Dance Department, University of North Carolina, Greensboro, 1992–1998.
4. Ron Kirby, "The Probable Reality behind Structural Integration," *Bulletin of Structural Integration* 5 (May 1975), and David Gorman's series of articles on tensegrity underlying postural support as utilized by Alexander Technique practitioners, http://www.learningmethods.com.
5. A good review of this concept can be found in the articles in Maxine Sheets-Johnstone, ed., *Giving the Body Its Due*, 132–58.
6. The first time the author encountered the term "kinesthetic anatomy" was in a course with Irene Dowd, New York, 1977.
7. In the summer of 1996, the American Dance Festival brochure divided the course offerings into "Technique" and "Non-Technique" courses, a division that caused its own rift among faculty and administration.

8. For a full listing of Dr. Fortin's writings, please contact *Département de Danse* (Department of Dance), University of Quebec at Montreal, fortin.sylvie@uqam.ca.

works cited

Alexander, F. Matthias. 1932. *The Use of the Self.* Los Angeles: Centerline Press.

Amazaki, Akira. 1996. "Reinventing the Body." *UNESCO Courier* 49 (January): 28.

Applebaum, David. 1995. *The Stop.* Albany: State University of New York Press.

Beavers, Wendell. 1993–94. "Locating Technique." *Movement Research Performance Journal* (Fall–Winter): 4–5.

Bernstein, Nicholai A. 1967. *The Co-ordination and Regulation of Movements.* Oxford: Pergamon Press.

De Spain, Kent. 1994. "More Thoughts on Science and the Improvising Mind." *Contact Quarterly* 19 (Winter–Spring): 58–74.

Dowd, Irene. 1981. *Taking Root to Fly.* Northampton, Mass.: Contact Editions.

———. 1992. "Modes of Perception: Finding Pathways through Inner Worlds." *Contact Quarterly* 17 (Summer–Fall): 51–62.

Feldenkrais, Moshe, and Mark Reese. 1985. "*The Potent Self: A Study of Spontaneity and Compulsion.* Berkeley, Calif.: North Atlantic Books.

Fitt, Sally S. 1982. *Dance Kinesiology.* New York: Schirmer Books.

Fortin, Sylvie. 1993. "When Dance Science and Somatics Enter the Dance Technique Class." *Kinesiology and Medicine for Dance* 4, no. 1: 3–19.

Gendlin, Eugene T. 1982. *Focusing.* 2nd ed. New York: Bantam Books.

———. 1986. *Let Your Body Interpret Your Dreams.* New York: Chiron Publications.

Gibson, James J. 1966. *The Senses Considered as Perceptual Systems.* Boston: Houghton Mifflin.

Gold, Lorenzo. 1992–93. "Gaining Grace—a Somatic Perspective." *Somatics* 9 (Autumn–Winter): 34–41.

Goldfarb, Larry W. 1989. *Articulating Changes: Preliminary Notes to a Theory for Feldenkrais.* Berkeley, Calif.: Feldenkrais Resources.

Grieg, Valerie. 1994. *Inside Ballet Technique: Separating Anatomical Fact from Fiction in the Ballet Class.* Hightstown, N.J.: Princeton Book Company, Publishers.

Hamilton, William. 1982. "The Best Body for Ballet." *Dance Magazine* 61 (October): 81–83.

Hammond, Sandra N. 1993. *Ballet Basics.* 3rd. ed. Mountain View, Calif.: Mayfield Publishing Company.

Hanna, Thomas. 1980. *The Body of Life.* New York: Alfred A. Knopf.

———. 1987–88. "What Is Somatics?" Part Four. *Somatics* 11 (May–June): 56–61.

———. 1988. *Somatics: Reawakening the Mind's Control of Movement, Flexibility, and Health.* New York: Addison-Wesley.

———. 1995. "What Is Somatics?" In Don Hanlon Johnson, ed. *Bone, Breath and Gesture: Practices of Embodiment,* 341–52. Berkeley, Calif.: North Atlantic Books.

Hawkins, Erick. 1992. *The Body Is a Clear Place and Other Statements on Dance.* Princeton, N.J.: Princeton Book Company, Publishers.

Heckler, Richard. 1997. "The Unity of Center: Action and Being." *Somatics* 12 (Spring–Summer): 10–15.

Huang, S., and Donald E. Ingber. 1999. "The Structural and Mechanical Complexity of Cell Growth Control." *Natural Cell Biology* 1, no. 5 (September): E131–38.

Ingber, Donald E. 1998. "The Architecture of Life." *Scientific American* 278 (January): 48–57.

———. 2000. "The Origin of Cellular Life." *Bioessays* 22 (December): 1160–70.

Johnson, Don H. 1980. "Somatic Platonism." *Somatics* 3 (January): 4–7.

Juhan, Deane. 1986. *Job's Body: A Handbook for Bodywork.* Barrytown, N.Y.: Station Hill Press.

Kelso, J. A. Scott. 1982. *Human Motor Behavior.* Hillsdale, N.J.: Lawrence Erlbaum Associates.

Knaster, Mirka. 1996. *The Wisdom of the Body.* New York: Bantam New Age Books.

Laban, Rudolf. 1975. *The Mastery of Movement.* Boston: Plays, Inc.

Latash, Mark L., and Michael T. Turvey, eds. 1996. *Dexterity and Its Development.* Mahwah, N.J.: Lawrence Erlbaum.

Levin, Stephen M. 1982. "Continuous Tension, Discontinuous Compression: A Model of Biomechanical Support for the Body." Reprint from *The Bulletin of Structural Integration* 8, no. 1 (Spring–Summer): 1–5, accessed 2007 at http://www.biotensegrity.com/tension.html.

Maisel, Edward. 1989. *The Alexander Technique: The Essential Writings of F. Matthias Alexander.* New York, N.Y.: Kensington Publishing Corp.

Maturana, Humberto, and Francisco J. Varela. 1979. *Autopioesi and Cognition: The Realization of the Living.* Boston Studies in Philosophy of Science. Boston: Kluwer Academic Publishers.

McKeon R., ed. *The Basic Works of Aristotle.* New York: Random House, 1968.

Musil, Pamela S. 2001. "Chaos Theory and Dance Technique: Studies of Wholeness in Motion." *Journal of Dance Education* 1, no 4 (April): 7–18.

Myers, Martha. 1988. "What Dance Medicine and Science Mean to the Dancer." In Pamela M. Clarkson and Margaret Skrinar, eds., *Science of Dance Training.* Champaign, Ill.: Human Kinetic Books.

Norkin, Cynthia C., and Pamela K. Levangie. 1999. *Joint Structure and Function, A Comprehensive Analysis,* 3rd ed. Philadelphia: F. A. Davis Company.

Peat, F. D. 1986. *The Philosopher's Stone: Chaos, Synchronicity, and the Hidden Order of the World.* New York: Bantam Books.

Pierce, Roger, and Alexandra Pierce. 1989. *Expressive Movement, Posture and Action in Daily Life, Sports, and the Performing Arts.* New York: Insight Books.

Port, Robert F., and Timothy van Gelder, eds. 1995. *Mind as Motion: Explorations in the Dynamics of Cognition.* Cambridge, Mass.: MIT Press.

Reed, Edward S. 1989. "Changing Theories of Postural Development." In Marjorie H. Wollocott and Ann Shumway-Cook, eds., *Development of Posture and Gait Across the Life Span,* 3–24. Columbia: University of South Carolina Press.

Reese, Mark. 1999–2000. "A Dynamic View of the Feldenkrais Method®." *Somatics* 12 (Fall–Winter): 18–26.

Ross, Janet. 1994. "The Right Moves: Challenges of Dance Assessment." *Arts Education Policy Review* 96 (September): 14.

Shearer, R. R. 1992. "Chaos Theory and Fractal Geometry: Their Potential Impact on the Future of Art." *Leonardo* 25 (February): 143–52.

Sheets-Johnstone, Maxine, ed. 1992. *Giving the Body Its Due.* Albany: State University of New York Press.

———. 2000. "The Formal Nature of Emergent Biological Organization and Its Implications for Understandings of Closure." *Annals of the New York Academy of Science* 901.

Simpson, Maria. 1996. "Dance Science: A Second-Step Approach." *Impulse* 4 (January).

Sparger, Celia. 1970. *Anatomy and Ballet: A Handbook for Teachers of Ballet.* New York: Theatre Arts Books.

Steinman, Louise. 1995. *The Knowing Body: The Artist as Storyteller in Contemporary Performance.* Berkeley, Calif.: North Atlantic Books.

Stinson, Sue. 1994. "A Feminist Pedagogy for Children's Dance." Unpublished paper presented at the Conference of Dance and the Child International, Sydney, Australia, July.

Suzuki, Tadashi, and Thomas Rimer. 1986. *Way of Acting: The Theater Writings of Tadashi Suzuki.* New York: Theatre Communications Group, Inc.

Sweigard, Lulu. 1974. *Human Movement Potential: Its Ideokinetic Facilitation.* New York: Dodd, Meade.

Tamboer, J. W. J. 1988. "Images of the Body Underlying Concepts of Action." In O. G. Meijer and K. Roth, eds., *Complex Movement Behavior: The Motor-Action Controversy,* 439–46. North-Holland: The Netherlands: Elsevier Science Publishers.

Thelen, Esther, and Linda B. Smith. 1993. *A Dynamic Systems Approach to the Development of Cognition and Action.* Cambridge, Mass.: Bradford Books/MIT Press.

Todd, Mabel Elsworth. 1937. *The Thinking Body.* New York: Dance Horizons.

Tuan, Yi-Fu. 1977. *Space and Place: The Perspective of Experience.* Minneapolis: University of Minnesota Press, 1977.

Watkins, Andrea, and Priscilla M. Clarkson. 1990. *Dancing Longer, Dancing Stronger: A Dancer's Guide to Improving Technique and Preventing Injury.* Princeton, N.J.: Princeton Book Company.

Winstein, C. J., and H. G. Knecht. 1991. "Movement Science and Its Relevance to Physical Therapy." *Movement Science: An American Physical Therapy Association Monograph.* Alexandria, Va.: The American Physical Therapy Association.

melanie bales

11 falling, releasing, and post-judson dance

During winter 2002, I was again fascinated by the kaleidoscope of bodies and stories paraded before us, courtesy of TV Olympic coverage. While I watched athletes collaborate, defy, mock, flirt, resist, escape, and surrender to gravity, I didn't give much thought to questions of underlying assumptions or values. I did find myself arguing out loud again with the ice skating commentators in matters of style, taste, and elusive notions of beauty and form. "So what if they fall down?" I ask from my dancer-viewpoint, choosing to ignore the essence of competition and focusing on the movement in and of itself. "A fall is just an accident," I argue, "it doesn't *mean* anything!"

the meanings of fall

Not until a few weeks later as I picked up a copy of *Sports Illustrated* did I think again about falling at the Olympics. The line under the article's title is not subtle: "It's easy to look good when you're on top of the world. The challenge is looking good when you're flat on your face—or bottomed out" ("Fall Fashions" 2002). It is not so much an article as a photo gallery, picturing athletes in various moments of disarray and disassemblage; a luger sliding off the apparatus onto one shoulder, legs flung out and up; an ice skater straining to catch herself with her hand as she falls back, one leg bent and inwardly rotated at an alarming angle; a skier shown on one side and plunging headfirst down the hill with obvious strain on her face; another skier viewed spread-eagle; a speed skater grimacing as she tumbles, her powerful legs helplessly flailing the air. It all spells trouble, a fall *off* the pedestal and *from* grace, unflattering echoes of the now iconic "agony of defeat" footage. To fall down here is to lose dignity, stature, conquest, the medal. Compare this to dance techniques where falling is an art: Doris Humphrey's fall and recovery, or Contact Improvisation, or the dancelike martial art of Aikido with its curvilinear swoops and rolls.

Counterexamples to the "falling as defeat" model exist, even in high-powered competitive sports. Perhaps not coincidentally, two such examples emerge from relatively recent history. Snowboarding was the big sensation at the 2002 Olympics. These athletes tumble in the air, making upside-down and off-the-vertical a good thing. The more confusing and confounding the stunt looks, the better; simpler and more extended lines of the body are not favored. Speed is not the issue; valued is the thrill of the trick, the personal style, complexity, and daring. Like the ski jumper, snowboarders fly, but they look less like soaring birds and more like hip-hop acrobats. Interestingly, these athletes resemble skateboarders in the slacker torso and more relaxed limbs. These are bodies that don't mind being thrown around, up, and over; they go with the force rather than straining against it. Falling on a landing or off the board would be "a bummer," but somehow not as tragic or as awkward as the *Sports Illustrated* photos of other sports.

Recalling the amazing ice-dancing pair Christopher Dean and Jane Torville yields a second example of alternative falling. At that time there was an increase in ice touching; skaters got down on their knees, caressed the ice, or dragged their partners across it. In the final moment of the ground-breaking *Bolero* choreography, Torville and Dean fell with ecstatic and almost reckless abandon across the ice and each other, splayed out rather than decoratively arranged. This final gesture followed Ravel's musical one of climax reached and collapse. There was something subversive about it too. The last movement created a more raw sexual tone than previous ice dancing, seemed to flaunt the conventions of the sport/art itself, where the big finish is usually cheery, presentational, and upright. Just as Dean had taken the form into new territory in other ways by his brilliant movement invention, here he chose simply to fall.

orientational metaphors

Offering ways to draw links between bodily states and other human experience, the authors of *Metaphors We Live By* have identified "orientational metaphors . . . (which) have to do with spatial orientation: up-down, in-out, front-back, on-off, deep-shallow, central-peripheral" (Lakoff and Johnson 1980, 14). These metaphors show that experiential bases for meaning are present in language. Words belie our cultural and human connections between the physical and the expressive: "But metaphor is not merely a matter of language. It is a matter of conceptual structure. And conceptual structure is not merely a matter of the intellect—it involves all the natural dimensions of our experience, including aspects of our sense experiences: color, shape, texture, sound, etc." (235). (To this list I would add kinesthesia and proprioception.)

Considering some of the up-down pairs from *Metaphors We Live By* can give us points of reference in order to test assumptions embedded in language (here, English). For example: happy is up, sad is down (high spirits, feeling down); conscious is up, unconscious is down (wake up, fall asleep); health/life are up, sickness/death are down (peak of health, fell ill); having control is up, being subject to control is down (on top of the situation, under my control); more is up, less is down; high status is up, low status is down; good is up, bad is down (high quality work, all-time low); virtue is up, depravity is down (upstanding citizen, a low-down thing to do); rational is up, emotional is down. The "physical basis" given for that last pair is because humans exert control over plants, animals, and some natural phenomena and, since humans can reason, control is up (on top), man is up and rational is up (17). I would also point to the fact that, anatomically and spatially, our head is above our heart and our gut when we are standing!

Lakoff and Johnson reflect on the fact that "verticality enters our experience in many different ways and so gives rise to many different metaphors" (19) In other words, the same bodily experience (such as our relationship with gravity, or orientation to the earth) can produce overlapping and even conflicting bands of meaning. An example given for this is: "That's up in the air" versus "The matter is settled." While those phrases are not coherent with "good is up" or "finished is up" (as in "finish up"), they *are* coherent with understanding as grasping—it is easier to grasp something if it is fixed or on the ground rather than floating (20). A consideration of these suggestions provides ample opportunity to connect values and meaning with examples from movement practices including dance, yoga class, or sport.

To this list, we could add the notions of *going* up or *going* down, phrases that imply movement not just position, motional rather than static. Following the Torville and Dean example, I might project into their descent the following implications or relationships: loss of control; emotionality; lower status (usually skaters want to be on their skates), even some depravity, as suggested earlier, or ill-health. Owing in some part to how these things added a layer of passion and risk, and to Dean's genius, the routine was a big hit.

Considering the oppositional pair, upside-down versus right-side-up (note the obvious preference in the word "right") is also evocative. Practically and anatomically, we are not meant to stand on our hands. Our structure doesn't support it, nor does our circulatory system or our balancing mechanisms. Upside-down can be confused, literally disoriented, the opposite of logical, or at least unusual as in "she turned everything upside down." Going a step further, upside-down has the idea of going against the grain, being off-beat, even subversive or mocking. Yet, upside-down is also miraculous, superhuman, amazing. We marvel at the acrobat, the trapeze artist, or the skateboarder.

The notion of going against, or defying, gravity is an important one. Gravity may be the law we cannot break, but we can die trying. Flying, floating, being lifted or thrown, feelings of elatedness and "walking on air" are experiences related to that notion. As above, those experiences describe a body in motion, in contrast to the static states of *being* up or down. Gravity reminds us that we live on our earth; it is the force that draws us to earth, and our reminder that we have limitations. On the other side, Mother Earth is reassuring, generous, life-sustaining. Being "down to earth" is a complimentary descriptor. Again, as Johnson and Lakoff point out, a range of meanings on both positive and negative sides can issue from a single experiential base.

techniques and judson dance theatre

Interaction with gravity is a core issue with regard to almost all aspects of dance in terms of technique (how to do it), style (what makes it distinct), and expressiveness (what it means or communicates). Any style of dance, or choreography, or single dance will make some statement about the gravity and the body. In light of this, it is interesting to look back at the creative and sea-change producing phenom in modern dance known as the Judson era. This refers historically to the years 1962–64, when works were produced at the Judson Church in New York City, and, less specifically, to the artists and trends associated with that period. There have been some recent events—such as the PastForward performance project, which produced revivals from that era—that suggest the time is now far enough back to elicit all kinds of examination, hindsight, and nostalgia.

"Judson" has almost become a synecdoche for an artistic worldview in dance, although the explorations represented a multiplicity of world- and other views from the onset. It is almost always inaccurate or useless to speak monolithically about a group of contemporaneous artists or artistic values, as evidenced by arguments about the use of descriptors such as "postmodern" to cover the Judson period and what came thereafter. I will, however, attempt to link some ideas in dance since the Judson (or postmodern) time to previously stated notions about falling and gravity, meaning and metaphor.

Another interrelated term to post-Judson and/or postmodern is "release technique." The term as used by dancers and choreographers is one that defies a strict definition, yet most dancers could easily identify certain dancers or choreographers as exemplars. Whether or not there is great agreement on who does or teaches release technique is another matter. Two 1999 issues of the *Movement Research Performance Journal* (the mouthpiece of "downtown dance," yet another label both handy and flawed) were devoted to demystifying or at least discussing the topic. On the cover of volume 18, editor DD Dorvillier refers to "the study of gravity . . . its limitations, its benefits" (1999, 1).

Several contributors or subjects reject the label altogether—even the very ones that are associated with release by many dancers. For example, there is a photo of Trisha Brown, former Judsonite and still an influential choreographer, with a caption that reads: "I don't have any idea what release technique is, my body moves how it wants to move."[1] Susan Klein, who developed concepts from Bartenieff Fundamentals among other things to become a highly regarded movement teacher for the past twenty years, writes, "Klein Technique is not a release technique" (Klein 1999, 9).

On the other side, Daniel Lepkoff, who studied with Mary Fulkerson of the Mabel Todd/Lulu Sweigard lineage (other movement theorists who impacted dance), embraces "release technique" and takes issue with others who would claim it (1999, 7). In brief, sometimes the release label is embraced, sometimes not, but the *idea* of releasing from many different things—old habits, old styles, tension, holding patterns—seems to be shared by nearly all the writers and responders who contributed to the journal. Another related theme revolved around the idea of movement efficiency: doing more with less, using momentum rather than force, along with Zen ideas of "getting out of the way" and "letting it happen."

Kirsty Alexander says of Skinner Releasing: "Releasing alignment is multi-directional and dimensional which implies suspension rather than support and therefore there is no up or down, nor no fixed centre of gravity" (1999, 8). In many somatic practices, the body's relationship to gravity is examined on and off the vertical axis, through exercises or experiences that require lying, sitting, or getting up and down from the floor. Alignment is not about standing straight or upright but rather about the changing relationships within the body, sensing balance, and avoiding unnecessary muscular holding so the body is open to possibility. Based both on my experience with these practices and from texts of the originators, all of those things can be said about Alexander Technique, Bartenieff Fundamentals, Bainbridge Cohen's Body-Mind Centering, Moshe Feldenkrais's work, Sweigard's ideokinesis, and Klein Technique.

Release technique(s) and the Judson period of the 1960s are related historically and aesthetically; people who developed or practice release techniques have roots in common with movement educators like Mabel Elsworth Todd, Lulu E. Sweigard, Barbara Clark, Irmgard Bartenieff, and F. M. Alexander, among others. This cross-fertilization produced new movement and dance forms, incubating both in universities and in the professional arena. A few examples: the coming together of Steve Paxton (Judsonite) and movement educators/theorists like Mary Fulkerson in the development of Contact Improvisation; the lineage of Margaret H'Doubler (university movement educator) to Anna Halprin (Judson foremother) to Deborah Hay, Simone Forti, and Trisha Brown (Judsonites).

Movement techniques that came out of the desire for a more "natural" use of the body developed alongside choreographic pursuits. It is no wonder that dancers began to investigate existing body techniques, extending lines of inquiry from figures like F. M. Alexander or Moshe Feldenkrais, or adopting practices from the East, such as yoga and Aikido (Wheeler 1984). Contact Improvisation represents an interesting crossroads where group process and democratic ideals transferred to the physical experience of giving and taking (of ideas and weight); and the highly skilled (Steve Paxton: Cunningham dancer, Judsonite, martial arts student) contacting alongside the less skilled, at least in the beginning stages. What followed was often an exploration of falling and recovering, risk management, trust exercises, and a thorough experience of the participant's relationship to gravity, including being off the vertical.

Falling or releasing into gravity with trust and playfulness, as in Contact, points to another "alternative falling" idea similar to those mentioned in the sports examples and offers yet another view of the up-down pairings. In this way of falling there is resiliency, the return of energy, and sense of rebound. In much of post-Judson or "release" work, the dancer focuses on dropping or falling into gravity and then catching the movement, and redirecting it through clear spatial intentions.[2] In her chapter on Judson entitled "Everyday Bodies," Deborah Jowitt remarks how the popularity of Eastern martial arts forms prompted movement ideas such as "acting without forcing" and being "alive in passivity" and underscored the notion of being more in tune with natural rhythms. These feelings are reflected in release technique phrasing where, as in Jowitt's references, "follow-throughs eroded into new windups" rather than clear or posed beginnings and endings (Jowitt 1988, 326). This looks very different from early modern versions of fall and recovery. In the work of Doris Humphrey or José Limón, the eventual shapes are held more deliberately, the falls are more controlled, and often more forcefully directed. Also, the serious tone of Humphrey's "arc between two deaths" is missing in more recent work where falling is featured.

Trillium, one of Trisha Brown's earliest dance works, was a study in getting up and lying down, built on "two movement themes: a sit-down fall and handstands" (Banes 1993, 121). Steve Paxton noted of *Trillium* in Banes's *Democracy's Body*, "It was odd to see people doing a handstand in a dance at that time" or "off their feet doing anything but a very controlled fall." Brown herself speaks of her engagement with gravity in non-struggle terms; fellow Judsonite William Davis found the dance "elastic and floppy" (121). She named the dance after a flower that wilted and faded on the way home from picking it. Like many of her dances since, the image refers to something soft, indulgent and yielding, curling in on itself. It is this delightful quality of resiliency and the playful attitude that is both so appealing and emblematic of the style. In one *Performance Journal* entry, the Trisha Brown Company had "a relaxed, easy quality (no strongly pointed feet or contracted torsos here) and favored quick bending of the joints and sequential movement initiated by specific body parts" (Moss 1999, 4).

playing it down

Much of the movement experimentation of the Judson era had to do with notions about falling and other forms of release and contributed to the distinction between dance of that era and prior eras. Judsonites reconsidered the technical and aesthetic ideas of their dance predecessors. They turned away from the angst and grand mythic scale of Graham, or the "dancerliness" of Cunningham, and experimented with human scale and the hyperpersonal or idiosyncratic. They disengaged (dropped out) from the idea of the artist as genius, and tried to be craftsmen, or in some dances, much less than that.

In a summary of her presentation for the 2000 Dancing in the Millennium Conference, and drawing on her experience as a dancer in the 1970s and director of the Bennington Judson Project, Wendy Perron produced several lists under the title "The Lasting Influence of Judson Dance Theatre." One of the lists is composed of "the aspects that I feel are still with us or that have evolved into a lasting influence." From that list: "*A new idea about the body:* Simone Forti left the Graham school because she was asked to hold her belly in. The JDT dancers required a more relaxed body to counter what Jill Johnston called the pulled-up rigidity of ballet. This fed into the development of release technique, both as a healing technique . . . and as an approach to choreography" (Perron 2002, 27). In so many of the Judson dances, and in work that issued from the influence, the high emotional affect so apparent in other styles as reflected in a held or expanded torso, was replaced by what Laban /Bartenieff theory would call a "relaxed body attitude."

> Posture and body attitude are most often used interchangeably, the latter generally incorporating the element of expressive content. In common usage, posture refers to total body alignment along the vertical axis struggling with anti-gravity forces. However, in common metaphorical usage, posture also indicates expressive content as, for example in the reference to "the posture" one assumes with regard to an issue. (Bartenieff 1980, 109)

So, exploring new relationships to gravity, or opting for a less formalized or held torso can expose new attitudes or "postures" towards the body and the world, as seen in the following examples.

In a self-interview originally for *Ballet Review*, Trisha Brown referred to her desire to work with dancers who can free themselves of certain habits like the "puffed out ribcage." A trained dancer "couldn't necessarily do a natural kind of movement, even a simple one. So what I looked for was a person with a natural, well-coordinated, instinctive ability to move" (Brown and Dunn 1979, 169). She then acknowledged that later she became more interested in working with "unnatural movement" (170).

In *Democracy's Body*, Sally Banes's account of the Judson concerts, a Steve Paxton piece is described. He had deconstructed some material from ballet that was "recognizable on stage by one of its essential components: a taut, charged body" (Banes 1993, 45). We can assume that it was Paxton's intention to personally inhabit the "taut, charged body" from either an ironic or ludic postmodernist stance, rather than a sincere attempt to become a *danseur noble*. These examples from Brown and Paxton point to the rejection (either by leaving out or making fun) of the heroic or grand posture, including a held or stilted torso.

Another Paxton solo, *Transit*, was "marked," the dancer version of *sotto voce*, or movement done with the least possible energy and usually in diminution. Not only does it render the doer less than presentational but, as Yvonne Rainer points out, marking "has a very special look tending to blur boundaries between consecutive movements" (1979, 146). Here, by dropping out the high affect of the trained dancer, Paxton transformed both the phrasing and the body carriage.

Robert Morris wrote about some of the early ideas he shared with collaborator Simone Forti: "I wanted to avoid the pulled-up, turned-out, antigravitational qualities that not only have a body definition and role as 'dancer' but qualify and delimit the movement available" (Banes 1993, 143). Rainer also attempted a human scale dance with *Trio A,* which is now, ironically, an icon in dance history. From observation of the recorded performance of Rainer in that piece and in versions by others, we can note the slack or relaxed torso, along with relatively uninflected gesture.

The more "everyday" posture or released torso signaled a change in attitude towards the world and the world of American dance in this case.[3] Many of the Judson dances explored the line between dancer and nondancer, questioning the purpose and value of dance technique itself, and deciding in favor of using found, pedestrian, or improvised movement. If looking like a dancer meant having to hold yourself (literally) up, then they let themselves respond to gravity in a different way. For this reason, I identify relaxed body attitude idea as a form of falling, even though the body may not be falling through space or down to the floor. The experience of releasing tension, or giving in to gravity is still present. This experience also suggests a metaphorical falling away from old ideas, limitations, and approaches, and may also suggest vulnerability, humility, or passive resistance.[4]

lma and passive weight

In Laban's Effort theory, the Weight Factor has to do with how the mover senses and activates his/her own weight, and is represented as a continuum from strongest (intense, highly charged, assertive, often driving movement) to lightest (delicate, refined, wispy, vaporous in quality) Weight. Effort theory is one part of Laban/Bartenieff Movement Analysis (LMA), which also addresses bodily and spatial aspects. The other three Factors in the Effort theory (Space, Time, and Flow) complete the variables that combine to create the myriad of movement qualities possible in human movement. According to Laban theory, movement quality is also inextricably linked to expression or intention, as seen in the Bartenieff quote above. This works in much the same way as Lakoff and Johnson's orientational metaphors, where a physical phenomenon is linked to a metaphorical one. For example, Strong Weight (forceful, concentrated use of one's weight) is associated with firm resoluteness of purpose.

Analyzing the Weight Factor is part of Laban dance style analysis, which can reveal intention, attitude, and meaning, and connects or distinguishes one style, one mover, or one movement from others. The Strong to Light continuum does not, however, include the concept of *passive* weight where the mover is involved in sensing weight, but is not really acting on it by intensifying (Strong) or rarifying (Light). Allowing, letting go, releasing, and falling are all experiences or expressions more related to passive weight, or weight sensing. We have seen how those concepts have played a vital role since the Judson era in dance, and could connect with my earlier examples from sport or other movement practices where explorations of upside-down, off-vertical, relaxed body attitude, and so on, figure prominently.

This is not to suggest that dances of the Judson era and the styles or choreography that issued from the Judson influences were *primarily* concerned with passive weight but that it played a bigger role stylistically than in earlier forms of modern dance, such as the Graham technique (often very Strong, Bound, and Direct). Perhaps this was also part of "keeping it real": no to floating angel moves (Light), no to the bold hero (Strong). Also, a body with less muscular tone or tension, and a more relaxed body attitude, will take on a different cast under the spell of gravity than does a body with held or high-toned physical texture. Movement may be more isolated to body parts, or ripple through the body one part at a time (successively), as opposed to movement where the whole body moves as one piece (simultaneously). A fairly extreme example of simultaneity with held body attitude would be a military march.

The movement descriptors above—more passive weight and lower tone—would apply to a significant body of work coming out of or after the Judson explorations. What started in some cases as the result of questioning (values of dance, role of artist in society), investigating (Eastern philosophy, theatre ideas, your own limitations), and creating (new strategies for dance, new forms of art) resulted in new styles of movement. Perhaps given the particular influences of the time, a *falling away* from tradition, whether in playful or rejecting spirit, was more likely than a storming of the Bastille. In any case, the legacy of that period is still shaping dance today—from actual movement style to the idea that any and all forms of dance and movement are fair game.

Wending my way through several tangential fields of inquiry and forms of physical practice, it is possible to see how an experiential concept can be a way into knowledge of multiple sorts. Seeing movement in its complexity with regard to context, bodily elements and possible meaning will eventually lead to more understanding, and less reliance on established routes. There are so many fascinating and affecting displays of the human body and human condition all around us, falling and rising in ways uncountable.

notes

1. See photo, page 17, in *Movement Research Performance Journal* 1999.
2. This is not to say that every Judson choreographer was as involved with negotiating gravity to the same degree or in the same way. Lucinda Childs's work remains fiercely vertical, composed mainly of step patterns and direction changes. In terms of Lakoff and Johnson's orientational verticality schemata, her work could be related to: up is

rational, having control is up, conscious is up. However, since that period, the change in body attitude and the willing release into gravity are two significant movement values that are still finding resonance today.

3. In an article on Africanisms in Balanchine's choreography, dance historian Brenda Dixon Gottschild suggests: "So much of what we see as avant-garde in the postmodern movement is actually informed by recycled Africanist principles. The coolness, relaxation, looseness, and laid-back energy . . ." (Gottschild 195, 99). I agree that those sensibilities were becoming more prevalent and valued during this period, as through popular music and dance, by mainstream white culture; and Judsonites were, for the most part, white upper-middle class intellectuals within a supposedly anti-intellectual counterculture. However, I do not think these "recycled principles" can be seen as the sole influences resulting in the released look. It is interesting to note that a relationship exists between hip-hop culture (Africanist), those same attributes Gottschild names, and the body attitude of the quasi-outlaw, counterculture skateboarders and snowboarders.
4. It is interesting to examine some of the values and assertions in terms of our up-down, falling-rising schemata. Going against the stream (the establishment, the military-industrial complex, the king, tradition) usually requires, as in the phraseology of Johnson and Lakoff, standing up for yourself, rising to the occasion, swimming upstream. Yet, in the 60s rebellion, people were dropping out, tuning in (to yourself) or tuning out (in meditation), letting go, letting it all hang out, trying not to be *up*tight. All of those expressions have a direction of going down or in: giving in to gravity rather than struggling against it. Here is another example of how seemingly contradictory metaphors can coexist.

works cited

Alexander, Kirsty. 1999. "You Can't Make a Leaf Grow by Stretching It." *Movement Research Performance Journal* 18.

Banes, Sally. 1993. *Democracy's Body: Judson Dance Theater, 1962–1964*. Durham, N.C.: Duke University Press.

Bartenieff, Irmgard, with Dori Lewis. 1980. *Body Movement: Coping with the Environment.* Langhorne, Pa.: Gordon and Breach.

Brown, Trisha, and Douglas Dunn. 1979. "Dialogue on Dance." In Jean Morrison Brown, ed., *The Vision of Modern Dance.* Princeton: Princeton Book Co.

Dorvillier, D D. 1999. Editor's Notes. *Movement Research Performance Journal* 18.

"Fall Fashions." 2002. *Sports Illustrated,* 25 February: 64–69.

Gottschild, Brenda Dixon. 1995. "Stripping the Emperor: The Africanist Presence in American Concert Dance." In David Gere, ed., *Looking Out.* New York: Schirmer Books.

Jowitt, Deborah. 1988. *Time and the Dancing Image.* New York: William Morrow.

Klein, Susan T. 1999. "A Movement Technique—A Healing Technique." *Movement Research Performance Journal* 18.

Lakoff, George, and Mark Johnson. 1980. *Metaphors We Live By.* Chicago: University of Chicago Press.

Lepkoff, Daniel. 1999. "What Is Release Technique?" *Movement Research Performance Journal* 19.

Moss, Diane. 1999. "Coming to Terms with the Release Technique." *Movement Research Performance Journal* 18.

Perron, Wendy. 2002. "The Lasting Influence of Judson Dance Theater." *Dance USA Journal* 18, no. 1.

Rainer, Yvonne. 1979. "The Mind Is a Muscle." In Jean Morrison Brown, ed., *The Vision of Modern Dance.* Princeton: Princeton Book Co.

Wheeler, Mark. 1984. "Surface to Essence: Appropriation of the Orient by Modern Dance." Ph.D. diss., The Ohio State University.

part iii

training stories

Part III includes sixteen training histories of dance professionals currently working in the field. Our initial idea in conducting these interviews was the notion of inserting short, one-paragraph thumbnail sketches throughout the book to provide personal viewpoints as mini-illustrations of the themes. But in the process of collecting the interviews, we discovered that each dance professional had an engaging story to tell, and that these stories collectively emerged as the text that could illuminate all of the main issues that we had identified in our initial discussions about current dance training. Our selection process was fairly random—we took advantage of guest artists in our respective university dance programs, or dancers and choreographers that we came in contact with in the profession during the two-year span in which the majority of the interviews were conducted. Our criteria were simply that they were or had been professional dancers or choreographers and that they met at least one of our guidelines for identifying post-Judson training (outlined in the Preface). Formats for these interviews vary from question/answer, to summaries, to narratives.

As expected, the themes of deconstruction and bricolage in dance training surfaced in almost every interview; some dancers stayed firmly in one mode or the other, while others had gone through intervals of both. A pattern of alternation between the two modes, with a period of gathering information or studying many different styles of dance, followed by a period of debriefing, or stripping away was also a common training strategy.

Falling under the heading "Deconstruction," we found that ridding the body of unwanted habits, holding patterns, or overworking was a universal theme, with almost all of those interviewed having studied at least one somatic practice. Modalities include Bartenieff Fundamentals and Laban Movement Analysis, Alexander Technique, Feldenkrais work, Klein Technique, Yoga, Pilates, and Gyrotonics, among others. Experiences in these practices varied from dabbling in various different techniques to a long-term investment in one modality, even leading to certification in some cases. Some came to the work from an injury, some fell upon it by chance, and others sought it out for a more in-depth exploration. Those who fell most clearly in this category include Chris Aiken, Kathleen Fisher, Mark Haim, Sara Hook, Iréne Hultman, and Bebe Miller. Eclectics in their approach to dance training included, but were certainly not limited to, David Dorfman, Angie Hauser, and Cynthia Oliver. Many of the artists interviewed related an early stage of gathering, or soaking up, many different styles of dance followed by a period of debriefing, stripping away—evolving to a stage of synthesis.

Other interesting subthemes within the Deconstruction/Bricolage dance-training model emerged as we spoke with the dance artists. First, the use of improvisation, not only as a choreographic tool or a performance art but as an essential training component, was discussed by a number of artists, including Iréne Hultman, Kathleen Fisher, Ralph Lemon, Bebe Miller, Angie Hauser, Sara Hook, and Contact Improvisation specialist Chris Aiken. Partnering was also identified as an important factor informing technical training by Stephen Koester, Miller, and Aiken. Several dancers brought up the significance of athletic training in their backgrounds, including Aiken, Hauser, and Hultman.

The majority of interviewees revealed the importance of ballet as a primary component of, or a through-line to, their training, even though they identified themselves as modern dancers. Janet Panetta brought ballet training to many of the modern dancers, most notably in the 1980s, although as a performer she transitioned from a ballet to a modern dancer. Shelley Washington, Angie Hauser, and Karen Graham were ballet-trained; many, such as Cynthia Oliver and Stephen Koester identified ballet as beneficial for "maintenance," Miller described it as "medicine," and Panetta as "vitamins." Many continue to take ballet, or at least *barre,* as a means of maintenance or refinement of their training.

A traditional conservatory training was also common among the interviewees—Kraig Patterson, Shelley Washington, and Mark Haim studied at Juilliard; Sara Hook at North Carolina School of the Arts, and Janet Panetta at American Ballet Theatre. Most, but not all, have university degrees in dance. And following the modern dance tradition, there were some that went through stages of rebellion and rejection after studying codified techniques.

Another theme that emerged, especially in speaking with several of the men, was the blurring of lines in the identification of the training period as separate from or preceding the period of professional performing. The notion of training as a preparation for a professional life in dance was not clearly defined in the backgrounds of Stephen Koester, Ralph Lemon, Angie Hauser, and Chris Aiken, for example. Likewise, several interviewees, including Stephen Koester, noted that they began teaching almost as soon as they began dancing, crediting teaching as a significant training element, and even as their own technical practice. Others, such as Tere O'Connor and David Dorfman, identified themselves as choreographers very early in their careers, challenging the model of establishing oneself as a dancer before becoming a designated "choreographer."

As discussed in the Preface, most interviewees reported that the model of choreographers training dancers in their style by teaching technique classes is no longer prevalent. Rehearsals have become the training ground, with dancers selecting their own technique packages. Tere O'Connor, for example, never recommends where or how his dancers study. There is more emphasis on learning by doing rather than learning in a technique class format and *then* doing. Some of the individuals interviewed, including Chris Aiken, Kathleen Fisher, and Ralph Lemon, described their personal practices, working alone rather than engaging in the established dance tradition of "taking class."

A recurring theme in the interviews was that of "circling back around," of rediscovering and reinvesting in one's dance roots, so to speak. In many cases, what attracted a young dancer to engage in a movement practice in the very beginning seems to be central in some way to who he or she is as a dance artist. In some instances, there is a rejection and a journey away from those first experiences. We found though, that many of the artists interviewed returned to at least a kernel of those established foundations that launched them into the dance or movement arena. Cynthia Oliver, for example, circled back to her Caribbean dance roots, not only incorporating this information into her vast array of experiences with a myriad of styles but embracing it as a central element in her work. Ralph Lemon, another example, was a runner in high school and now, after many years of dance classes, running has once again become a major part of his movement practice.

It seems that interviewing is in the air. At least two books have come out during the writing of this one that feature firsthand accounts from performers and choreographers: *Re-inventing Dance in the 60s,* edited by Sally Banes, and Brenda Dixon Gottschild's *The Black Dancing Body.* It is our hope that the words of the dance artists that follow will be informative, illustrative, even entertaining. Besides giving a "day in the life" description from a sampling of professional dancers, these interviews serve to give a broad picture of the post-Judson contemporary dance world from the studio, where the "meat and potatoes" of dance is practiced.

— Rebecca Nettl-Fiol

12 training stories

chris aiken

from an interview with rebecca nettl-fiol, june 2002

Chris Aiken is a leading international teacher and performer in the field of dance improvisation and Contact Improvisation. He is currently an Assistant Professor of Dance at Ursinus College, Collegeville, Pennsylvania.

rnf The first question is to discuss your dance training history, from the beginning, until now, especially the defining moments, or the things that had the most impact on you as a dance artist.

ca I'll talk about the most important teachers I had, and then go chronologically. Probably one of the two most important teachers was Nancy Stark Smith, who is one of the cofounders of Contact Improvisation. I could tell right away that she was a master teacher, and she is somebody that I have always held as the model of how I want to teach as I get older. She was important to me because she not only showed me the basics of Contact but she also showed me how what you think about, the images that you think about and use to prepare yourself as you're working, completely change your body state.

rnf When did you study with her?

ca This was 1986, -7, -8, -9. My first dance class was in 1980. But I didn't seriously get going until 1983. The other person that was important was Andrew Harwood, and he's from Montreal. He's one of the second generation of Contact dancers. What Andrew did was to model and speak about a way of moving that was spherically oriented; in other words, it was Aikido-based, and the idea was that one developed movement capacity in all areas of one's kinesphere. And that the movement was always connected to the center of the body, which is very martial arts–like. And he introduced me to a lot of the inverted work, being upside-down. He also was very acrobatic in the way he would dance and partner and do Contact. In my early days, and still to a certain degree now, I always appreciated sheer athleticism—people who could really launch their bodies into space and recover.

That's something to point out, going back into my training, I had probably fifteen years of athletics—I did many different sports. My main ones were swimming and running, but I also did wrestling, lacrosse, tennis, gymnastics, and fencing. When I first came to dance in 1980, it was because I had met these ballet dancers when I was camping, and I was just amazed at their physicality. They looked to me like they were eighteen years old, although they were probably thirty. Their bodies were in perfect condition. And I just realized that there were other ways to stay in shape besides doing sports. So I thought, "Well, maybe that would be interesting, to take some dance classes." So I went into ballet. And very quickly I thought, "These guys don't move," and besides, I didn't like the music. I also realized that I was starting so late that I didn't think I'd ever really be good at it. But I met some folks in Boston who were part of a community called Dance New England. And that was a community of people who gathered periodically to improvise, and they're the people that introduced me to Contact. Their physicality was at such a high level I thought, "I want to do that!"

Another important element in my training was that I went to a workshop several times called A Cappella Motion. It was a fantastic workshop, with high-level professionals from all over the world, and one of the people there who had a profound influence on me was Sue Schell, a teacher of Authentic Movement. Sue was a powerful teacher because she had this amazing presence that could generate a sense of safety and support for exploration in a room of people. In terms of models for my teaching, Sue was important because I wanted to create a safe environment where people could really explore and yet not have it be just an amorphous new age, touchy-feely kind of experience. She had the ability to get a roomful of people doing amazing work that was very deep and powerful, but keep it centered. It wasn't just the words, it was her whole presence and being, and so it was not a technique, it was who she was as a teacher that inspired me. Karen Nelson and Alito Alessi also were early Contact teachers.

One of my first improvisation teachers was Bart McCarthy, and what was good about Bart was that he was an actor, so he approached improvisation as a choreographer from the very get-go. He taught me simple compositional principles. Since I got that at the beginning of my training, along with Contact, I had a somatic and compositional base right from the beginning, and that's been essential to who I am as an artist.

Then there is another layer. After I'd done a lot of Contact work and the compositional work, I was also studying bodywork. And that gave me understanding about anatomy and physiology, and began to introduce me to the whole notion of somatics. Even though I was doing Contact, nobody ever talked about somatics; we were just doing it. But I really didn't get to another level of that until I met Eva Karczag. She is a dancer who used to dance with Trisha Brown, and she introduced me to release technique and Alexander work. I look at that as being introduced to my bones.

Skipping back to improvisation, Simone Forti was another person that I met at the time that I was learning improvisation, and Simone was quite a powerful influence because of her blend of incredible intelligence and capacity to work in a stream-of-consciousness way. She would tell stories and improvise at the same time in ways that were amazingly intuitive and nontechnical, but highly virtuosic.

When I moved to Minneapolis I started working with Patrick Scully, an action theatre–based artist. That kind of improvising is largely about improvised text, or storytelling with movement. That was good for me because it represented a form for exploring extremes of emotion. That was really influential.

Another person, obviously, was Steve Paxton. I had met Steve numerous times because I would attend these jams called the Breitenbush Contact Jam. Steve's work really influenced me, not only because of the Contact work and the Aikido training that informed that work, but also the spherical movement awareness that I was talking about earlier. He also made me conscious of the power of the mind to influence how you move. He does all kinds of exercises that are perceptually oriented that get you thinking about how you perceive.

Let's see if I can think of any other things. I've probably had fifteen to twenty "technical dance classes" in the jazz, ballet, and modern world. And they all happened when I was between ages twenty and twenty-two, twenty years ago! Part of the reason I didn't pursue that was, first of all, once I found improvisation, that was my love, that's where I felt I could express myself and it really engaged my mind in ways that the other dance forms didn't. Another reason is, I'm partially dyslexic, so I had a hard time learning quickly. And I found that incredibly frustrating. I felt I was never dancing. I was just marking movement, approximating it, imitating it. And having come from an athletic background where I knew what it was like to fully move my body, it was just not interesting to me. If I couldn't really move, I didn't want to do it.

rnf You answered most of my questions. I was interested in knowing whether it was a conscious choice not to study the more traditional techniques. But I think you answered it.

ca It wasn't, "I'm not going to do that." It was, "I'm interested in *this*." When I started dancing, I never had any intention of being a dancer. I just started pulling on a thread. It was an interest I had, and I just kept growing in it. And the truth is, as a male dancer there were opportunities for me to perform very early, when I didn't know what I was doing. Part of what kept me going was that I really did love performing. But I think if that were the only thing, I would have stopped. What I really came to love was the practice of moving with people, the collaborative process. And somehow, that was one of the most sustaining things—that you could actually cooperate with other people and make something seemed a miracle to me.

One of the interesting things in my development is that when I was about three years into dancing, it's going to sound blasphemous, but I started teaching. The reason was that in Boston at that time, there were very few people teaching what I wanted to learn, which was Contact, and later, improvisation. So what I started doing was coteaching with my partner at the time, Olivier Besson. I realized very early in my dance career that teaching was a way of research, because as soon as you start teaching, you realize what you don't know. That was seminal in the development of my becoming a serious artist and a serious dancer, because at that point I realized that I really wanted to learn, I really wanted to get to a high level in my movement, and in my artistry, and that the way to do that was to bring in people from the outside. So I became a producer. I would bring all the best people that I knew into Boston to teach workshops. By producing them, I would spend time with the artists. And that was critical. When I moved to Minneapolis in 1989, I did the same thing. That ten-year period from 1989 to 1999 was the richest period of my artistic development, other than the early training. That's where I took the training and made it my own. I also started going outside of dance to research other fields, to draw new information into my body and into my mind. And one thing, again, that's important to my development that I want to clarify is that Contact was never an aesthetic practice for me. It was a somatic practice. It was a physical and emotional practice, but it was not about making art.

rnf Like a technique?

ca Yes, exactly. It was a technique for me. The only thing different about that is that Contact is one of the most integrating and therapeutic things I've ever done in my life. And I don't do it for therapy. But to not acknowledge that it's healed parts of me that I didn't even know needed to be healed would be ignoring the obvious. Through doing the practice I realize how touch-deprived we are in the world. And as we grow to be adults, the exploration of touch, and just touching, in nonthreatening or nonsexual ways, or nonfunctional ways—it just doesn't happen. It happens less and less as we get older, and Contact made me aware of that.

But in terms of Contact being a technique for me rather than an aesthetic practice, my aesthetic practice was influenced by Bart McCarthy, who made me aware of basic principles of choreography and theatrical expression and development. But most of my aesthetic training was not in dance. Certainly I was influenced by watching other artists, but I never had any composition teachers.

rnf And you didn't dance in choreographed works?

ca Well actually, I did. I was in Synapse Dance Theatre and then I was later in Prometheus Dance Company, both in Boston. But what they were doing was not really at the core of what made me the artist that I am today. Another thing that is important is African-American music. That's the reason I became a dancer in the first place.

rnf You mean popular music, or jazz?

ca No, I mean in particular, soul and funk and like, Aretha Franklin, Stevie Wonder, and Marvin Gaye. When I heard those voices, and those rhythms, I wanted to move. When I was young, when the rock and roll would come on in a dance party or a dance club, I couldn't dance. I wouldn't even try. But as soon as the black music would come on, everybody would clear the floor, and that's when I would go out to dance. Because that was the only music I could feel. There was something about the phrasing in the jazz and the blues and the soul and funk, that, it wasn't just rhythmic, it was also the way they would work the melody, the sense of songfulness and soul, for lack of a better word—that's what made me move. That's what I wanted to convey as a mover, was that level of connection to your heart and to your emotion.

rnf I have another question. It's about your recent interest in the Alexander Technique. I'm curious about what attracted you to the work, and if you feel it will influence or does influence your dancing.

ca Yes, yes, and yes. First of all, as I said earlier, I was introduced to Alexander Technique through Eva Karczag years ago, and actually, I believe Neal Katz was the first person. But what was important in my early training was the idea of moving efficiently, and moving with as little unnecessary tension as possible, so that the body would become more expressive and more energized. As a technical practice, that's something I had worked with for years. Then when I met Eva I started to realize how a deeper understanding really could help you do that. Then when I moved to Minneapolis, I started studying with Elizabeth Garren who was also a Trisha Brown dancer. The few lessons I had with her gave me my first real introduction to poise—the sense of poise and balance. I had felt, in my experience with a number of Alexander teachers, that there was an attempt by a lot of people to hold on to their poise and balance, and so they became stiff. That's the total opposite of what they're after. But Elizabeth wasn't like that at all.

I would be missing something if I didn't mention Body-Mind Centering. Bonnie's [Bainbridge Cohen] work has had a profound influence in the Contact world for years, and so although I haven't studied it, I've read her work, and I've worked with people who have worked with her. The whole notion of working with the body systems is really important in realizing that you have body systems that are more than simply your bones and your muscles and your skin and your nervous system, but that you also have your digestive system and your glands and all kinds of things. While I don't pretend to be an expert at that, there is the realization that you can burn out certain systems in your body by overusing them. So for example, if you are continually working in your nervous system, you don't get information that comes from other parts of your body. So as an improviser, if you're always improvising from your nervous system, it's difficult to actually relax in your body, and to get the release and the touch sensitivity that you get when working with other systems of the body. So you tend to be tense, and you tend to be hyper-alert all the time, it's difficult to access a multitude of emotional states. And so as a way of freeing up expressive range I have realized that I have to free up how I'm using myself. And that's very much linked to Alexander work and the whole notion of habit.

In terms of somatic work my understanding is that it is necessary to see the relationship between words and belief and somatic reality. It isn't just physical and emotional things that are creating our somatic reality; it isn't just gravity and your habitual use of yourself; it isn't just your emotional patterns that create holding; it's also the way you think. And that's what Alexander's work is all about in my mind. It isn't just about posture. For some people who teach somatics, it never gets to the level of how you think—it stays at the level of function and efficiency. But the passionate kind of life force that I recognized earlier in soul music, for example, that does not come from functional, efficient focus. It comes from spiritual and soulful expression. I think that that's a huge part of somatics that's not really dealt with often. If being functional and efficient is a model, it's a model of a way of being that has very severe limitations. It is not scientifically geared to make you perfect or make you correct or objectively efficient, because you can't separate the emotion from it. Certainly—I'm not saying that science isn't important, it's vital, and I love the things I've learned about my body through science and the scientific foundation of somatic work. But that's not enough, and it's not an aesthetic training. And I need both of those things to be an artist, or just to be a healthy human being.

david dorfman with lisa race and jennifer nugent

from an interview with melanie bales, march 2002

David Dorfman is the Artistic Director of David Dorfman Dance, which he founded in 1985. He is also Associate Professor of Dance and department chair at Connecticut College and teaches as a guest artist at universities throughout the United States and abroad. Jennifer Nugent and Lisa Race are members of David Dorfman Dance. They also each produce their own work and teach as guest artists at summer dance festivals and throughout the country.

mb I would be interested in hearing from you, David, about your journey into dance.

dd Well I have this distant memory, tugging on my mom's apron strings when I was probably about eight or something, and saying, "Mom, I want to start a dance school. And I know I want white shirts and black pants." I think I'd seen probably like Peter Gennaro or Gene Kelly, or kind of jazzy show dance on TV like the Judy Garland show or something. But I put those so far under the surface, those desires, that I just played sports and got good grades and all that. I learned all the social dances when I was a kid. And I would go to parties and dance the Monkey and the Frug and the Jerk, but I didn't know what dance was, really, and that you could study it. I took a junior year leave of absence from Washington University in St. Louis to go to U of I[llinois]—I grew up in Chicago—and I wandered into a beginning level class, and it was very free. I think it was required of theater majors, so there were really talented, funny people in there. I think that next summer or two summers later I studied at Gus Giordano jazz dance in Chicago. I was dancing disco dance and teaching disco dance right away, to anybody—youth groups, seniors, anybody, private parties.

mb A social animal.

dd Well, there you go. But also I think what's important is that I learned social dance more importantly, or earlier, or more passionately than I learned modern dance or experimental dance. Being exposed in the Chicago area, and even at U of I, to a lot of experimental theater, I started seeing different ways to make plays, or to present theatrical ideas, but I didn't see that in dance. I hardly knew what modern dance was. So I just thought like you disco-danced around basically, and kick-ball-change was god. Then I returned my senior year to Washington [University], and they had an eclectic base there: [Alwin]Nikolais-[Murray] Louis influence, [Merce]Cunningham influence, and [Martha]Graham influence, and I didn't do very well at any of them. But I noticed the thing that I could do was to be lower to the ground, be more athletic and almost primitive. But I enjoyed it and being in comp classes and making up early compositions, some of which had gestural stuff, humor stuff. When I started to more seriously study, two years after getting a business degree from Washington, I went to Connecticut College for an MFA. I studied under Martha Myers, and she was astute in many different body techniques. And Mark Taylor was one of my first modern teachers. He was teaching a very flowy form of Cunningham-style technique, but with a little bit Limón-y in there. I didn't get exposed to that much floor work at that time, but I'd been experimenting a little bit with rolls and Aikido-based stuff, just from my athletic background.

mb But you didn't study Aikido, or study any martial arts?

dd No. People always think that I have been influenced heavily by martial arts. And in a way I have, but I've never studied it. I remember getting so much scar tissue under my shoulder blade from practicing an Aikido roll with no training over and over and over. I got shin splints right away because I didn't know how to jump. I also studied with a woman named Colette Barry, who to my knowledge was Susan Klein's original partner in the beginning of release technique, quote unquote. That was one of my most influential early trainings. We would be in a hung-over position for sometimes forty minutes, with little breaks. And we would do just carving with the shoulder blades and the hips and that was a whole class, very much the beginnings of that technique. So that, along with learning steps and social dance through Daniel Nagrin when he was doing jazz styles and teaching all those forms.

mb Where were you exposed to Daniel Nagrin?

dd At Connecticut College summer program after ADF moved, and then at ADF. And so I took extensively with Daniel, he became my dance dad and Martha my dance mom. So, I was getting some technique, a little more towards Cunningham more than anything else. I was getting social dance through my interests and also through Daniel's classes, and was exposed to some bigger definition of "release technique" through Colette's classes. Basically I avoided ballet because I was afraid of it, I didn't do well in it, and I thought, "Boy, what if I get really discouraged and it's just going to get me down on dancing?" I took just enough to get by and it wasn't until I was in New York probably five years later that I said, "It's about time, Dave," going to teachers I felt safe with, like Ernie Pagnano and Cindy Green. I love the ideas and the technique and the feeling in the body of ballet. I also kind of crusade against it in its purest form, because I don't think it allows—in the worst-case scenario—a certain openness that I look for. But then I look at ballet companies that I adore like Frankfurt where they can do all ballet stuff and all modern stuff and I just drool, you know? Or I see Pina's [Bausch] company, "Oh, those guys are just good at telling jokes and walking around in heels." And then you see them do everything and it's wonderful.

So, that was my collegiate stuff, and then I got to New York and I had a scholarship at the Cunningham studio. I knew I would never get into the Cunningham Company, but I was at that time at least good enough to dance with folks that have that kind of technique, and I loved training my body in that way. But, left to my own devices, I would hear "Well, you know, you're really improving in all that technical stuff, but it's the more idiosyncratic stuff, Dave, that I'm drawn to." So I tried to keep bringing that up: that confluence or combination of learned techniques *and* your natural oomph, or motivation to dance.

mb Where did you find the opportunity to show the oomph, self-generated stuff? In composition class, or were you making dances already?

dd Composition classes encouraged me. I also thought that I would never be good enough to perform with anyone, so I ought to learn how to teach and choreograph. And then I just absolutely fell in love with performing and really drove myself to train so that I could be appealing to other people and in my own work. I performed early on with Kei Takei's Moving Earth, and with Susan Marshall and Company. Then I danced in some early dances of Stuart Pimsler's. Stuart introduced me to Martha Myers.

mb When you were dancing with Kei Takei or Susan Marshall, were you taking class and if you were, what was it or what were you doing for yourself?

dd Kei would rather you take karate or a martial art or train with her in her series of exercises, but I was doing Cunningham because I was a scholarship student. I wanted to get a wide training. A little bit later I started taking ballet classes as well. I remember Doug Varone seeing an early Yard [a performing arts colony on Martha's Vineyard] performance in which I danced for Susan Marshall and he said, "Oh, I really like your off-balance work." I thought that I had a decent sense of taking a risk and being physical. Now I'd like to also train the lines of my body more, so I looked for that in classes. I remember David Parsons at the 92nd Street Y. I could do it but it was hard.

I remember when Lisa [Race] and I were doing our athletes' project in Paris. David Zambrano was teaching there. We used to see each other at ADF, David and I, and it just reminded me of what I really loved—the in and out of the ground, the animalistic movement, the sheer joy. David was highly influenced by Simone Forti, whose major theory is letting your self come out—a very animalistic approach, in the most positive way. But as far as what's in the company, these guys [Race and Nugent] have influenced me and become part of what I do in a way, as much, if not more sometimes, than my own impulses.

mb You can't draw the line exactly.

dd These things are very appealing, teasing questions. I remember once you [referring to Race and a former company member] came up to me on the subject of teaching and asked, "How come the classes you teach," meaning me, "are different than our choreography?" And at the time I was in a choreographic phase, we used to joke about it: "Let's not lift our legs high! If your leg goes over parallel, there's a fine!" Not because it was wrong, but as a limitation. I think I just wasn't finding vocabulary in me that I wanted, and I thought by limiting maybe I'll find something—rolling, running, tackling. I think I was also influenced by some parts of European physical theater, and at that point my class was more exercise-oriented.

lr It was very Cunningham.

dd I thought we needed to find our balance and that kind of thing. But from that era on, things started to change. As I did more community work, I just found teaching a Cunningham-based class or any strict type of format useless in that context. So I think doing more community work, and realizing that what I was teaching in class was different than what we were actually choreographing, made me start to shift in the way I wanted to teach.

I was thinking about how there seem to be two uses, or approaches in teaching. One is teaching certain kinds of range: a class for those that already have a certain level of technique, whatever technique that may be. The other way of teaching is almost starting at ground zero, not necessarily in the community but maybe with beginning dance students, and focusing on skills like balancing on one leg, or getting a straight line. But then, it's funny, if you're teaching the technique of a handstand to advanced dancers that have no technique at handstands, that's kind of a blend of the two. I may get their ribs and arms moving in a different way, where if someone was a social dancer or break-dancer or whatever, they'd get that in two seconds but couldn't do a *fouetté* turn. I remember Martha [Myers] discussing things like this at ADF: "Are you teaching a dance style? Or dance technique?"

mb Do you think, David, that your experience and what you're developing in teaching is going towards some sort of codified collection of material, or that you've narrowed down certain experiences to support your choreography?

dd I would say moderately.

mb You're not interested in making a codified technique.

dd It has been a passing thought, but pretty fleeting. I think I'm a little afraid of it on a kind of an ego level—the idea of a David Technique. I think the way I dance may be, even on my body, a little bit surprising. Whether it's the weightedness or flow or the fact that a short squat guy is going to get his leg up. I choose company members for their unique expressivity and their incredible dancing, for the way that they look doing the phrases I make up, and I love to make up phrases. I also ask them to make up stuff from the get-go, so both those things are really important. So, when I ask people to make stuff up, particularly in collegiate situations, I might say, "You know, the beginning and the ending are looking really unusual and surprising to me but the middle—I recognize that—it starts to say *attitude* turn. Now that's a value that I hold, that things should be maximally idiosyncratic, maximally expressive, and personal.

mb So, something like that is a tricky and different matter than teaching some other things.

dd That's why I choose to begin all classes with some kind of expressive exercises, with improvisation; I feel I'm doing improvisation and composition in a technique class. That's why I've been calling them dance classes or dancing classes, rather than technique class. Then right away I am up front in saying: "This is the kind of class that I will be giving, and I hope that's okay for you and if not, it's okay to stretch for that hour and a half or two hours." When I'm teaching I am starting to express certain values: I like to spin, I like to go in and out of the ground, I like to jump. Over the years I keep seeing wonderful people like Lisa and Jen who inspire me, and I think, "I want to make a longer phrase. I want to do things that are less symmetrical." I'll look at a phrase I made and wonder how I could improve it.

mb I would like to hear from Lisa in terms of what you share of those values and something about your own teaching.

lr Mmmhmm, I think I've been strongly influenced by the social aspect of David's classes. My technique class is probably more of a straightforward technique class. I do tend to continue to use certain exercises that I've developed and that I like, maybe slightly different variations, but the same warm-up. But also, within that warm-up, I like to have people partner with each other. I feel like that's really important, just to help people get out of that staring at the mirror, fixed kind of focus. That just drives me insane!

mb Isn't it also practical in terms of touch and weight and those things that they're going to be doing?

lr Yes, and also, David's choreography and my choreography are strongly influenced by Contact Improvisation, and doing lots of physical partnering, and just being comfortable with another body. This is particularly important when we go around to colleges where there are really different kinds of training at different schools.

mb Do you train with anyone else now? Or do you just do the work and help other people through it?

lr Yes, for me in a way, giving a class is my way of kind of working through some stuff. One of my main missions in teaching—for the style of dance that I do—is to just get people to drop their centers.

mb And boy, that's just the biggest difference between you and everybody else in the room. That is just something I see right away—and the suppleness. You have a grand range of movement, not just in being able to get your pelvis down, but also—because your style is so much based on momentum and follow through, and the agility of catching momentum—that somehow you seem to get more momentum because your range is so large.

lr I think that another thing I'm really interested in, in capturing that momentum, is about kind of being able to harness circular energy, and transforming that into the physics of momentum and pathways in space. The warm-up that I do is a lot about rolling and circles and spirals. I feel if I can get people to really allow their bodies to travel through the circular space which often gets cut off, then—even if it's not a real wide range—it takes the whole path in, rather than cutting it off, and that really helps set up a lot of the later stuff in class. Also, for me everything comes from using the fold, hinges, hinging joints to try to capture momentum without a really held physicality, or a held musculature. That way, you're also letting gravity do some of the work, and allowing a lot of what I like to do start to happen.

dd I believe you try to avoid bound flow.

mb I would call that a value too. The way we're talking right now is more physical-level, or body-level, I guess. I believe body-level stuff feeds into more human values, or has an interaction that is interesting. Lisa seems very engaged in investigating movement, how to teach it and how to personify it. How do you, David, see that in terms of your idiosyncratic thing?

dd I thought about the word "subverting," when I said earlier how I was running and rolling and not doing more leg extensions and stuff like that.

mb The anti-technique?

dd Yes, a little bit. What Lisa does in a way is turn technique upside down. But there are all those incredible extensions and there's what you were talking about as range, hip joint range, range of leg, range of reach, range of energy. A lot of it is either completely upside down or inverted or beginning to fall.

mb But in a way, isn't it just another technique, rather than one is technique and the other way is not?

dd Right. Absolutely. I just saw the Frankfurt Ballet a couple months ago. Some of them have had as much modern training as ballet, and some are more ballet trained. But even within the ballet idiom, if they do something that either releases or falls or something, that becomes a little bit more personal or idiosyncratic. When you see Lisa just drop to the ground in two seconds, or all of a sudden doing a circular turn the leg just goes up there—to me that becomes a Lisa signature, or idiosyncratic. Not because of its display of technique, but because of its surprise. What I like about Lisa's and Jen's dancing so much is that aside from all the physical stuff there's heart with a physical and emotional openness, a dramatic quality, even facially: all of that harnessed to these incredible limbs going everywhere. I just adore that.

mb Is it just a coincidence that Jen, whose dance background has jazz as well as modern and ballet, hooked into this style, or does she have another spin on it—no pun intended—that you, David, have blended in?

lr Jen's got the down-to-earth thing, and she's got the spiral thing like neither of us have going on.

dd Which is so gorgeous. In her class yesterday, she emphasized a turned-in walk across the floor. Certainly people have worked in parallel for a century now, but it made me wonder again: is it idiosyncratic, is it a gesture? The way that Jen grasps space, and the kinesphere around her is amazing—also, her use of the head, and the ability to throw herself into space and into the ground, which she works on in class.

mb And how do you [Jen] work on that in class?

jn I guess what struck me are all the little incremental details that contributed to how I learned how to move my body. I think that's what I work on in class. Going back to the first summer at ADF, I didn't understand how they [Dorfman company] were suddenly falling through space. I had just started taking Contact [Improvisation], and that summer I took Alexander [Technique], and all the things that helped me understand: my weight is what I teach. I concentrate a lot on being supported by the floor, being supported by the space—floor and space, and focus and direction.

dd I think one of the lovely things about dancing as long as all of us have, is that, maybe we're not going to get each technical moment right, but we're used to imbuing the physical movement with imagery. Jen and Lisa and I all try to use imagery that we've gained from people like Sara Pearson and Danny Lepkoff and Colette Barry way back then and all that, so that it's like we're finding our connection into the universe, as sappy as that might sound. One thing is to use all the little bits of techniques. I think we all probably try not to use any exact exercises that someone teaches in class but if we do, we edit, taking the key elements that have inspired us, and then mix it with our own desires and try to inspire a new generation of dancers, trying to get all that collective dance knowledge. But I was also referring to literally connecting into forces around us. I do exercises where there is someone in the middle of a circle and we call that person's name. I encourage people on stage to pretend that someone is calling their name on stage, instead of just thinking, "I'm going to accomplish these movements." Your body is being motivated, that's why I'm saying the forces of the universe. There's a crisis in the Middle East, there's a flood over here, there's a tornado last night, you have a loved-one that's sick, you're absolutely overjoyed, everything is going well. How can things like that inform your dancing?

mb I am interested in what you're saying about bringing these things into your teaching that are sometimes borrowed or extended from your pasts, whether it's a deeper contribution as with Lisa or Jen to you, David, or whether it's a more momentary thing from a student or workshop participant.

dd There is very little of doing the master any more. When I think of the Cunningham company and those big institutions—Merce cannot do his movement fully now, he's hardly walking. He's generating it with computer and all that. Now the folks are less like him, and more like really highly skilled ballet and modern dancers. I think that there are certain precepts that his teachers are teaching, about what is a curve and a spiral and all that. Some people have the leg here, some here, and they have their own little bit of expressiveness. We saw the company last summer, and I don't think there's a way of doing Merce now. There are still companies at our level where the choreographer does give out all the movement and you will hear comments like, "Oh, that person looks a little bit more like the choreographer," but I find that that's more in the minority today.

If I think of the way I move today right now, because my name is on the company, it will be assumed that I've done this careful consideration in making that happen. But sometimes I don't know where these guys [LR and JN] have influenced me and where I've influenced them. As Jen was saying—when she first came in and she was looking at us move—that pushed her in a different direction. Now she pushes me in a direction.

mb Thank you so much! You said a lot of fine things.

kathleen fisher

from an interview with rebecca nettl-fiol, march 2003

Kathleen Fisher is a dancer, teacher, and body worker. She was a member of Trisha Brown Dance Company from 1992–2002, and has performed with Jane Comfort and the Bebe Miller Company.

rnf Could you trace your training history, especially the defining moments, or things that had a lot of impact on you?

kf When I was really young, I did have a little bit of tumbling and then a little half-tap, half-jazz class, at a local studio, and it was just fun.

rnf You remember it?

kf I remember it. I kept doing tumbling for a while after we moved, but there was no dancing school. I did dances with my grandparents, those big Polish festivals, where everyone's doing the Polka. All the old men danced with me, I danced the whole time. And my parents did ballroom dance, and I did go to their lessons with them; the teacher would throw me up in the air, and that was really fun.

And I did little things in high school like swing choir, but I wouldn't say that was dance training. But people were encouraging and positive to me.

When I got my license, I drove to Peoria, and I took ballet classes. I don't know if those classes were anatomically very good, but I was just in love with the whole thing, with dance. And one woman, Eleanor Colon, was so lovely, and she had such a love for what she was doing. She had never been a professional dancer, she started dancing very late in her life, but she was very musical, and had a real love for dancing. That was encouraging to be around someone so positive.

Then I came here to the University of Illinois to be a music major, and the first semester I also took dance classes, among them ballet with Robbie Dicello. The second semester, I transferred my major; that is really how I got started. I remember doing things in your [Rebecca Nettl-Fiol] class, where we would fall. I always liked the lyrical parts and the falling.

I actually did go to a ballet camp the first summer, because I felt so far behind. And then I came back, and I think it was during that year that I lost interest in ballet. At the camp I lost interest in ballet because I thought there was such a head-trip with all the young women. They were young and all so worried about their bodies, and they were ridiculously fine. And then physically, I was enjoying other things more than I did ballet, the actual experience of other things became more pleasurable after a while.

I know I remember taking your class and Renée's [Wadleigh] class, and I think those were the biggest influences here, even though we had guest artists. Although I loved Loretta Livingston—she seemed so supple to me, even though she was much stronger than I was, and in a very different kind of body. She was so intriguing, the way she was able to move like a cat. And Stephen Koester. He was very positive in terms of being open-minded about what technique and dancing were.

Also, every summer I was here, I did workshops. I went to ADF [American Dance Festival]. Technically, I don't think that was so great an influence. More importantly, it was filled with dance and dancers, and some of the teachers were very kind. I was still trying to learn basic patterns, so it was good to challenge myself technically. The summer after that I did Bates [Dance Festival]. Around my sophomore or junior year I was introduced to Contact [Improvisation] and that was a big influence because I think it helped my technique. I couldn't ever really let go of my weight at all, or find the weight of my limbs. I am sure I had the capacity, but I hadn't found it yet. Seeing the athleticism of some of those dancers, yet in very different medium, as in Chris Aiken's dancing: it is tremendously technical; it's just that the choreography isn't set. I liked the animal quality and I was pretty amazed by it. In my sophomore year, I started to do the Alexander

Technique. I remember that my knees hurt me a little bit. I never missed many classes, because I never made too big a deal out of it, but they did hurt.

rnf You studied Alexander for several years here.

kf I think studying Alexander really helped me start to figure out how to be more efficient—a way of dancing that I liked and that I thought I could do. There seem to be certain temperaments and body types that are compatible with it, if you know what I mean. It seemed like a way I could dance fully and not injure myself; I was beginning to find that out. I started to become aware of a more subtle way to move, rather than just doing the movements. That's a big shift. I was working on the movement in a different way. After that, ballet classes seemed very fast to me, even though I could learn the patterns.

So the training I had here, and the Alexander Technique and then getting exposed to Contact—those were the major influences. Obviously seeing Trisha's [Brown] work, and doing a workshop with the company was another big influence. The way those classes were taught was interesting to me: someone would just teach repertory, but they taught quite slowly, and sometimes they didn't talk at all.

rnf You just followed along?

kf I had to look very closely, because in a sense, it was a new vocabulary to me, it was almost like seeing something for the first time. After a long time in the company, seeing some things are a lot easier than it was the first time, because you know some of the habit of it, the way things tend to go together.

rnf Once you moved to New York, what did you do for training?

kf I tried to find an Alexander teacher right away, and I had lessons from June Ekman. She has been a great teacher for me and has really helped me with certain movements I just couldn't figure out how to do. So that's been a central part of my training. I also continued for a few years with Contact and with other kinds of improvisation, which I think was really good training for me in how to enjoy being in a piece. Ensemble improvisation, as with Danny Lepkoff, for example, helped me be in choreography. In the choreographies I was learning, you had to do your own thing but at the same time pay so much attention to everything that was going on. Improvisation gave me tools for that to be interesting and fun.

rnf You didn't take class . . .

kf I would occasionally take class with Bebe Miller and a couple other choreographers that I liked. While I was in the company [Trisha Brown], I warmed up every day. I was very disciplined. I spent at least an hour in learning the new material; even though her [Brown's] material appears easy, it's actually quite difficult. For instance, a lot of it is low to the ground, and in and out of the floor, which for me was a different vocabulary. I'd spend a lot of time stretching, or doing Constructive Rest, or just basic things on the floor and then move around a little to warm up if I felt I needed to. Or maybe I would dance around and improvise a little.

rnf And then you had several hours of rehearsal.

kf It started out as five, and then later on we switched it to six.

rnf That doesn't leave much time for taking class.

kf I know of some dance companies where they rehearse that much *and* take class. Maybe they teach class, too, but I don't know how! Often, I wonder if I am innately just not that strong of a person physically. I had shows where I danced almost the whole show and was in the theatre for six hours before that. I guess it's just a choice. Later, when I started working on my voice, I really felt that helped my dancing a lot. My last year on tour, I did a vocal warm-up before each show, for at least half-hour or an hour, along with my physical exercises. I felt like it warmed me up internally in a way. At night I might stretch, or in the morning for just fifteen or twenty minutes, and then before the tech[nical] rehearsal, do another twenty minutes of something. Usually, some time during the day, I would spend an hour doing a vocal/physical warm-up, and then right before the show we'd all just improvise on stage or run parts of the dances.

rnf It's different from the old model that used to exist more, where you'd have company class.

kf I think a lot of companies do. I also think that the company thought I was crazy.

rnf Not to take class?

kf No, no—with the vocal warm-up. Some of them didn't warm up at all, but some of them got hurt so . . . I have to think that the two are connected. Honestly, there is a problem if people are not able to pinpoint some interest in training themselves; the dancing gets kind of complacent because they are not working on anything.

rnf But you were just self-motivated and worked on your own.

kf Yeah, and kind of in my own way.

rnf I think that's unusual, really.

kf I think it is too. I think a lot of independent artists are like that, but members of companies still have class.

rnf Do you think that your work with the Alexander Technique was instrumental in your success in Trisha's work?

kf For me personally, yes, because I was so interested in it. And the Technique was also my way into solving a lot of bits that were problematic for me. I used the Technique as a tool to help me notice what I was doing and attempt to change it. I also used the Technique to find a good support system. Trisha's work is sometimes quite vertical, but in some pieces there is a lot of off-balance work. So I needed to find a support system for that. And for me, I think that sort of lightness and the "up" has a corresponding down and connection, so that you really have an energy going in and out of the floor. I think that was really necessary for Trisha's work.

karen graham

from an interview with rebecca nettl-fiol, april 2003

Karen Graham is a dancer and assistant for the David Gordon/Pick Up Performance Company. She has also danced with Baryshnikov's White Oak Dance Project. Her own choreography has been produced in New York, Minnesota, and Illinois.

rnf I would like to know your training history, starting from the beginning.

kg It's one of those classic stories: my best friend was taking ballet, and I was probably eleven or twelve, and I started going to class because of her. It was Rockford, Illinois, I forget the name. . . . Debbie's Ballet School, I think. I started doing that and my body took to it—I had a facility for it. And I did that for maybe three or four years, and then began studying at the Rockford Ballet school and a few months into that I started taking modern. What happened is that I saw a modern teacher dance a solo, and she was a bigger woman, she was not the dainty ballerina type, nor was I. So I responded to that, and there was something so free about it, and sort of juicy. And so I started taking modern. There was no particular kind of technique that they were teaching, it was fairly eclectic. That was my first training. But it wasn't until I came here [University of Illinois] that I realized it was something serious for me. I think until then it had been a kind of fun, physical pursuit.

rnf But you didn't consider being a dance major when you were going to college.

kg Well I did, but for various reasons that I still don't quite understand, I just never chose to. My first creative outlet had always been writing. I'd written short stories and poetry from a really young age, so I think I still had an attachment to that. And probably my parents' influence of, "Well, you can't have a career as a dancer . . . so get a degree in English literature, that'll be great," you know? (laughs) I don't think I had the ability at that time to really confront the issue and say, "No this is really what I want to do." I was on the fence. And so I was taking a lot of dance classes; other than composition and dance history, I took as much as majors were taking. What was so great about the department at University of Illinois is that they bring people in that are working professionals. For example, Jan Erkert was a frequent guest at that time and her whole thing of swinging and momentum and being upside down was really important for me, because although I had taken modern, I'd had more ballet, so I was kind of held in my body—it was a little bit upright. And she's also just a great teacher, so she really influenced me.

Anyway, getting different kinds of techniques and also the sense of the larger dance world was really important. During this time, it became clear that this was something I wanted to pursue. And that was partially because the training was so diverse, so I just started to feel like I could spend a lifetime trying to explore this.

rnf From there did you move straight to New York?

kg Yeah, I graduated in '84, and actually lived in New Jersey, so it was a two-hour train trip to take class, which was challenging and expensive. And I didn't know the city, so it was a rough first year. But I started going to a place called Peridance. They had good ballet teachers, and also Jennifer Muller's company was teaching there at that time. I can't remember the name, but a male dancer with Jennifer Muller was teaching there. He had that full-bodied way of moving—very luscious but definitely including the need for ballet training—really strong technique. And he also took me under his wing and told me where to go. So I started taking classes all over the place: ballet—Jocelyn Lorenz and Christine Wright were the well-known ballet teachers for modern dancers. And I went there and met a lot of people, and then people in class would come and say, "I'm doing this project—would you be interested?" So I started doing projects like that, and that went on for a while. I was taking ballet three times a week or so, and then trying different modern classes—everything from Jennifer Muller to eventually Wally Cardona, more release-based work. I went to Barbara Mahler's a few times, but it didn't make sense to me completely. People who studied with her really moved beautifully, but it didn't happen at the time in my life where I could really engage with it. My version of that was yoga. I started studying yoga because I had some back problems and somebody suggested it. I think it's connected to the release work in that it's a slower way of warming up. It's also the idea of bringing breath and energy and attention to the parts of your body, particularly the spine, to begin warming up, and how much that actually does for you, instead of fifty *pliés*. You know what I mean?

rnf It's more efficient.

kg Yes, and that was a big change for me, and it really helped the injuries I was dealing with. Yoga also coincided with a time with David Gordon where we were working with actors in a theatre piece. This whole conversation began then, about motivation. And I was in the studio for the first time with people who were going up to David and saying, "Well, I understand you're asking me to say this and do this, and it doesn't make sense, and I need to know what you're going for." This whole other kind of conversation was happening in the studio. It was a conversation about the work, and he was sharing a lot more than he ever had with dancers, because he had to.

rnf Dancers just do it.

kg That's right. Just observing that changed the way I started to think about performing. I was talking to the actors about how they think about things . . . and we were using text, so I was also speaking for the first time. That was a big change and I think somehow those things are connected. You know yoga is also about going inward, and noticing what's happening in your body, giving it respect and attention. And quieting it in a way, so that you can reopen and reveal who you are. The process of working on that theatre piece at the time really was doing that too, so that David needed me not to just be the dancer doing the steps, but rather, "Okay, this is your character, and I need to see this character and it needs to come from someplace that you truly understand from the inside and not just kind of a veneer that you're putting on." So I connect these two things in my experience as a really pivotal moment in terms of performance and how I approached dancing.

rnf And do you still do yoga?

kg Yes.

rnf Now that you've established your training, and you've been dancing for a long time, what do you do to keep yourself in shape technically?

kg I should be taking more ballet classes (laughs).

rnf Why do you think that?

kg Well, I don't know. When I started working with David [Gordon], again it was an ongoing process like I mentioned earlier with Jan Erkert. Ballet had been established in my body, it was really clear in the way I approached movement and line. And David was interested in human beings doing extraordinary things with their bodies, so that you're not carrying yourself like a dancer, but like a human being. He's also interested in spontaneity, as if you're just walking down the street and you're inventing the movement, as you go, not just performing the steps that you've been given. So I felt like that was another version of trying to change where the movement was coming from. So I stopped taking ballet because I felt like I needed to let go of some of it, and try to find that more—pedestrian's really not the right word . . .

rnf It's a different body attitude.

kg Yeah. And I studied a little bit more of the release work at the time. But your question was why do I think that I should be taking more ballet now? Because I feel like now I just need the strength. I believe very strongly that ballet is the only thing that can really give you that kind of foundation. But it's hard to find the balance between that and this other thing I'm exploring which is about letting go. Ballet is about holding. But I believe in both, so I'm trying to find a balance.

rnf By both you mean yoga and ballet? Or something that will release or free the body?

kg And still have that strength as a foundation to move from. I think that they work well together, but you have to keep both of them going.

rnf So for you, yoga's really been your main way of doing that.

kg Yes, it has. And it's interesting, when I studied with Wally [Cardona], he studied with Barbara Mahler, so that's a big influence for him, and he speaks about the anatomy very much, and cells moving and all of that. And I see it as just a different way of doing a similar thing which is going inside and trying to listen to your body, and warm it up with a kind of attention, energy, phrasing the breath, and getting to know it so that when you start dancing, it's not a disconnect between you and what you're doing.

rnf Which is what all the somatics are about.

kg Exactly. Alexander, too, I've studied, a little bit with Jennifer Kellow in New York, and that has been one of the more amazing experiences for me because it's so mysterious. I mean probably because I don't know that much about it, and she's not one of those teachers that explains a lot, she just puts her hands on you, and talks to you, so it's just this mysterious but very potent interaction. I'm sure it changed my dancing, but I think even more, my performing, because of that idea of bringing attention here and now that changes things in your body, and focuses you in a very simple way. So I really use that a lot before I go on stage.

rnf What does David [Gordon] think about training for his company? Does he train his dancers?

kg It's really interesting because, you know his first dances were about saying, "walking is dancing," to put it very simply. And so the first dancers that he used were sometimes not well-trained dancers; in fact he was not a particularly well-trained dancer. But he knew how to move. So it was that way for a while. And then, he got to know Misha [Baryshnikov] and started doing ballets. He did a ballet on ABT (American Ballet Theatre) and at some other places, and he began to work with highly trained dancers. And I think got interested in it. Then the people that he started looking at at auditions changed, and what he wanted changed. I think I auditioned just at the right moment for him, because he had become more interested in technique.

rnf So David didn't provide the training, he just gathered people?

kg Yes, exactly. There were a couple people in the company when I first joined that had been there for awhile, and they were trained dancers, not a lot of ballet training necessarily. And then there were people in the company who took everything from ballet to Tai Chi, to release technique with Barbara Mahler. So it was very mixed. And I think he felt that since he wasn't providing a technique, he couldn't say, "I want you to do this technique." He was in fact, interested in the differences and he used those different ways of approaching movement.

rnf Any final thoughts?

kg I feel like my training post–U of I was more about performance than about physical training. It was about opening myself as a person on stage and being available to truly be present in that moment of performing the movement that I had learned to do. So in a way I guess I consider it an emotional training to add myself to my dancing in a strange way.

You get so wrapped up with trying to accomplish the physical tasks that you're asked to do, and struggling with the things you're struggling with physically. Not everybody wants to be a performer . . . some people are training to be teachers, but you can forget that you're working towards being on stage. And what does that mean to you? Do you want to relate to the audience? Do you want to not? My feeling has become that I want to be as available as possible. Not that I'm playing to them, but that I'm just as present as I can possibly be, with myself and with the other dancers, and with the movement. And it's a lot easier, also, I found, performing that way.

mark haim

narrated by mark haim, june 2001

Mark Haim was Artistic Director of Mark Haim and Dancers from 1984–87, and the Companhia de Dança de Lisboa from 1987–90. He has created works for dance companies and been guest artist at universities in the United States and abroad. He is currently Artist-in-Residence at University of Washington in Seattle.

tap

This was my first experience with dance. As I was a young classical musician, this style of dance made perfect sense to me, as it is based in rhythm and musicality. I loved feeling my body as a musical instrument, creating rhythms and dialoguing with the music. For me, dancing was all about expressing myself in relation to music. I loved moving to music; it was the driving force behind my dance. In many respects, this continues even now.

jazz

While in high school, I became involved in the drama club's annual musical. As I knew my right foot from my left, I was cast as a dancer in all the productions. I loved the performance aspect of this form—the style and the expression within the larger theatrical picture. It was here that I began to learn the necessity for flexibility (got to get those legs up in those kicks!). When I began to take jazz classes at the neighborhood school, I learned a stretch routine and did it very often in my bedroom to disco music. Much of it consisted of bounces. I was introduced to physical pain (i.e., while stretching) and quickly saw the benefits of stretching: capability to kick my legs up high and do splits. As I had never been very interested in competitive sports, this stretching/exercise routine took the place of athletics for me.

ballet

I was introduced to ballet while a liberal arts student at The New School for Social Research. I first took an introductory ballet course, learning the basics of rotation, positions, simple ballet steps. I found this technique to be completely inorganic and after a few weeks, pulled a calf muscle. I gave it up for a while but found myself still practicing at home.

I also studied introductory modern with a former Erick Hawkins dancer. There, while sitting on the floor, I was introduced to the ugly curve in my back and my inability to straighten it! I thought it would never change, but it slowly did.

In the spring of the same year, I took an adult evening ballet class at the Joffrey Ballet School and enjoyed it more. I had a very encouraging teacher, who used to put me in the first group across the floor, and tell the other students, "look at him! He's only had ____ classes!" For my audition to NYU/Tisch School of the Arts, I recorded myself playing a Schubert waltz on the piano and did a big jump combination across the floor for my audition piece. Needless to say, I was not accepted. I was accepted, however, to Adelphi University, where I had the foresight to choreograph something more modern, with my own personal vocabulary—a music visualization to the third movement of Ravel's *Piano Concerto in G.*

ballet, modern and everything else

In the summer of 1979, I went to the Harvard Summer Dance Center. By this time, I knew I wanted to be a dancer. At Harvard, I took four classes a day: ballet, modern technique, composition, and tap. I quickly moved up two levels in ballet class. (I was always too ambitious and trying to progress too quickly—what can you do?) I studied the Limón technique with Gary Masters and enjoyed it for the most part. But with my classical background in piano, it was ballet that resonated within me mostly: the discipline and the routine. Tap continued to be a pleasure, and they were the last classes I ever took. A shame, because I was a really good tap dancer and enjoyed it so much.

In the fall of 1979, I was miraculously accepted to the Juilliard School, and that began my professional training. At Juilliard, I studied modern—Graham and Limón techniques—ballet, and some jazz. I was very ambitious. Having started relatively late, especially in relation to my peers, I pushed very hard to progress quickly. Ballet and the Graham technique were very much based on strength and shapes, and I soon began to feel that my body would never complete the required shapes in the way bodies around me were able to. My musicality and intelligence were acknowledged, but I somehow felt that they were in compensation for a fundamental inability to "look like" a dancer, having spent most of my childhood playing the piano and studying books. I was not an athletic person, and this lack of athleticism led to trying way too hard to prove myself all the time, resulting in injuries—most of which were not addressed by the faculty there, as they were from the old school of teaching: if you repeat what I do for a long time, your muscles will respond and you will not hurt yourself. If your muscles are not responding well, then you shouldn't be a dancer.

With that in mind, I gravitated towards choreography. If I can't do it, then I'll make it on others. The only problem with this is that deep down I felt I was a very good dancer, even though on the surface I never felt adequate. This constant struggle to feel adequate, much of it due to self-imposed perfectionistic expectations, led me to a very inconsistent approach to dance. If I had been a girl, I am sure I would have been a prime candidate for anorexia nervosa: I binged, then starved—both in terms of food and in terms of work ethic. Juilliard left me injured and frustrated. Yet somehow, through all of the injuries and frustrations, I managed to graduate with a solid knowledge of technique, line, style, and strength.

I had my first exposure to a different way of approaching movement while at Juilliard (although I was hardly ready to hear it!): the Alexander Technique. I met Jane Kosminsky, a teacher of Alexander Technique and movement for the Drama Division and a former Juilliard alumna herself. Jane often spoke about ease in movement, finding the right way to do something, moving with muscular efficiency. It felt terrible to me. Having lived so long in the mode of needing to prove myself, this idea of ease and efficiency made no sense. I was afraid I'd be boring. Or lose what little strength I had so "intensely" struggled for. Not being able to ease up and change my way of thinking, and having studied three techniques that were mostly about bound flow and strength for the past four years, I ended my last year at Juilliard injured with a lower back problem that would plague me for two years.

Post-Juilliard was initially a time of recovery. I spent the following year trying alternative therapies to cure what had become a chronic lower back problem. I began seeing a chiropractor, and I began frequenting a Pilates studio in my neighborhood which was highly therapeutic. I began swimming as a way to maintain some aerobic shape. I also toyed with connective tissue massage and vitamin supplements. I tried some private Alexander lessons with Deborah Kaplan, but was still not ready to "not do." All these elements contributed to my healing; the most important one of them being my commitment. I began to learn how to maintain the healing/recovery process, without giving up at the first sign of a relapse. Eventually, I felt strong and confident enough to return to classes and began studying Zena Rommett's Floor Barre technique. The floor barre helped me to establish strength lying down so that by the time I stood up I was more well placed and connected. As I was no longer at Juilliard, I found teachers more to my liking, teaching ballet for modern dancers—among them, Ernest Pagnano, Cindy Green, Jocelyn Lorenz.

One teacher who influenced me greatly at that time was Christina Bernal, a former dancer with the San Francisco Ballet. A fleeting spark of a woman, Tina had developed her own principles of placement, many of them influenced by the locally renowned ballet teacher, Maggie Black. She placed a lot of importance on the alignment of the ankles and legs in parallel and rotation and the weight distribution over the legs. She believed in keeping the weight quite forward and evenly distributed on the two legs ("50-50!!" she would yell), which caused us to nickname the *barre* "white knuckle" as you would grip so tightly to stay in the center of two legs and forward. I felt some changes in my placement with her, and found myself able to move, jump, and change direction more quickly.

I took Tina's approach to the classical technique with me to Portugal, giving ballet class as company class and getting everyone up and forward. While there, I also invited Jane Kosminsky to come guest-teach and expose everyone to the Alexander Technique. It was a revelation to all. We all began talking about the principles and applying them to our class work in ballet and the repertory.

It was there that I began to experiment with the idea of giving myself inner directions while dancing, trusting that they were "working." I did not have to work so hard and try and control everything, assuming that nothing would happen without constant vigilance. I remember one afternoon, in particular, giving myself a *barre* in the studio overlooking Lisbon, and just repeating "yes" to myself and my body as I gave it direction. I found myself crying throughout the *barre*. Somehow, with the relinquishing of control, the hurt and pain could come out and be washed away. This has been a through-line in my life—giving up control—and I can see it very clearly in my dance training's progression.

Once back in the States, I began to make a move toward modern dance in my training. I studied with a few teachers who influenced my technique and my teaching. One was JoAnna Mendl Shaw, a former Bill Evans dancer, former artistic director of Danceworks in Seattle, and recent transplant to New York City. Her technique class's progression, from the floor upward, initially utilizing exercises related to Bartenieff Fundamentals, influenced my warm-ups both in class and on my own. It also spurred me to take a workshop in Bartenieff Fundamentals at the Laban Institute for Movement Studies. Another teacher who influenced me was Barbara Grubel, an exceptional and loyal proponent of Susan Klein's studio in New York City. I learned about deep connections through slow stretches through both her classes and a few with Barbara Mahler at the Klein studio itself. I also took private yoga classes for a while with Paula Macali, who was in the midst of studying Ashtanga Yoga. The series she taught me was virtually impossible for me to do, and gave me a taste of serious yoga, not simply easy stretches. I opted for the easy stretches. . . .

In 1995, while choreographing the *Goldberg Variations*, I tore my right calf muscle. For recovery, I chose the Pilates technique again, studying privately with Lisa Love. There, I learned more about pelvic placement and how it affected the use of my external rotators, hip sockets and hamstrings. While recovering, I found new connections. This happened once again this year: with the onset of chronic hip tendonitis and a damaged long right thoracic nerve, I returned to the Pilates reformer and Cadillac, this time with Pamela Pietro.

In many respects, looking back on my training, I'd say that the important people are the ones in which I've had a dialogue and worked with one-on-one. Perhaps that is due to the years of studying classical piano, where one has a one-to-one relationship with one's teacher for a few hours, and then goes home to practice the rest of the week. There are people who have given me much to think about in one instant, in an intensive setting, and others who I've felt comfortable studying with in one capacity or another over many years.

In retrospect, I must admit now that my frequent battles with injuries during my dancing/choreographing career have been a blessing in disguise. It has led me to seek alternative techniques and modalities that have so deepened my body's awareness of itself. That, and the endless hours of practice time on my own while making my eighty-minute solo, *The Goldberg Variations* which gave me ample time to be in my body and explore it. There is always more to do, even as I have entered my forties. As long as I'm alive, may it never stop.

angie hauser

from an interview with melanie bales,
october 2004

Angie Hauser is a dancer and performing improviser, teacher of Contact Improvisation and dance technique. She is a member of the Bebe Miller Company and has danced in the companies of Elizabeth Streb and Liz Lerman.

mb Can you give an outline or trace your training from the time you started dance until now, with highlights or turning points, and the things that seem most resonant?

ah I think I have to go chronologically. I started quite late for a girl. I started dancing officially around fifteen or sixteen.

mb So no ballet, tap, jazz—nothing as a kid?

ah No. I did have a trampoline as a child. I spent a lot of time on and truthfully, I think the trampoline, in terms of building the alignment in my legs, was totally key—and the spatial awareness because of the flipping.

mb No gymnastics or anything?

ah No, A tiny bit, but no sports. A lot of tree climbing, just outdoors stuff, always super physical. But then I started taking ballet; I should give my mom credit because she was very specific about the kind of school. She didn't want it to be a school that had recitals. She found a good school in Columbia, South Carolina, and my training there was classical for sure: extension and multiple turns and beautiful feet and you know, really turned-out fifths.

mb Not attached to a company?

ah There was a regional company, but the training was pretty clear. Anita Ashley who ran the school was my primary teacher and had a healthy body image and clear alignment and knowledge of the vocabulary. I was *blessed* with some good training early. I still had issues about puffing up my ribs because as a teenager, no matter what your training is, you get weird body stuff with ballet. I joined the regional company; I danced with Ashley Tuttle, a principal dancer with ABT [American Ballet Theatre]. I stood beside her in *Bayadere*! Then my first year of college I just stopped because it just felt too precarious, the performance part felt restraining to me.

So I stopped dancing for a while, went to college. In college I met a woman who was an Alexander teacher and an LMA [Laban Movement Analysis] person, and got involved with her. We made a solo together and a duet. I look at it now and it seems really simplistic in terms of the vocabulary, but what happened in the solo for me—and I'd been in the corps and this was a modern solo—my first situation where expression was in the foreground. It was my first interaction with a director or choreographer where I actually had say! Right away the piece was created from both of us. She was not giving me steps, she was giving me ideas and then I was doing them. I fell in love with the idea of translating a choreographer's vision. Then I started doing Alexander. I got enough of a seed that really has resonated with me for a long time. I did take ballet still sometimes back at the studio, but in limited amounts; I was searching, my training was inconsistent then. But, I went to ADF in the summer, and it was a total eye-opener.

I took from Donald McKayle, total modern dance. He did counts and rhythms and things that I just had had no experience with, and he's a large personality, so it was exciting to be a part of that. And Gerri Houlihan; I thought I had to take Graham, so I took a little bit and hated it.

mb Did you see a lot of performances?

ah I saw Paul Taylor, and a company from Spain I still remember so well. It was the first dance theater I had ever seen. Then I saw Trisha Brown's company and I decided, "Oh, I'm going to go to New York and dance with Trisha Brown!" It was this great physicality, and the clarity—I just fell in love with the idea of partnering and . . . I didn't know what it was, but I was very excited by it! The other part during college that absolutely changed my life was attending a weekend workshop in Atlanta with Nancy Stark Smith. I didn't even know what Contact Improvisation was. I drove three and a half hours to a workshop in a gym with Nancy. I didn't know it was *Nancy.*

mb One of the founders of Contact Improvisation.

ah I never did pure Contact after that until much, much later. But what I learned in those three days from Nancy—I learned the principles of it and carried them with me to my work.

mb So you kept something of that.

ah Absolutely. I think it also clicked right in with what I had already, in terms of interest and how my body works and how I perceive myself in the world with other dancers. It wasn't all new information, but it tempered the information I already had. I went to the Contact thing with Nancy, and I think I wore a unitard! I was still very much in ballet. That was the only idea I had about dance.

Then I moved to New York, right after college. Trisha Brown was having classes at Battery Dance; she didn't have her space yet. I went and I did love the material. I stayed for a month. But the personality of the room didn't fit with me. I loved the movement, but there was something very precious. It was very quiet and reserved, because the work is very specific. It's "Your foot goes here, your knee goes here, where is your weight"—they're so amazingly precise about it that it was fascinating to me, but I couldn't get into it in terms of where my heart was about dance. It just didn't click with me. I was fresh to New York and that was pretty high-end practicing at that point for somebody that was coming mostly from ballet.

mb And were you also taking some other classes then?

ah Those were the first classes I took, then after a couple of months, I got a job dancing with a Butoh company. It was amazing and insane: amazing because it was improvisation. I can't remember what the structure was, but at the first rehearsal, he gets up and he puts on a CD and dances for ten minutes straight—this amazing, crazy solo. Then he sits down and gestures to me. He just wouldn't say anything, just kept looking at me, so I got up and started dancing. That was the way it worked: you danced until he told you to stop, then he would slowly shape it, but he didn't make up one step. Some really amazing stuff would happen because all the dancers that he was working with were really invested in what they were doing, so some great performances were coming out. Finally, he would structure these pretty tight choruses, where four or five people were doing the same thing, with wild, improvised solos or duets.

At that time, I was taking ballet with Jackie Villamil at Dancespace, and some modern classes, but I kept getting frustrated because I didn't know at the time how hard it is to find a good modern class. I was acclimating to the city. You just need somewhere to go to actually take class and learn. Her training, the ballet, was where I hooked into the idea of energy—line as energy, not just line as shape. It's exactly what has evolved in my understanding of technique in dancing and performance. I started doing Iyengar yoga a few years later, and I brought what I learned from Jackie, in terms of lines of energy, into the yoga.

mb Did you think that knowledge was in the yoga you were taking, or did you bring it to that?

ah I don't think it's emphasized, because often the language around the yoga is more about bringing the muscle into the bone, and the way I envision it is lines of energy going outside the sphere of the body.

mb Less body referential.

ah This is tricky, but I've always worked muscularly, and in my teaching I realize that working through your muscles gives you information. There's a sensation that you feel when you're working through your muscles that helps you understand proprioception, and where you are in space. The yoga helped me engage, not just in my limbs as in the way I'd thought about it in ballet, but all the way through my back, through the muscle system. At the same time I was using ideas of energy lines, so I avoided getting tight and muscle bound. I did do a gymnastics class for a while when I worked with Elizabeth Streb.

mb And where did you start working with her?

ah I saw her work at the Brooklyn Bridge Anchorage: an amazing piece called *Look Up*. They were scaling down this wall, and I was really blown away by it. She had an audition and I went, then to the callback, then to a two-week training program for a few people she was interested in. I did a couple of performances with them over a two-year period, but I was always somewhat peripheral. I really wanted to dance but I didn't really understand the ins and outs of a company, but I was into the work, and that's where I discovered my upper body—being able to pull and push, which would later completely influence my Contact work. I also discovered the ability to go in and out of the floor with power, and eventually with suppleness. Her work is very impactive. The impactive nature of that definitely taught me something about line and traveling through space. It changed my body a lot. My arms and my shoulders got really big, much more muscular than I had ever been.

I began thinking about going to grad school. I was also dabbling around in release work in New York, taking classes from Wally Cardona and Vicky Schick and Barbara Grubel. It would be hanging over, stretching, alignment of the legs, then rolling up and down and aligning the whole spine, then into phrase work: one big phrase, you don't reverse it and there's no music. It was that time in New York: no mirrors or music! Again, I was acclimating to the whole scene, taking it in and responding well to some of it, being confused by other parts. I was probably doing it, quote, wrong, unquote, doing it ballet-style, or my idea of what they were doing.

mb Do you remember how it felt or what you thought they were trying to get at? Did it seem like the Trisha Brown studio?

ah A little bit. The truth is I was just on the top layer at the time, and so I didn't really know. I remember taking from Wally Cardona, and he said something that I would later hear from Barbara Mahler, about hanging over and being back further on your heels, more into your hamstrings, then aligning your pelvis right over your heels. I didn't really understand it, but I did it and I kept at it. It was just practicing, exploring and practicing. So, I am doing improvisation with the Butoh group, very physical work with Elizabeth Streb, gymnastics and yoga, and then ballet for structure, emotionally and physically. At the same time, I would go to modern class and I just wouldn't get it. There were periods of real frustration, and I stopped going to modern technique classes in New York, because I just wasn't getting anything. Slowly I began to sort of assert my own personality, and I decided to go to grad school.

I'd never been in a structured dance environment for school. I came to Ohio State with a performance focus, because that was my experience. I had not been making work, but I was already beginning to think of myself as a dancemaker because I realized right away the work that I was doing with the choreographers, especially with the Butoh, was coming directly from my point of view, from my aesthetic, from my physicality. I was making the choices about that material. My work with Elizabeth was about training, and physically being able to do it. It was about endurance and limits—huge, motor movement that I hadn't done before, like jumping off of a platform into a line.

mb And kinesthetic feeling, like your trampoline maybe?

ah Absolutely. It totally engaged in the kinesthetic.

mb At OSU, is that the first time you'd had formal composition courses?

ah I think I may have done a workshop or something, but I had not done any composition. And I took Vickie Blaine's weight studies class; I was her TA, and I was her TA for that class the next two years.

mb So you got a really deep experience of that.

ah For me that class was about being able to make decisions about qualities of movement *while* you were dancing, or creating something, or had set material to perform. She wasn't explicit about a lot of things, but she has a very intense personality and you know she wants you to do something, but there is space for you to find out what that is. For me it was great because a certain notion began to crystallize: the idea of training went from steps and pathways to qualities, and using the same brain for particular qualities or states that you use to articulate particular steps, moves or shapes or patterns. It is that other realm of training as a dancer and the practice of—

mb Presence?

ah Presence, yes, but not just performance, but Effort with the big E [from Laban Movement Analysis] and weight qualities: the layer in movement that naturally good dancers have.

mb Inflection and dynamics.

ah Absolutely. I came to a place where I thought, "Okay, you can train this, this is how you train dancers for performance." At an advanced level, not the way to train a fourteen-year-old dancer.

mb Maybe that comes in when you're secure about some other things.

ah The reason I was able to go there is because I had a really strong structural base with technique, alignment, the muscular systems that I had talked about, and the introduction to the idea of efficient release, a skeletal approach. I did finally have a strong base that was very clear to me, I understood it, so I began to add on and make choices and then take away and put back in, but never editing out anything altogether. I never said no to ballet.

mb Many people we've talked to go through many phases or years of feeling like they're adding things to their palette, taking on this and that and the other. Then, at some point in their training or in their careers they start to unpack or to deconstruct, and say, "You know, I don't really need *that* anymore," or "I should really re-investigate *that,*" or "I'm going to stop taking that class or stop moving in that way or having that as my goal," and they have a feeling of starting over.

ah Well I do have some of that, but really I kept redefining. I kept redefining what ballet was to me, and what it did.

mb So you didn't have to throw it out to redefine it.

ah No. When I started dancing with the Bebe Miller Company, I did stop taking ballet for about a year, because Bebe and I move very differently. She is very earthy and grounded and deep into her weight, and into her legs and pelvis in a very different way than I am. Lightness is an affinity of mine. I knew that quality wasn't going to go away, so I did stop taking ballet to get deeper into Bebe's work, but then once I felt like I had a decent grounding in it, I had started taking ballet again. I realized over that year with Bebe that she loved the ballet legs and the feet and all of that. She loves that.

mb It's part of who you are.

ah I was able to pour that back in, because I have more of a handle on how she works in that physicality. We work so improvisationally in the company, it was mostly a question of letting my body open itself to new patterns and new ways of moving. If you overload your body with a particular style or technique, it will come out when you're improvising, and I like to keep the mix happening in terms of the material. I realized that my way of moving with lightness was coming out a lot in the improvising. At first I thought of it as an anxious quality from being in a new situation emotionally and psychologically, but I just needed a little room to let that settle into my body.

mb Have you studied Contact since you graduated about four years ago?

ah I started taking Contact with K. J. Holmes a little bit in New York, and then started working with her on a duet. This was the last couple of years. Then when I went back to Bates—I was there with Bebe two years ago—I did Nancy's Contact class. It was great to go back and revisit that material. Also, I've read *Contact Quarterly* a lot, read what Steve Paxton wrote. As far as training now: a steady diet of ballet, Contact, yoga, with variations in terms of how heavy in one or another. And working on my own in the studio which is part of being an improviser. Sometimes it's very specific: rolling from my shoulder up to my head onto my hand or just pathways that I'm interested in. Other times it's more conceptual.

The other thing I wanted to say about training, I just realized that in grad school studying Cunningham technique with Karen Eliot is really where my understanding of turnout came: that it's not static, and how to engage turnout in movement in order to move powerfully through the space. It goes with this energy idea, because I was at a sophisticated enough place in technique and alignment that I wasn't just going to crank it out with my muscles, but with the idea of energy and muscles—and bones. Many people have told me I dance from my bones. I love to imagine the bones moving by force of an idea, throwing or tossing or pulling in or hiding. It might be an idea about air or about direction. Unlike working from muscle, I can't be in a bone mind-set and be thinking anatomy. I have to be thinking metaphorically or in images. But, I never stay in one place. I never *always* work a certain way. I'm a real dabbler: I like to quilt things together, and get impressions. I have studied a little Chi Kung and Tai Chi, but even with my superficial dabbler's approach, the energy work means something to me. I feel I can take a seed of an idea and it can become very strong. There are some things I'd like to go more deeply into, but sometimes you just graze up against something, and it can be really influential.

mb A catalyst for something.

ah I believe you can get a lot from just a very quick impression of something, as when I worked with Nancy for those two days—it changed my dancing for years and years. At this point in my dancing, my body is really smart. I can just be in the room with someone dancing and absorb some of their ideas very quickly. There is something to that, but it is not the only way. There are some things you can only get by going deeply.

mb As you said, if you have a base or a core, you have the facility to be more experimental and open.

ah Yes. I and other people ask this question: are dancers technicians? Is that what they do? Are we artists? I've tried calling myself different things, a choreographer, for example, but really it comes down to the fact that I'm a dancer. I include a lot of things in that: artistry and creativity and activating my imagination in performance and in improvisation or in teaching. I never think of dancing as only working in the studio, training my body, learning positions in order for a director to give me steps.

mb You've been practicing that approach. Someone makes a suggestion—you take it and go with it.

ah Something I practice in improvisation is getting to the essence of another dancer while I'm dancing with them. Or, if working with a choreographer, sometimes I want to try to do it specifically the way they want it—to really get inside their idea about it. Other times I want to depart from their idea and see it through my lens. It depends on the situation.

sara hook

from an interview with rebecca nettl-fiol, october 2005

Sara Hook danced in the companies of Alwin Nikolais/Murray Louis as well as Jean Erdman, Pearl Lang, and David Parker. She directs her own company, Sara Hook Dances, and is an Associate Professor of Dance at the University of Illinois, Urbana-Champaign. Hook is a Certified Movement Analyst (CMA).

rnf Can you tell me about your early training—a brief sketch, starting when you were very young?

sh I started ballet lessons when I was in around third grade, for a year and a half. My mother took me to Marcia Dale Weary's studio, a very famous school that has produced several dancers in New York City Ballet. I didn't last there very long at all because they put me into a much more advanced class than I should have been in, just by looking at my feet. That was really a shame because I had no idea what I was doing, but I could fake it. So they put me into an even more advanced class, where kids were just dancing rings around me, and I was mortified. That experience turned me off of ballet for a long time.

Later I discovered a class at Gettysburg College in my hometown. A guest teacher taking the class was Jackie Hand whom I consider an important mentor, because up to that time it was just dabbling. Jackie recognized that I was passionate and she started her own studio and I worked with her for about a year. She is trained in LMA [Laban/Bartenieff Movement Analysis] material, so I was getting some Laban principles in the way she taught, even in ballet. She is also the one that sent me to American Dance Festival for one summer when I was sixteen and I just got so carried away: I thought: "Okay, this what I want to do." I loved it! My mother knew about North Carolina School of the Arts (NCSA). I did a last-minute audition, and got in even though I really didn't know what I was doing. I was part of the first high school class in the modern department, the class with Mary Cochran [dancer with Paul Taylor]; it was a wonderful group of peers that both intimated and inspired me. I was there for my last year of high school. That experience was kind of shocking culturally—being around a bunch of crazy artists, and realizing that I had so far to go, so much to learn. I studied mostly Graham with Dick Kuch and Dick Gain, and also with Marcia Pleven who taught Graham and Limón techniques.

Then I went away for a year to try a liberal arts setting at Goucher College in Maryland. That was a good experience because, rather than struggling in the back, I became the one who was getting attention, which helped me gain confidence. After returning to NCSA for the summer session, I decided to transfer back there for college. I had Graham technique, and Dianne Markham was teaching Nikolais-Louis technique, and we had various guests. We had ballet, which was taught by people on the ballet faculty who I felt were uninterested in modern dancers because they didn't really respect modern dance and thought it was too late for any of us. Again, I just faked it.

After that I left for New York to study with Maggie Black, mostly because a guy I was dating at the time told me that I should. I did some Pilates training because I had surgery on both knees while in college. I had a plyca and cartilage that had to be removed because I was injured at a young age, which was good in a way because it led me to study somatics. At that time it was Pilates, later on other things. Maggie Black's classes were great but there was a herd of people and I really needed more attention, so I began to study with Cindy Green who introduced me to the concept of space in a way that I could understand and could be applied to ballet. I began to learn the steps based on what they were doing spatially and that made it easier for me.

After about nine months, I got a scholarship at the Graham school, studying there intensely, and also dancing with Pearl Lang and Jean Erdman. I also took workshops here and there with various people, a few classes at the Cunningham school, which I was not attracted to at that time. Then I got into the Nikolais company.

rnf So your goal in going to New York was probably eventually to get into a company.

sh Yes, coming from the conservatory environment—I think it's changed a little bit now—that was the expectation. You know, you go dance with a major company. The major company that I really wanted to dance with was Paul Taylor's. They didn't have a school at that time until I had been in New York for three years or so, but I studied there while I was still dancing with Nik and studying with Cindy Green. That was an odd mix!

At one point Paul Taylor said to me, "you know, I think you're a great performer but you're not strong." I was pretty devastated; he had me understudying for a while, but that was the only time he ever let me know directly what was worrying him. My mother, a singer, was studying with someone teaching voice through Alexander principles, and she must have said something about how I had been so devastated by Taylor's comment. Her voice teacher recommended I study Alexander Technique and gave me Jane Kosminsky's number. I studied with her for at least two years. That was really revelatory because I learned that my strength was going to have to come from how I connected, because I just didn't have brute strength or a natural athleticism.

rnf I love that idea that someone recommended Alexander for developing more strength, because that's not commonly understood.

sh No, it's not. At that time I was willing to try anything to get into the Paul Taylor Company. But now I thank him and that experience because it opened a world up to me both physically and creatively. I developed more self-awareness and understood with detachment and reason why I wasn't compatible with the Taylor repertory. I loved it because it was so musical and was the kind of dancing I wanted to do, but I realized that I just wasn't that compact . . . So then what did I do? Studied Alexander and started to do my own work. When I left the Nikolais company, it was Jackie Hand who encouraged me to do the Laban program [certification in LMA].

rnf So she was the link.

sh That was completely revelatory. I had a really good faculty in my program, including Janice Pforsich, Jackie Hand, and Clio Pavlantos.

rnf So you went there not really having had much Laban education?

sh I had taken the intro courses in [Bartenieff] Fundamentals and the theory, and really liked it. I had a little spell of auditioning for musicals at that time after I left Nikolais (laughs). At some point Jackie, who is also a connective tissue therapist, began to work on me, and I mention that because I feel a big part of my somatic education was getting her to work on me. At the Laban Institute, I did a creative project for my thesis that gave me confidence enough to continue to choreograph. I also started to study with Zvi Gottheiner; I could connect the Alexander to what he was doing. He was very good with injuries, and I had been plagued with a chronic back injury in the Nikolais company. I based a lot of my early choreographic work on somatic experiments.

rnf Now you've incorporated a lot of that in your own technique teaching. I don't know if that happened quickly or gradually, but how have you made those connections?

sh I think that happened very gradually. At first I did floor work based on the Nikolais floor and the Fundamentals. I experimented with that at Rutgers University, my first teaching assignment. I taught at Zvi Gottheiner's studio where there was relatively low visibility—I didn't have that many students, a lot of them were just my friends or people dancing with me—so I could take my time experimenting with things. Because of my injuries I was exposed to Feldenkrais [Awareness through Movement] and cranial-sacral work by the well-known physical therapist from the NYC Ballet, Marika Molnar. Also, I studied some Gyrotonics that, at the beginning seemed to be hurting me and irritating my back, but I got back to that more recently. That was the beginning of finally healing my back, which I don't think I did until I got here [teaching at the University of Illinois]. Other things that have helped me here were Linda's [Lehovec] yoga class, because it was all about stability, and working with Kim Hardin [physical therapist] when I discovered degeneration happening in my back. I began to cope with the fact that I have the kind of body that really does need to work on stability and strength all the time. Pilates has been helping that. I wish I could study more Alexander.

rnf Right, and I remember that you discovered through Alexander lessons that you had been overusing your abdominals and had to struggle with learning to let go of a little bit of that.

sh Yes, that was really helpful.

If I could do anything over, it would be not being as afraid of ballet. For some reason, because of those early experiences, I got the idea that ballet was something that some people really understood and some people just didn't, unless you'd studied it when you were really young. As far as the Nikolais class, we worked on concepts that might go into the choreography, but I didn't find it a versatile, functional technique class. The thing about ballet that I'm so fascinated with now is *épaulment*—I just can't get enough of it because it seems so fundamental. I just didn't understand it; I never memorized the names of the positions, as some kind of defiance. When you're not good at something you tend to decide that it's not something you need. I remember Mary Cochran making a comment to me about a class I was teaching. She asked: "Could you give us some arms?" (laughs) I think I was so interested in the back and the butt and the legs, and I wasn't coordinating arms with it. Marcia Plevin at NCSA used to ask, "Why are you looking down at my feet? Look at the whole body." I still have to really force myself to use both the arms and legs at the same time.

rnf Could you say more about the Laban/Bartenieff work? It seems to be integrated into your thinking all the way around: in your technique class, and your creative work too. Do you feel that?

sh Definitely. The spatial aspect really opened me up creatively: how to move bigger and locomote through space, to be aware of space rather than making always self-referential gestures. It forced me into a level of physicality, and also forced a kind of specificity. Immediately I began to focus on how it was going to be useful to me as a creator, or as a performer, teaching or choreographing.

I turned my certification project into a piece, and one of my other early pieces that I did here was all about Bartenieff Fundamentals. Making a creative thing out of the Laban work was a way that I could take ultimate responsibility for the material—how I could own it.

rnf That's such an interesting idea—learning a principle or something technical by exploring it choreographically.

sh Right, but it always seemed natural to me.

rnf Going back to technique teaching . . .

sh After Rutgers, I did something at Zvi's studio where Zeva Cohen saw me teach and hired me to teach at Princeton, mostly because of my Laban/Bartenieff background, which she thought would be perfect for non-majors. I developed a warm-up for them that was based on simple Bartenieff coordinations. I continued taking things like Irene Dowd's spiral course, integrating some of those principles in my warm-up too. I continued working out a technical problem in a creative context. I would work on things that I thought they needed to develop in, and try to analyze how my aesthetic was developing. I had done so much solo work that I could figure out something about myself stylistically and then try to build it into the technique class.

rnf Do you think the Laban framework gave you the tools to be able to do that?

sh Absolutely. There is no other training that gives you a language for analysis, not only that but also being able to devise movement sequences that would relate to what I was seeing. There were also times when I would incorporate the Gyrotonic stuff into my technique classes, and then my technique class would inform my next piece, and so I couldn't tell if it was the chicken or the egg anymore.

I think it was really useful for me to have to work with beginners at Princeton—I was forced to figure out what is fundamentally important. Zeva Cohen was a great role model because her class emphasized the things that were really important to her, such as a luscious *plié,* and undercurves in space. When I saw that her warm-up connected so much to her style of dancing and what was important to her as a choreographer, I realized that that was a really big opportunity.

rnf To develop your values, and your stylistic and aesthetic interests.

sh For example, I started to realize how much I enjoyed twisting and how important it was to look at ways to get in and out of the floor—to look at that technically because I hated it when it was awkward choreographically. Yet it was really easy for beginners to learn the basic principle of head-tail connection and pelvic forward shifting. I realized I needed to integrate that into my warm-up.

rnf It's interesting how you did the Nikolais work and the Laban work but yet they didn't come together.

sh Right, they were totally separate tracks.

rnf Did you see the relationships?

sh I do now. I feel totally ashamed that I didn't understand the relationships sooner. I remember when I left the Nikolais company I told Nik about my doing the Laban Certification program, and I asked, "Do you know much about that?" (laughs) He looked at me like I was out of my mind! I wasn't aware of the historical connection between the two, but when I got deeper into it and saw those connections, it made sense considering my choreographic lineage that I'd be attracted to studying Laban after having danced with Nikolais. There is a Graham influence in my classes too: the spirals and the love of the floor, and attention to the upbeat in the rhythm, the attack or the phrasing.

rnf We talked about the framework that Laban gives you, both in your choreography and your technique teaching. What about your composition teaching?

sh I would like to integrate more Laban into that. So far I have done mostly really simple things like make a Laban spatial scale and do a map of movement to it. In the same way that it worked for me, it helps students inhabit more space and physicality. In Milwaukee a couple of summers ago I did a class that was basically LMA as compositional inspiration. We analyzed a combination they made the first day based on what geometric form they were dancing inside of, then they re-created the same phrase inside another crystalline form. It taught them so much about their preferences and how they could expand. LMA also informs the way I write, I think.

rnf Your writing about dance?

sh Yes—having more descriptive ways of dealing with movement.

iréne hultman

from an interview with melanie bales,
october 2001

Iréne Hultman is a Swedish-born dancer and choreographer. She danced with the Trisha Brown Company for five years before forming her own company in 1988. She is currently the rehearsal director for the Trisha Brown Company.

I started to dance thanks to gymnastics. I grew up in a very small town, Borlänge, where they didn't have dance. I especially loved the floor-work and that led me into dance. Dance gave me a feeling of being whole, complete. I remember when I was a teenager I used to dance by myself. I used to skip lunch and go down and dance in the gym instead. I did it as self-expression, as a need—otherwise I didn't feel good. When I was about fifteen, a jazz teacher came to my hometown, so I started to take jazz once a week in the afternoon. He came from out of town in a sports car with a drum machine, a dog, and sometimes a girl. He was very Swedish and very blond. With him it was eight down, eight up, and it was something about that downbeat that is still in me from that experience.

In Uppsala as I studied to become a laboratory technician, I continued my jazz—Dunham studies with Regine. I also started an improvisation class with Stephen Goldin. I really don't know why I started that class, but I loved it and it has had a very important impact on my life. After my studies I moved to Stockholm to work at the hospital and I rented an apartment from Nina Lundborg who later danced for Trisha Brown. It was just a coincidence that it happened to be her apartment. In retrospect, it was a very bizarre coincidence. We are still friends. In Stockholm I continued with the improvisation course that I adored. I also did ballet since I had heard that everybody should do ballet. I danced five days a week in the evening, as a hobby. As a hobby! I was working in the hospital laboratory in the day and dancing in the evening. It was a happy time.

I was almost twenty when I got accepted into the Ballet Academy. It was a total surprise since the reason I auditioned was so I could dance for free for a month. My ballet teacher at that time thought I was great and she begged them to take me into the school, even though I was not their body type. That's how I started ballet at the Ballet Academy, which was a very traditional school—jazz, ballet, and modern every day. No theory, no writing, no alternative sport thing. They invited different teachers, so we got exposed to Graham, to Horton, and Cunningham techniques. In the end I felt I was wrongly trained, with muscles in all the wrong places. My problem was that I could do three *pirouettes*, through pure will and muscle power, not with technical knowledge. I also learned how to stand differently according to which teacher I had: toes back or shoulders back, shoulders forward: learned behavior based on pleasing the teacher. It's very bizarre, I think, because it has nothing really to do with education. I was longing for everybody to dance together until we got really tired and couldn't walk!

Then I took a one-year leave of absence to work in Copenhagen with Eske Holm, a former principal dancer with the Bournonville Opera Ballet. It was a fabulous time. We did Stravinsky's *Rite of Spring,* and also *L'histoire du Soldat.* I was so amazed that I got the job, not really aware of what working entailed. At that particular time I loved to put myself in a trance so I could get a sensation, a feeling of oneness. I wanted to be in that place and I didn't want to leave it. I wanted to return, and I wanted to be there alone. I stayed in Copenhagen after the work was done, just for myself, for self-discovery.

I finished school, planning to work with my Cunningham technique teacher, Kjell Nilsson. He made socially critical dances. One was to *Carmina Burana,* in tons of newspaper, and at the end we put the newspaper underneath the unitards as disfigured fat human beings but still functional. "Beauty: where does it lie?" was the question he posed. It did not work out with him so I went to New York. The only thing I had done continuously for myself during this time was improvising. I always improvised, I never really thought about it or the reason why.

At that same time, I was introduced to Simone Forti who changed my life. I studied with her at Eden's Expressway, and we just danced. I really appreciated the whole feeling of not knowing what to do, and then suddenly getting involved with some little movement of the elbow. I still remember the sensation of discovery. She was the initiator and she gave us space to discover. I have a tremendous respect for Simone. She asked us, "Well . . . what do you feel, what do you think?" which was new to me: "What *did* I feel?" You had to learn about it for yourself. I also did the ball-work with Elaine Summers [Kinetic Awareness]. I wanted to retrain my body from school. I was acutely aware of that. I retrained my body and it was very painful. I don't wish that on anyone. I still think the academies today don't have enough anatomical and physiological information. It still seems to me that the old rule rules, it's got to be pain if you do it right. Maggie Black, a ballet teacher also has meant a lot to me, helped me tremendously during this time. I was having a bad time with an old back injury and she gave me invaluable corrections. Improvisation was very important during that whole period because it was then when everything started. We used to improv all night long, with Peter Rose, Tim Miller, Ishmael Houston-Jones, etc. Then I went back to Sweden again and started doing my own work.

In Sweden I met my life dance partner, Per Jonsson. We were equally obsessive. We had gone to the same school and we were drawn to each other, and used to get really inspired by Lucinda Childs, dancing all night long, just he and I. When I left Sweden to go work with Trisha [Brown], he did his first piece for the opera and became very well known.

I came back to New York at Christmas '82 with a grant to study further, and I met my old "work in the restaurant" buddy, Yoshiko Chuma. She had said, "Oh, come back and do a show with me!" That's how I happened to be in town when Stephen Petronio (who also performed in it) told me that Trisha Brown was having an audition again. I had auditioned for her before. I had seen rehearsals with the old company thanks to Nina Lundborg, including Elizabeth Garren,

Eva Karczag, Lisa Kraus, and Nina [Wiener]. I didn't know at that time whether to be old school or new school, should I point my feet or not! I was especially interested in her concepts; everything I was interested in, she had already done. At the audition I remember a diagonal phrase, which had been set on Eva. It was a little like a *chainée* turn ballet thing with very fast footwork. Since I have a really good eye and was so relaxed I could pick it up really fast. I noticed that the company noticed and I think to this day, that got me the job. I wasn't nervous because I didn't really want the job. I just wanted to dance the movement. I really felt at home in her movement. But when I finally got the job, I didn't take it. I went home to Sweden, but quickly changed my mind. I had cried all the way home. I was doing my own work and I was really into myself, having a good time. But then I thought: "Now this is ridiculous, Iréne. Who do you think you are? Go and learn from this fabulous woman. Take it. Treat it as you're going to school for three years."

I hurt myself in the fourth month of employment, because I was so incredibly tense. I used to warm up by running around, and I'd jump up and I'd throw myself on the floor. The contradiction of my tense muscles and Trisha's loose joint work twisted my hips and spine. I got chiropractic treatments to correct myself short-term, and Alexander Technique to correct myself long-term. Other dancers in the company were doing a lot of Alexander Technique and going to the gym. [Susan] Klein wasn't there when I was there. She came through Diane [Madden] and Diane took me to one of Susan's classes, but it wasn't for me. I was too built up in my shoulders already, and when I did the Klein technique I just got tenser in that respect. My interest in martial arts has always been there, so I did quite a bit of that, and lying on balls, and then Alexander Technique with June Ekman. I wouldn't have continued dancing after my injury if it weren't for June. When I started Alexander initially I couldn't mix it with dancing. There was too much of new information and directive thinking. But you can do both after your body responds to your thought pattern—my body didn't respond to my thought patterns in the beginning. If it was a fast ballet class, my old pattern took hold.

When I was rehearsing with Trisha, you were expected to come warmed up, so sometimes I went to the gym and sometimes I did Tai Chi. Other times I would need to go to a dance technique class and nothing else. I really felt my body going in circles and I learned to listen to the rhythm of my body and where it was taking me. Thank God we toured, because I learned so much about my body through the touring. I had books, I stayed in my room going through different Chinese disciplines to know my body and learning to use some thinking devices on stage. You are not 100 percent all the time, and you have to find ways to go on. Trisha's work is not psychological; you don't exactly need to interpret a role. I always felt instead I needed to go deeper physically, or deeper within myself. I started with knowing my skin, and then through the next layer and the next layer in. Through all of the alternative views—with the ballwork and with Alexander, with the Asian practices, and Japanese imagery exercises—I went deeper. I wanted to feel whole, learn more and also, of course, prevent injuries, but mainly to research. You're doing research: that's what it is. If you do the same *plié* thirty-five times, you really find out something! Once you feel the *plié* in your left knee, and the next time in your little toe, and sometimes you discovered something when you performed and you went back to the hotel the next day and you explored it.

I stayed with the Company for five years, although after three years I did feel that I needed to go on somehow: it had to do with my own development. I wanted to explore something else. I had to make up stories all the time on stage, from a literal standpoint. So I just had to quit, and I didn't know if I would ever be on the stage again.

I wasn't sure I wanted a company. I did want to be in the studio by myself. So that's what I did: on unemployment and getting teaching gigs here and there. I had taught before I came to Trisha's. I can't quite remember much about that, but I know it was full of swings. I remember knowing about making material from the big muscle groups and then to the small muscle groups. It was physiologically correct. When I started with Trisha and after my injury, I had to change my own way of moving. My objective was to be warm, so that's what I told the students: "I'm going to teach you to be warm." My frustration with classes was that I was rarely warm. A class may develop coordination, or this and that, but if you're going to really learn you have to be warm first. I really strongly believe you can learn technique through the material and through repetition. My objective was to really warm up by developing perception and learning to see, through a positive attitude. I taught myself to talk along with the class because I found I didn't want to stop the flow to explain. I wanted to keep the momentum, the warmth of the body and I also find it thrilling for myself in some way, an external/internal relationship. My own learning through teaching was to further develop my perceptions.

I continued teaching in New York and in Europe. I never made an effort to teach, but people kept asking me so I kept teaching. I developed things that interested me—focusing on joints and finding center—things from my own experience, from what I found important. My mantra at the beginning was to have everybody able to warm themselves up—to realize what they needed so they could go home and never have to come back to class again. I considered other art forms—how musicians train at home, and how opera singers train at home. Sometimes dancers don't have a sense of themselves as individually valuable, but I always felt that each dancer is a voice and has the interpretational skills as a character similar to a theater actor. They need to take responsibility for their own bodies. There are dancers who have taken ballet classes for a long, long time, and still can't do one *tour en l'air.* Then I think something is wrong. They don't take responsibility for that, but say to themselves, "I can't do it."

These thoughts were precursors for my interest in choreography. But I have always made work, even in Sweden and before I started Trisha, but I never saw myself as a choreographer. I enjoy the research and so forth and after I finished Trisha, I spent time in the studio alone doing work, and then I realized I wasn't quite happy. The fairytale trilogy came about on an airplane hearing Jack Nicholson read "Billy Goat Gruff," and I was thinking: That's the material! That's what I'm doing! I realized I needed two dancers, to get a grant, and so it starts. In the beginning I was interested in the movement vocabulary. I wasn't interested in the dancers contributing as much as I am now. I was interested in researching myself, the rhythm, and the emotional expression it makes.

The piece I did recently in Sweden was also created through improvisation and guidance, so in some ways I'm a dance director. I did phrases with them taken from improvised material I had worked with for *Black Tie Optional;* I just transported that material. So they had something from me, but interspersed movement of their own, so I feel it was more like directing.

In *Love, Betrayal and a Bowling Trophy,* I worked with an actor who needed different input in order to click—he needed the intention behind it. Then the dancers could not at all create from that. They needed something else—adjectives like heavy. I always believed that the movement and the expression is created from the intention and direction of your thoughts. I'm still like an interpretive dancer, but on a larger scale. I still believe in the trueness of the movement and the rhythm. If you don't have the exact rhythm, you have a different expression.

stephen koester

from an interview with rebecca nettl-fiol,
may 2003

Stephen Koester was co-artistic director and dancer with Creach/Koester, a dance company based in New York City. He choreographs nationally and internationally and has been a guest artist at numerous universities. He is currently Associate Professor and Director of Graduate Studies at University of Utah.

rnf Tell me about your early dance training. Did you dance as a child?

sk I never danced, not even at dances. At high school dances, I was a wallflower, petrified to get on the floor.

rnf So when did you begin?

sk My first dance class was at the University of Utah—this is full circle. The school paper had an ad for the national touring cast of *Hair,* and I auditioned and got called back. I had to sing and dance. I was told, "You know, you sing flat and you can't dance to save your life." Which just goaded me on to take my first non-majors class; and actually, the whole thing was a sham. It was some guy with money looking for boyfriends.

rnf I didn't know that you went to the University of Utah.

sk Yes, I took a year and a half here, as a non-major sneaking into majors' classes.

rnf And do you remember if it was a certain style?

sk I remember I had a grad student teacher, and I think I took rhythmic analysis with Betty Hayes. Eventually, I quit because I was doing other things. My majors were psychology and architecture.

rnf What happened next?

sk I took two courses in Russian studies, one at Ohio State, which was five weeks in the Soviet Union, and then University of Northern Iowa, which was also going to the Soviet Union. Then I went to Canterbury College of Art and to the University of Minnesota, studying architecture, and almost finished. Later, I picked up some courses at the Pratt Institute, which transferred back to Minnesota—I finally received my degree about ten years later. In Minnesota, I had a summer job that fell through at the last moment, so I had nothing to do. I decided to take a dance class—a summer workshop with the Nancy Hauser Dance Company. Very little training of mine was in a university.

rnf Did you go right into taking company class?

sk It was a studio, with a regimented program. There was composition, improvisation, and technique. No academics in dance, or grades. It's amazing that I teach at a university, because I never went that route, and I like the way I went.

rnf How long did you do that?

sk I must have been there about five years, and I supplemented that experience with workshops. At the end of year two I was in the company, taking the advanced class.

rnf So you started feeling serious about it?

sk Yes—because I realized I was going to be a lousy architect. Some people have a gift for it, but it was just so much work for me, figuring it out. I was good at design stuff, abstract design, but I realized that I was better in one thing than the other, and I felt a passion for it [dance]. During that time, I went to study with Hanya Holm in Colorado, and the University of Minnesota had summer workshops.

rnf So you were doing mainly modern technique.

sk Yes, the Holm philosophy was to keep ballet and modern as separate as possible.

rnf Then you were dancing professionally, and your training foundation came from those modern classes.

sk Right away I was teaching class, I think within my first year, even before I joined the company. I find teaching to be as good an education as taking a class. And we were encouraged to choreograph as part of the apprentice company, so I was choreographing from the very beginning. We learned through doing.

rnf Very integrated.

sk Yes, it was great.

rnf Once you began to dance more and more, did you keep training?

sk Oh yes, the whole time.

rnf Did you search out classes?

sk I went to New York, taking classes on a regular basis, starting also into ballet. And that was pretty much just technique. I was working as soon as I got to New York, so it was busy.

rnf Yes, with Jamie Cunningham. And did he give company class?

sk No.

rnf You had to find your own training. Did you feel it was necessary, or did you just become interested in taking ballet at some point?

sk I just wanted to. Well, I was terrible; I was starting from scratch again. It was just horrible. But I was also taking other classes from whomever I wanted, so it was very eclectic: Viola Farber, Dan Wagoner, Limón technique with Ruth Currier, Gerri Houlihan, in the Lubovitch style, and quite a bit of [Alwin] Nikolais technique, as well.

rnf So no one was telling you, "You should have more of this or that." Now it is very common for people to do other things beside dance techniques. Did you ever do anything else?

sk Not really. Now, I go to the gym. I started that in the later years in New York, when I stopped taking class regularly. I ended up just doing ballet, as maintenance, and going to the gym.

rnf So none of the somatic practices really came into your training.

sk No, I mean I had just the briefest little smattering of several. At the time, those things were too subtle for me. I just liked to move. I didn't care how; I didn't want to know the refinements. Technically, I did—I wanted to be good. But as far as understanding all the details, and the deep work—I didn't get it. Walking around trying to feel your psoas, for example, then forgetting to dance. I just dance. I have worked backwards in a way, particularly in having to teach early on. I am an intuitive mover, a big mover. Having to teach, I have had to figure out more and more about the articulation. In having to describe something, I go deeper, and that starts to influence my movement, which I then need to describe even further, as to the articulation or how one joint relates to the others, or about how the initiation of one body part leads to the next movement. Finding the connections in your own body, instead of someone telling you, is a different way of learning. I think most of my training has been me figuring it out, rather than having someone guide me.

rnf I can see that. And probably your choreographic work prompted that kind of discovery.

sk I think so. When I teach technique, particularly when I throw in a little partnering, I always honor how partnering has taught me more about the way I dance as a soloist than anything else has: the use of momentum, about gravity, about having to let go, because you can't be rigid and partner. A large part of my education, too, was the Creach/Koester experience. We commissioned many choreographers to make duets for us. Every duet involved the three of us: Terry [Creach], me, and the choreographer. That process is nothing like being a corps dancer—being in the studio with the two of us and Bill T. Jones, or Peter Anastos, or Bebe Miller, or Jane Comfort—that's pretty deep.

rnf When those artists were setting work on you, did you train outside of the rehearsal setting? Or take some classes in whatever style you were working with?

sk No, we just did it and learned through that. You know, I actually think I understand a lot of the somatic stuff, if not on the verbally articulate or theoretical level. I enjoy taking little parts of it, and I start to integrate a little of that into occasional warm-ups, or designing a floor *barre,* for example.

rnf Could that be part of your process of trying to figure out how to explain things that you already know, to other people, your students?

sk Well, I do try to make it have relevance to their dancing, such as being clearer about joint articulation, not using excess energy, about letting go. I might also throw it in if they look really tired, as a different way to approach things, for variety, or to bring more ease into their work, or to focus on specific bodily aspects. I use it more for investigation than for warming up, or maybe a combination of the two.

rnf At the present, for your own training, you go to the gym?

sk Occasionally, I'll take other people's classes. Right now my own work is it—planning class, teaching class, that is my class.

ralph lemon

from an interview with rebecca nettl-fiol, september 2002

Ralph Lemon danced with the Nancy Hauser Dance Company and Meredith Monk/The House before forming the Cross Performance/Ralph Lemon Company in 1985. He dissolved the company in 1995 and has created projects dedicated to new forms of performance and presentation. His recent project, The Geography Triology, was an international project that culminated in three evening-length works.

rnf Could you talk about your training history—how did you begin?

rl In high school I did track and I was on the wrestling team, and running was something I did, that was my favorite thing to do. And it's really interesting now because now that's what I've gone back to, that's what I do.

rnf You run?

rl I just run, and I stretch. That's my training. But really the first dance classes I ever took were ballet classes, at the University of Minnesota. Then someone suggested the Nancy Hauser studio, which was Hanya Holm/[Mary] Wigman training. As I discovered much later, it is a very grounded, old modern dance technique, which I imagine I still carry with me in my movement principles now.

After Nancy I moved to New York and I was working with Meredith Monk—actually I moved to New York because I was so fascinated with Merce Cunningham. Viola Farber had come and worked with Nancy Hauser in the early seventies, and I was part of the company. That technique was mind-blowing because it was so hard, and I don't think it was even my revisiting this idea of ballet, it was about the legs being straight, and *battements,* and *jetés,* but in this really broken, fierce kind of way, which I found really engaging, but intimidating. That wasn't what we did at the Hauser studio. But the energy of it I found really very sexy. Merce came to town, and Merce was on TV, and he just became a hero, an idea. So I wanted to move to New York and work with Merce Cunningham—not the technique part, but just the art part was really interesting. But I didn't! Meredith came and she and I connected, and that was interesting because it was so different, technically. And yet at that point, I was a young dancer and my training was young, and so there was this momentum I got by being in the studio, training, taking ballet *barre* and being in the classroom. I wanted more of that. My body became aware of needing more information—not art, or even dancing *per se,* but just about standing on your leg, and pointing your foot—that you could control that. Not only flexibility, but the expression one could have in different parts of the body. So when I moved to New York it was a watershed in terms of classes and students and places to go.

rnf You studied at various studios?

rl It was a lot about studying, which was interesting. I found a segue into "super-technique," via Zena Rommett, the floor *barre,* which seemed to have a Hauser connection, and yet alternative enough to fit into my work with Meredith. And then I started doing ballet, with ballet teachers or studios that were home to a lot of modern dancers, where there seemed to be a real community. If you were a modern dancer, you studied ballet: this is the early '80s. There were other things going on that I wasn't privy to so much, because I think that, for me, ballet training seemed an obvious, conventional choice—maybe not the right choice, or truthful—but an obvious conventional choice to train the body, getting the body stronger to stand and move.

rnf But you didn't go to the Cunningham studio?

rl Didn't go to the Cunningham studio. Taking class with Viola [Farber], as incredible an experience as it was, was so intimidating. I think that for the first time in my young dancing life, I became aware of "not so good," "good," "real good," in terms of myself as a dancer. I never really thought of myself as a good dancer. I was attracted to what my body could do. And it wasn't as clear then as it became later, that I wanted to be a creator versus a body in a creative situation.

Ballet seemed anonymous. I could stand at the *barre* and I could leave early, and I could hide behind someone. In Viola's class, you are right there, and she is really looking at you! And at one point she asked me to join her company, but I said no.

rnf Why?

rl I thought about it a long time; "Why am I saying no?" It had been after Meredith, and I felt that after I left Meredith, I really wanted to do my own work. The whole classroom situation in my modern experience was very judgmental. But whether it was Nancy, or Viola, or Meredith, in those situations I was seen as someone learning a technique, but also someone who is an artist. In ballet I was just learning technique. It's the difference between the messiness of being a creator in the modern training situation, versus the clarity of just going and doing a *tendu,* or a *plié.*

When I started doing my own work, I was taking ballet classes and Zena Rommett's floor *barre.* And that went on for a number of years. Then my work started to grow and change and at a certain point in the late '80s, some of my dancers were not doing ballet anymore. They were finding all these somatic alternatives and some in particular were studying with Susan Klein and Barbara Mahler. Before my rehearsal I would give everyone forty-five minutes or an hour just to get into their bodies. And that also changed things: being more serious about making dances meant that there was less time to think about training.

rnf You training your dancers, you mean?

rl Yes, and training my own body. Also, the community of the company shifted priorities. Having dancers that were interested in different kinds of training really disrupted the whole idea of what was possible. I would watch them come in and hang over, and ask them what they were doing, and experiment with it. I took a few classes with Barbara [Mahler], and there was something about it that connected for me. Around the same time, I started meditation with Barbara Dilly at Naropa [Institute]—something called Open Space. It is an improvisational practice about personal awareness. You sit and meditate, and then you move, then you go back and sit and meditate, then you move; and I brought that back into the company. Before rehearsals we would do an hour of Open Space. A lot of stuff started to affect not only training, but affected work and ideas, particularly through the body, and that changed my practice. Then from there, I started yoga classes, moving further and further into this alternative way of thinking about my body and moving and making dances. This went on until I disbanded the company in '95, which was about re-looking at my whole dance history—everything. And I started traveling.

I traveled to Africa, and to Asia, and of course that just turned the whole idea of training upside down—how other dance cultures deal with the idea of training is very different. I learned a respect for those ways, and that raised questions about my own dancing, in the process of communing with these other kinds of performers. So, the work changed. I used to make dances where everything was set, and particularly on my own body. Now I only improvise. That's really interesting to me, what that means—that shift. I don't go to class anymore. I jog, and I stretch, and I find a discipline: something much more open and that fits in with my own personal creative politic right now.

As I go into the third part of this trilogy [*Geography*], my work is centered around parts of the [American] south, so I'm doing living room dances, engaging relatives of old blues musicians. I bring recordings of old music I've been listening to, where the artist is long gone, but the relatives are still alive, and I share some of what I've been doing with that music with the relatives, in their homes. Also, I'm doing physical performance rituals at lynching sites. So, my stage has changed, my studio has changed, my warm-up space has changed. Often I'm warming up in hotel rooms, which is not necessarily limited, but demands a certain kind of practice. Dancing in these really emotionally charged spaces doesn't call for dancing the way I used to dance. So for me, it seems that a lot of my training has been predicated on what I'm interested in psychologically, or in creative processes, as much as what the body might need. When I do go into a more conventional studio and work, it is hours of stretching and moving around, moving to music. There was a long period when it wasn't about that, but now, I am moving as basically as I can.

rnf And you don't have anything to do with the training of the people you're dancing with?

rl Now I am working with performers who do *Odissi* or West African technique, for example, so trying to train them in anything would be absurd. However, in all these situations we still had rehearsal periods where we shared physical information, and of course those were very complex and difficult. But they were ways of communicating beyond language.

rnf When you had a company, did you ever consider trying to train them in your way of moving?

rl I was never really good at that. In the beginning we all took classes at the same places. I think I eventually worked with dancers who began to expand, and at the same time my work and thinking about my work was expanding, so it became impossible to do communal classes, because everyone was in a different place, and some people in the company were still going to ballet classes, for example. Other people were just rolling around on the floor. All that brought something really rich to the process, so I wasn't going to disrupt it. It was very valuable.

rnf What intrigues us [Bales, Nettl-Fiol] is that the model has really shifted from the early modern dancers. Being in the university, I'm always looking at what's going on in the professional world, and wondering if we are perpetuating an old curricular model that's no longer valid. Should we synchronize with what's happening in the profession, or do we have a different responsibility?

rl I find these issues of training really interesting, and I think that they are still importantly and boldly practiced: the idea of training in many different categories of what is modern dance now. For example, Paul Taylor dancers, I suspect, go to class; there is a technique behind it. And Trisha Brown—she might never say this—but that is a technique now, too. They actually have a school.

rnf And now you've really gone full circle from running to running.

rl I was running around the park the other day; the sense of weight and aerobic breath are things I find really important now. Movement I'm interested in now is connected to an idea of history and how people moved when they were just social dancing in America, particularly in the South, and particularly black people, when dancing was part of the culture. Perhaps it's the place that is most comprehensive to my new relationships with African friends and Asian friends. This is a generalization, but I've discovered that they don't really separate their performance dancing practice from their lives. Our idea of training is really abstract, because there is an important separation. I imagine many of the dancers I am working with have taken class, and do study and have teachers, absolutely. But there is a stronger relationship to the larger scope of life.

rnf Do you think doing the technical study removes you or prohibits you from being able to do the other?

rl Actually, I'm finding that it adds a nuance to the going back, that I find useful.

When I'm doing my lynching site rituals, or my living room dances in front of an audience of passing cars, or an old woman sitting in a chair, I'm sharing something with them, and simultaneously considering all that I know about my modern, or post-postmodern dance. Everything that I've learned I access, I'm engaging when I move. I'm thinking about ballet, about straightening my leg, about bending my knee, flexing my foot. I'm thinking about jogging, about breathing, or about "How do I feel?" I'm thinking about how delightful it is, or if I will hurt myself, or if I am warmed up enough. I might even be wondering if it is all that different from being in a ballet studio, or being on stage. All that becomes part of my moving.

rnf So you bring it all with you.

rl I feel like I'm dancing now in such a different context than I did before. And as I'm dancing I'm asking questions.

rnf Issues of the body are both so simple and complex.

rl And also life! I think what becomes really important is embracing that larger perspective. It is about straightening your leg—and also about not necessarily knowing why you are doing that.

bebe miller

from an interview with melanie bales, 2001

Bebe Miller has been Artistic Director of Bebe Miller Company since 1985. She has choreographed for companies throughout the United States and abroad. She is currently a Professor of Dance at The Ohio State University in Columbus.

mb Let's start with when you went back to New York, your home, after graduating from Earlham College. You were there for a couple of years, working evenings and taking classes. What were you thinking at that time as far as professional aspirations?

bm That was in '71 and by then all I'd had was [Alwin] Nikolais [technique] and this one Merce Cunningham class, and then dancing in an improv class at school at Earlham. I had had folk dance too, and then African came in around college time, back in New York in the summer vacations. My older sister was very into African culture and I studied with Gus Dinizulu, who taught West African dance. I did my first professional gig at that time, though, substituting for a dancer with Phyllis Lamhut who was doing these outdoor pieces. I guess Nikolais, or Murray's [Louis] company was what I was sort of hoping for, but I don't know if I even articulated that to myself. I'd seen them perform since I was little.

mb Then in 1973, Vickie Blaine called you with an opportunity to come to Ohio State on a fellowship.

bm I had auditioned and I still remember it. I did this improv that was all about "interior space/exterior space," very Nikolais. I wasn't even looking at anything on a cultural level—being an African-American coming in doing abstract modern dance. As far as technique, I really had no experience with the [Katherine] Dunham/[Lester] Horton tradition. I had seen [Alvin] Ailey in the '70s when he came to Earlham. They did *Revelations* and it made a big impression, but it was still not me. Without even talking about it overtly that much back then, I knew I was coming out of my whiteground—my whiteground!—I mean my background was all white. There was a sense of choice that I wasn't talking about, but I was definitely making one. Once you align, I guess you can go back and forth, but I felt that I was going to stick with what I wanted to do. It had a lot to do with self-expression, but on a really political level.

So I came to OSU, and the technique—I was terrible. It was standing technique, which was fairly new to me. Phyllis had taught some standing classes, but with Nikolais you start on the floor with bounces, very modern, broad, with a lot of spatial emphasis. I was very good at across-the-floor and rhythm, and I could pick up combinations like nothing. What was hard about being at OSU was getting what was the essence of these standing techniques, like ballet, where you stand here and there's a gesture. The stability against gesture was very foreign. At that time at OSU, it was mostly Cunningham or [Paul] Taylor-based, not using the kind of language of space and energy and dynamics that is very much what Nikolais does. I may not have been as bad as I thought I was, but I was trying to find a way to perform it, and really couldn't figure that out, being overwhelmed by finding balance—you can't cheat when you're on *relevé*, you're just there. I think that I really didn't understand muscularly or alignment-wise what was going on. I was there working against myself, and didn't know how to find that support in the body, just there hoping I don't fall over, hoping to stay on one leg, gripping. I remember Lucy [Venable] taught Fundamentals, and it was wonderful, but I couldn't figure out how to integrate that, even though I knew that was the goal. Then what was also important about OSU was that Nina [Wiener] came.

mb So after you graduated, you stayed in Columbus for a bit.

bm Nina was here as a visiting artist for two quarters, so I saw her a lot. She had just left Twyla [Tharp] because of an injury. I took her class and it was hard, but there was a way through. I should say also that Lynn Dally was another important link for me from OSU into Nina's work. I worked with Lynn for a year right after I graduated. We performed at Ohio University and then took the show to New York in the spring. I worked with her, and I think she liked what I did! And it was the rhythm, but also funkiness—she worked to music of Randy Newman, Rolling Stones, it was all sort of contemporary, and you were yourself. It was a stepping-stone into the personal, and into how to shape a personal story—that your own sense of style and dynamic is what you are really cultivating. That was a huge transition now that I think of it! So all that continued in working with

Nina: the jazz shoes, yes, but also the sensuality, sexuality and the rigor of it. I don't know why I was really ready for something that was technically hard, but she showed you a way out of hard, that it will take you someplace. Nina talked about the interior monologue as you're performing, as you're learning. "Okay, prepare for the arm here. No, this balance is how the arm is working against the leg here, and be ready for a balance, now let it go. . . ." No one had ever said it like that before. There was something you were feeling that made the exploration good and that was what you were revealing. You didn't have to mask it. You are your whole interior—which makes me think about Steve Paxton and how he shows his process. When you watch him that is what I think he is doing.

mb Did you see her works then, her choreography?

bm She didn't have any. It was just her class, the teaching of her movement. We did an aggressive floor, *battement* phrases from Albert Reid [former Cunningham dancer] and I remember a way of going across the floor with *battements,* just so you could figure out *battement.* It might have been boring, lots of repetition, but it wasn't, because you were the one trying to enliven it. The subtlety of it was fascinating, big things against small things, the whole counterpoint of sensibilities in the body. If you look at the early Tharp stuff, too, a little shoulder thing and then a foot here, it was all these little tiny pieces that added up to something really nice and slippery, silky, subtle, and female. And Nina wore a little headband and low-slung sweatpants—you wanted to be her, she was very cool. I was in maybe her second company. The first piece she did was at DTW [Dance Theater Workshop], right before I got there. Working with her meant a lot of rehearsing, daily rehearsals—a long day and no money. It was before the economics of the whole situation changed—rehearsing for four months to perform twice. It upped the ante tremendously to work with Nina, about what a work could be.

mb What else were you doing at the time, in terms of training?

bm Ballet, with Maggie Black, later with Jocelyn [Lorenz]—and some with David Howard—scary ballet people! I wasn't good, but Nina was my way in, they paid attention to me because I worked with her. She encouraged me to do it, to get better at it. Rehearsals were making up variations and learning phrases, so that was a lot. The idea of going to the diva, immersing yourself in her class and then in her choreography—that was the old model, Nina wasn't teaching a daily class.

mb So what was the next phase after dancing with Nina?

bm I think because we were so involved with Nina in the making of her work that making my own work just seemed inevitable. Something I didn't really foresee was that a year after I left Nina, I worked with Dana Reitz whom I met at the

Colorado Dance Festival while I was teaching there with Nina. That was the first time I had gone back to improvisation since I was about twelve. At that time, early '80s, I was making my own work—jazz shoes, solos and groups, popular music—Reggae and whatnot—that kind of loose, Tharpish, postmodern stuff. Dana and I hooked up with two other soloists—Sarah Skaggs and Maria Cutrona—and had a yearlong thing where we performed at BAM and went on a European tour. The idea of rehearsing an improvisational process for three months was mind-boggling. Going into the first day's rehearsal—I did a *barre* to warm up, Dana was pacing the room and Sarah was lying on balls. That was new to me, the first time I saw that kind of warm-up. During that time in New York, I was still doing ballet, there wasn't much modern, the Movement Research class series hadn't been started yet, so unless you went to the Cunningham studio, there weren't many places to study. You worked with your choreographer to get your training—especially with the new forms of dance.

mb With that group did you have the shoes on or off?

bm With Dana? Off. Nina, on—very much on. I remember Dana saying, "You're not using your feet! You're not using your toes!" With shoes, you turned, went up and down and you slid and that was reflected in the work. Dana was grounded, literally, because of no shoes. No turns. No touching either. With that kind of improvisation you are examining your body, in a way the aesthetics of the anatomy. My way was very different, but that experience took me right back to what I had been doing way before, to Nikolais, it was a circle back to my early training.

mb When you started making work with other people, how were you thinking about training or technique then? Obviously, you had made some big changes and developments since the early times.

bm Actually ballet was what took me all the way through to [Susan] Klein [technique]. Different ballet teachers had different subtleties with how to approach the body: like Jocelyn and Maggie and Nadine Revene. Also, Elizabeth Caron was one of the dancers in my early company, in the mid-'80s, and she studied with Klein.

Habit of Attraction was a piece I made in '87 where we took off our shoes, and Scott Smith, who was a Contact Improviser, was working with me then. We didn't start with Contact, per se, but I pushed the partnering because of Scott. I made phrases and they made variations, so there was improvisation in the sense of catching material and then finding ways to develop it. It was the beginning of another language. I would make a phrase, and then we would make variations and see where that took you to the next thing—the transitions, the connective tissue was partnered—which was a new aspect for us. That was also one of the pieces I set that I was not dancing in. Other things were taking hold. I was studying with Klein, along with [Stephen] Petronio's company at the time, my company, and Trisha's [Brown]. It was mystifying, but interesting: no shoes, grounded, emotional force. Klein was the first class I had been to where nothing happened. You didn't dance. You rolled down and asked yourself what you felt—nothing about space, totally interior. It showed me all the tensions that I didn't know I was carrying, the habits I didn't know I was carrying through. Learning to direct energy through the skin. But in learning that, I didn't go into the "release mode." I went into partnering. Then in '88, we started going to Bates [Dance Festival] where there was a big improvisation, Contact thing going on. That was new to me, but it brought back Dana, and an earlier version of myself as an improviser again.

Other influences came through Bates too: Alexander through Shelley Senter, Larry Goldfarb and Feldenkrais, Ann Rodiger [Alexander Technique teacher], Glenna Batson [somatics]. All this plus Klein gave me a place to start looking for something else in the work, I think. All of my injuries or weaknesses are on the left side. And suddenly I thought: "Why? What is going on? My varicose vein, my fibroid, my eye, my bunion, everything." It became much more psychological, or the whole physiology of that imbalance became personal. Klein work was also a way of making that visible.

mb You had a big change in 1993, a turnover with the company.

bm Yes, huge, it was very painful for a year. Then another group eventually formed. With company number two, there was an emotional distance that maybe made it easier for me to say: "Let me see this, let me shape this, choreographically." Then also because of that distance, they rely on themselves in a different way so that their interactions become more formative and something interesting surfaces. We didn't start off with phrases or catching, we started off with improvising.

mb Going back to the bodywork and the kind of information that brings to the dance artist, is there anything else you can say about that?

bm I think that work has the potential for going inside and clarifying in a way that is not about moving in space. It either makes you so internal that no one wants to see you, or it can, as it did for me, release you into a direct channel with other levels of emotion.

With Alexander, for example, comes the idea that you recognize what you are using, anger or force, not that you don't use it at all. It felt that sometimes literally we hold each other harder and rougher because of this kind of work—that the tactile experience has changed. When you literally put your weight behind a gesture, it can go further on the spinal or neurological level, where the movers meet each other in a raw way. Then my job is to shape that artistically, aesthetically. And that's where the theater comes in for me.

In a related thing, ten years ago when I seemed to be doing a lot of master classes in performing arts high schools in inner city neighborhoods, a lot of black kids came in with a "hard-skin" style and I was giving information about "let go." They knew I was a black woman out there with a company, so they followed me. But I was talking with Cornell West about this and he pointed out, "Well, Bebe, they don't have the luxury of just letting that outer tension go, letting their backs be soft," so there seems to be a survival aspect there as well.

mb The work you are making now—the work you just made [*Verge*]—how was that in terms of being more conscious of relationships and the theatrical or dynamic possibilities of people's movement?

bm It started with passion, all about touch. It started with animals, actually, the idea of animals!

mb It seems that when you started investigating the improv and the partnering more closely, that it took on a life of its own rather than so directly being related to your personal, bodily experience. Is that right or am I just reading that in?

bm I think that once you give up a certain part of the process to other people's input, you kind of lose that center, and that has been both a good thing and a bad thing in the work that I have done. In the first company, the making of phrases around my material was different than improvising around—I had more control. But I think what I always do and what I'm interested in, is how to shape something with the personalities that are in the studio. That really affects where I am going—I'm always looking for that dialogue.

tere o'connor

from a conversation with melanie bales,
may 2001

Tere O'Connor has created over thirty works for his company, Tere O'Connor Dance, as well as numerous commissions for dance companies around the world. He taught ballet at New York University's Tisch School of the Arts from 1990–99, and has been artist-in-residence at universities and dance festivals throughout the

United States and abroad. He is currently a Professor of Dance at the University of Illinois, Urbana-Champaign.

At SUNY/Purchase, when Tere was there as a theatre major, the curriculum included Grotowski and Alexander Technique for actors. After two years in the theatre program, he switched to dance, studying with Jacques d'Amboise, among others, for ballet, and major modern techniques with other faculty. In New York City, he continued ballet with Marjorie Mussman, and Jocelyn Lorenz until the early '90s. For three years, he took Klein-based stretch classes with Scottie Mirviss. He began his own work in 1981 and danced in it until 1996.

He is unusual in that, although he danced for other choreographers such as Rosalind Newman and Matthew Diamond, he began choreographing almost as soon as he became serious about dance, unlike many artists who dance first and then transition into choreographing. Because of this, his training influences are innately interwoven into making dances, and perhaps partly from his theater background, he looks to human gestures and situations as much as to dance technique for his material. Other art forms also inspire his imagination, such as filmic ideas like long shots, close-ups, framing, and abrupt editing cuts.

Tere sees dance as a metaphor for thought processes: idea-oriented movement versus material from a "danced body." He is intrigued by the "potential significances" of movement, the multi-layered nature of a gesture. For example, a body hunched over could be: a Graham contraction, vomiting, an old lady. An erect posture might refer him to a classical attitude or to the "hyperpersonal" stance of his father. An early work called *Construct-a-guy* drew from his family's gestures and mannerisms. He likes to juxtapose things familiar or standardized—ballet, high fashion—with things that are distant or exotic, or to mix raw or thrown-off movements with highly articulate or ornate steps. High contrast, illogical sequencing of his earlier work has given way to "exorcisms" where repressed voices are given free rein and then shaped.

As the director of his company, Tere never recommends or suggests where or how his dancers study. He has noticed that when people stopped doing Pilates, their bodies seemed less tense and their extremities were more released and articulate. He is concerned about dancers getting stuck in "technique concepts" and focusing excessively on physical aspects, class sequences, or getting an adrenaline high. He feels that the expressiveness of dance can be undermined by reducing things to "hot bods doing cool things" as an end in itself. He wonders if virtuosity, or the pursuit of it, is often compensatory for the lack of political or individual power that dancers feel.

cynthia oliver

from an interview with rebecca nettl-fiol, june 2003

Cynthia Oliver danced with the David Gordon Pick-Up Performance Company and Ronald K. Brown/Evidence. She is also a choreographer, performer, and scholar. Oliver is currently an Associate Professor of Dance at the University of Illinois, Urbana-Champaign.

rnf I would like to hear about your training as a child: your dance, sports, and physical training.

co I wasn't very athletically inclined as a child, but because I was the last of six and because I think my mother just wanted to get me out of the house, she enrolled me in dance classes. At the time we were living in New York. She took me to Ron Davis Dancers. I studied ballet and jazz, and I remember my very first performance was in a gymnasium and we danced to Hugh Masekela's music. It was my first taste of performance and very fun. We then moved to the Virgin Islands, to my father's home, and at about age seven or eight, I began taking Afro-Caribbean dance with Monty Thompson from Trinidad. He was part of Theater Dance, Incorporated, which was run by Atti van den Berg Bermudez, a woman from Holland who had danced with Kurt Jooss in the original "Green Table." She had moved to the islands in the '50s and established this school of dance. She taught the ballet and brought other artists in from various places in the world to expose the kids on the island to other different forms. We got a real smattering of styles and aesthetics.

After about two years with Monty, I began to take class at Theater Dance, Incorporated, taking ballet and dancing more seriously. With Atti, we did something called, "inner-dance," a form of improvisation that perhaps also came from Kurt Jooss. At the time it seemed innovative: we did environmental dances. We danced on the beach, on the rocks, in the woods. She gave us imagery to work with. Sometimes we moved with our eyes closed, interacting with each other. Improvisation was a major part of my training, along with ballet and Afro-Caribbean dance.

Eventually I started doing modern dance. I remember Homer Bryant [of Dance Theater of Harlem] came and also, Jean Destiné, the Haitian dancer. I stayed with Atti until I graduated from high school. My last year of high school,

Monte had broken off from Theater Dance and had created the Caribbean Dance Company, and I was one of the students who went with him. I managed to straddle both things—Theatre Dance and the Afro-Caribbean Company—juggling both. Atti encouraged us to study somewhere else during the summers, so I went to New York to take classes at the Ailey School, at Dance Theater of Harlem, and ballet with Nadine Revene, whom I loved. So I have a lot of ballet in my background. You'd never guess it, maybe, but I use it a lot.

rnf Is college the next thing that happened?

co Yes. A number of schools had come to the island to recruit me, and I chose Adelphi because it was close to my big brother who was in New York. At Adelphi, I studied with Norman Walker, Regina Larkin, Nancy Lushington, and May O'Donnell. Graham work was the core of the program. Our electives were ballet and other styles of modern, including Viola Farber's classes, and Renée Wadleigh's. Renée's classes blew my mind because I had never seen anything like that before—the quirkiness of it, the timing; it was really inventive. Working with Renée and Karen Levy was really exciting for me, and on the weekends, I would go into the city and study [Lester] Horton [technique].

I was a maniac; I was a dance maniac. It wasn't enough that I was dancing in every production at school and dancing all day long! I studied Horton with Debbie Lukitch, who is ingrained in my memory because she had the most amazing facility. I remember just going to class so that I could watch her. I had never seen anybody who could move like that!

When I got out of school, still in New York, is when the real experimentation began. I took ballet, and occasionally for fun, I would take a jazz class. I studied ballet with various people: Cindy Green, Maggie Black, Christina Bernal, Janet Panetta, and Pam Critelli. Then I would go off and rehearse with various companies, and the styles varied tremendously.

rnf You felt that ballet gave you a basic foundation?

co It was like the root. I knew what I was going to get. I knew that I was training myself well, and it would enable me to do other forms. It's funny—I didn't graduate and go back to improvisation, for example, maybe because the companies I was interested in were technically demanding, and I thought ballet would serve me as a foundation.

rnf Then how soon were you in David Gordon's company?

co I got into David's company in 1986 after graduating in 1982. Prior to that, I danced in other companies and did industrial shows, which was fun. I didn't know much about David. I just saw a notice in *Backstage* for women 5'8" and over, and I auditioned. It was still that period of time historically when you could be in a company working full time, with health benefits. Full time meant Monday through Saturday from 12:00 to 6:00. So in the morning, several of us took ballet class, and then rushed to the studio for rehearsal.

rnf But he didn't expect you to take ballet, or did he?

co I think he would have been happy if some of us had decided to take Cunningham technique, because he reveres Cunningham. Whatever would help us do what we needed to do in that room; and ballet was helpful for the footwork, the articulation of the feet, the change of direction, and with musicality, because his work had a certain musicality, whether from language or music. And you did need to be able to hit a certain kind of line, so I thought, "I had better take a class that will get me there."

rnf Did Gordon teach class?

co No, it was up to you. As an adult, you were expected to figure out what you needed to do for your body to be able to work for six hours, six days a week. On the road, we would give each other class sometimes, or do our own thing at the *barre* before rehearsal. He didn't dictate any of that. Also, he was interested in the particular qualities of each individual, and left it to us to manage our preparation for the work.

rnf How did that differ from the experience with Ron Brown, in terms of training?

co Actually, I managed to leave something out. In the mid-'80s, I trained for some time with Jennifer Muller. That experience helped me prepare to dance later with Ron, because he had danced with her company briefly. That's where I first saw him, on stage at the Joyce. He blew me away, knocked my socks off. I went running back stage and said, "Who are you, and how come I don't know about you?"

During that time I would do occasional workshops with people. One person I loved dancing with was Louie Falco. I studied with him in the early '80s. I did some summer study with Twyla Tharp too. I would insert modern where I could, but there wasn't any one style that I was really attached to. After I left my years of Horton, and went on to other things, I think I experimented with a number of different styles. For instance, Jennifer Muller helped me with Ron's work because of the particular kind of suspension and breath and the drop of the weight in the floor. I find that her technique has a ballet foundation, but with a modern twist. Like David, Ron was interested in dancers for their particular abilities, and he also trusted you to take class where you needed to.

rnf I remember you telling me one time about how you would go dance in the clubs, and that was your training in a certain way.

co That was a tremendous part of our training. And you know, I danced with a repertory company for a while, directed by Nanette Bearden. We would hang out in the clubs after, which is interesting because that experience really fed experiences later with Ron Brown. Some of the gay guys in Bearden's company took me to this club in mid-town: a black, gay, underground club called "Better Days." Later, when Ron started work on pieces addressing gay issues and was recalling that club, I could relate because I'd been there. On the road with Ron's company, after dancing all day long, we would go to a nightclub and hang out half the night in these gay clubs. It was kind of a parallel or complementary life that was going on simultaneously with the daytime formal, academic training.

rnf And did he expect everyone in the company to do that?

co No, it really was about whether it was your nature, or your inclination. I always took my sneakers because I knew that I wanted to do it, for my own enjoyment and release.

rnf Were there any other significant training issues after that, between then and now?

co I started going back to my roots, and I don't know if it was partly because Ron was exploring African, and Afro-Caribbean material, or if it was something that happened separately. But I started going to evening Afro-Caribbean classes, with Richard Gonzalez, and Ricardo Colon. So that's where my training went after the mid-'90s, and I still do that whenever I can.

rnf Now that you are teaching at a university, how do you maintain, or further train yourself?

co Interesting you should ask that, because I was recalling a certain point around 1998 when my back was bothering me, and I started going to an Iyengar yoga class. Dancers in New York had been fiendishly attaching themselves to yoga and really leaving ballet and other kinds of training behind. I didn't buy it when the whole exodus was happening. I stayed with ballet. It was much later that I found yoga. I found it really useful, but I didn't abandon traditional technique for it, I considered yoga to be a complement to dance training. When I came here [University of Illinois], I continued a bit, I did it on my own mostly.

Then I found that there was a Tai Chi master, Yang Yang, in town, so I started studying Tai Chi. Also, sometimes I take master classes, like the Zimbabwean class that was offered several years ago, even though it is hard to take class with my students; that's how I am trying to keep up.

rnf You take *barre* sometimes.

co I try to take ballet as much as I can. Yes, it's my mainstay. As far as this interview, I feel like I should try to be more . . .

rnf Sequential?

co Or at least connect the different lives that were going on simultaneously, like dancing in the club, and then going to ballet at ten o'clock in the morning! I think the climate that we exist in here now, was starting then. I feel like my moment with David Gordon was like the end of an era; companies really started relying on the dancers to get their training somewhere else, and then to walk into the studio and go for it. Dancers are required to be so versatile these days.

rnf And a lot of choreographers are interested, as you said, in the individuality of the dancers. They aren't necessarily trying to make everyone dance like they do.

co Yes, I think David is that way. I think that really influenced me, too, in my choreography. I'm interested in people of different backgrounds, not a homogeneous group, but there are some things that they have to be able to do. For example, they have to be able to point their feet and stretch the backs of their knees!

rnf So there's an expectation of ballet technique?

co Yes, but at the same time, I look for a grounded, "rootedness" that African and Caribbean dance requires.

rnf It seems then that you've had no time off; you've just kept plugging away, from one dance technique to another since you were five.

co I retired once, in 1990 or 1991. That was when I was managing Urban Bush Women. That experience prompted a shift of perspective for me; it was probably the beginning of my going back to my Caribbean roots, by watching how Jawole [Willa Jo Zollar, director of UBW] was combining dance forms. I didn't start dancing with Ron until 1993, but at that time I was looking at the way African-American choreographers were looking to the Caribbean and Africa for source material. I thought, "Hell, I'm from the Caribbean! Let me just call up what's there." That was a turning point.

It's interesting too because I feel that the style of dancing that I teach now draws from all those different perspectives, which wouldn't be the case if I had just decided to leave the roots behind.

janet panetta

from an interview with rebecca nettl-fiol, november 2002

Janet Panetta danced with the American Ballet Theatre as well as many contemporary companies. She has trained dancers in many of the major American modern dance companies such as Paul Taylor, Merce Cunningham, and Trisha Brown, and has been a guest teacher for many European companies such as Maguy Marin, Compagnie DCA and Anne Teresa de Keersmaeker. She is ballet mistress at the Tanztheatre Wuppertal of Pina Bausch.

rnf I know that you've taught many modern dancers. I'm interested in why you went in that direction rather than teaching more traditional ballet dancers.

jp When I made the change from being a classical dancer to a modern dancer, it was so freeing, because my personality was allowed to be there, as it never was as a classical dancer. When I started to teach, I felt it was the same kind of thing. When you teach modern dancers, you're teaching about being human, and you do it in a human way. When you teach ballet dancers, it's about being superhuman. Sometimes I teach ballet dancers and they like it, and I like them—it's ballet. I change what I give them.

rnf You do?

jp I do. They need a different vocabulary, actually. My modern dancers want to focus on really basic placement. And my ballet dancers should be focusing on that, but what they really want to focus on are the tricks. So the vocabulary has to include the tricks, and we move backwards from there into why they can't do those things. I was a ballet dancer in [American] Ballet Theatre, and I stopped being a ballet dancer when I was twenty-five, not exactly because I didn't want to be a ballet dancer any more, but there was all this stuff going on that was interesting, and I started to look at it and began to think, "hmmm . . . I don't think I was going to be a ballerina"—I didn't have the personality for it. I started looking at the dance downtown. I danced with people who danced for [Martha] Graham, like Paul Sanasardo, with people who danced with [José] Limón, like Libby Nye, and for people who danced with Merce [Cunningham] like Robert

Kovich, Albert Reid, and Neil Greenberg. From there I went to postmodern, but I stopped before release. That kind of work spanned a couple of decades, and was way more of my career really. Relatively little of my adult life was spent in ballet.

rnf While you were dancing in those companies, where did you train, or did you?

jp For a while I continued with Alfredo [Corvino]. And Margaret Craske, [Anthony] Tudor. I kept going to ballet class. Also, if I worked with Paul Sanasardo, I would take his class. If I worked for Libby Nye, I took her class. That way I got on-site training. I think because of the way I learned ballet that I was capable of learning other techniques. I wasn't locked into anything. I could see where the movement came from which was helpful.

rnf Why do you think so many modern dancers study ballet, sometimes exclusively?

jp I actually find that fewer dancers go to ballet now than they did in the '80s. I think what is asked for in contemporary dance now is less technical or less linear. I find people go to yoga more, or they study Feldenkrais, or Alexander—things like that. Except in Europe—there, they all have ballet class and it's mandatory, even for company members. Studying ballet keeps your body in a certain condition and allows you to go into a lot of different techniques, which I think is probably true. I experienced that myself. In the postmodern era, you didn't really have to study a technique. It was about going away from a kind of outward movement, back into pedestrian movement, about letting go and being more natural, as opposed to studying technique.

rnf Do you have many modern dancers coming to study with you now?

jp I do. I had the whole Cunningham company in the '80s. Right now in New York, I have two from that company. I've had some of the others because I taught at [SUNY] Purchase, but I don't have them now. I have one or two Trisha [Brown] people, which is really rare. I have a couple of Limón people. The rest of my class is made up of people who are doing project work—that is the majority. In my class, I see what would be relevant to the kind of work people are doing. For example, I have taught for companies like Ballet Preljocaj from France. They consider themselves to be a contemporary company, but I consider his [Angelin Preljocaj's] style enormously linear. The class I teach for them runs faster than any other class I give. There is very little breaking things down—it is really a straight ballet class. Whereas, when I teach a company like Rosas [company of choreographer Anne Teresa De Keersmaeker] who do a lot of floor work, we go down to basics. We do some ballet—they want to know where "on your leg" is and how to get there—but then they can go off of it. But do they want to stand there with their legs up in second position for a long time? Probably not. They want to be able to pass through some of those things, but it's about the movement, so the class becomes about how to facilitate movement.

I have been teaching for almost twenty-eight years. People in New York used to really study. I had people come to me five days a week, for ten years! Those classes were much more rigorous and advanced than the classes I give now, where I see people only once or twice a week. They can't afford to study, and they don't have time. Their whole idea of studying is different. So what do I do with them? My class is much easier than it used to be.

rnf If you were to set up a good training curriculum for a dancer nowadays, what would it be?

jp The experiment that Anna Teresa did in Brussels is very interesting to me. She started from today, there is no historical modern: no Graham, no Limón—nothing. They have some ballet. They have a lot of different contemporary teachers who are mostly release-based, more or less. But at least it's about movement—it's never . . .

rnf . . . hanging over?

jp . . . hanging over your legs for hours. It's always more movement-oriented which is a choice they made after the school had been around for a few years.

rnf They also have ballet, you said.

jp They have ballet, although I don't think they consider those teachers very traditional. They also have a yoga class. Each year, the focus shifts to something else: yoga or Pilates or maybe Alexander. They always had an anatomy teacher. The alternative tools are built right in the syllabus. And it's very interesting—the dancers improve enormously. Enormously! To watch how they come in and they go out two years later is impressive. I think they produce really good dancers, together with a strong focus on creativity. But even though the creative work is very structured, every once in a while someone will do a piece that's so reminiscent of something from the '70s or something from the '80s, or something from the past. Does it make a good dancer for today? I think it does. Does it make a well-rounded mind about the whole world of dance? I'm not so sure.

rnf Let's come back to the relevancy of ballet in the work you see today. Since you continue to teach it, I assume you still feel it does have relevance.

jp I feel my class is relevant. Would I say, across the board, all ballet classes have relevancy? There is enough knowledge about anatomy out there, so that should be reflected in the class, in a logical way. But you never know where the dance world is going. Ballet became very popular for a while, but I think it's sort of finished. Then at the height of the release technique's popularity, no one wanted to do anything else. It feels good and it is a good tool by being anatomically healthy. It is almost like getting bodywork. I would say that's fine, but then you don't know five years from now, what will be in the dance world. Actually, what I see coming is way more physical work. I think ballet is what keeps you. . . . It's like vitamins. Not that as a professional modern dancer you need to do it every day, all the time, but it is really good to have it in there, in what you do to take care of your body.

rnf My colleagues and I talk about this a lot too. We have the expectation that people that are at an advanced level can do certain things. They understand their leg in second, they understand how to jump, how to point their feet—those things that you call "technique." But some people don't seem to have much interest in that anymore.

jp No, they don't. They may never want to stretch their legs and point their feet. Okay, you don't have to. That's a choice you can make. But not being able to and making the choice not to—those are two separate things. The more you know, the more choices you have.

rnf And people who do release, I wonder, releasing from something—obviously, that's a reaction to something. So if they never had something—holding, for example—would they have something to go from?

jp It's a really unfortunate title. But the original Trisha Brown dancers—did they study release? They came out of a really well-rounded, rigorous curriculum such as [SUNY] Purchase, where they reached a certain technical level, and then chose not to use it. That's a whole different ball game. I remember being in class with somebody—I was actually taking one of the Twyla [Tharp] dancers' class—it was a ballet class. I was already maybe forty-five, forty-six years old—it wasn't a hard class. She gave a very nice movement phrase—those classes generally had one movement phrase at the end. There was a girl in that class, who asked every five minutes, "Could we sit down on the floor? Excuse me, I need to sit down, I need to feel my bones on the floor." It was so annoying to me. The movement part of the class was maybe twenty minutes, but for twenty minutes this girl couldn't stand up and move! I asked her, "How do you expect to perform anything? Do you really think every five minutes you have to get down on the floor and take a break—what is up? This is training for you, this nice, easy phrase. If I can do it at age forty-five, then you certainly can do it at twenty-two, without throwing yourself down on the ground every five minutes!" Oh, I was livid with her (laughs). But I think there's an idea that stretching—I don't mean stretching passively, but lengthening—is bad. Or that jumping is bad for you. This is absurd, really absurd. And if it's gone that far, then . . .

rnf Or finding a line. I've fought about that a little with some people who don't really want to go into some form. I had to convince them that something was missing.

jp Then you know you've gone too far. Yoga, for example, is wonderful. In my studio we have yoga classes, every day. Do I think it's an exercise and movement for people of all ages? I do. Do I think you can become a dancer from just taking yoga classes? No, I do not. Can you make pretty lines? Yes. Will you learn to move? No! I feel the same way about aerobics too. Is aerobics good for you? Great for you. I wish I were there now—a great tool to build your stamina, get you warm. Could you become a dancer from aerobics alone? No. The tools come along, and unfortunately I think release is a tool. But is that, or anything else by itself, going to make you a dancer? No.

rnf So technique classes should involve some kind of dancing.

jp Is technique class going to make you a dancer? It's not. It's a nice foundation. It's not going to make you a dancer. But technique can be taught. What makes you a dancer is probably something that can't exactly be taught.

So you take all those tools that are there to give you choices, and range as to what kind of dancer you can be. Choosing only one tool will limit your range. When I was dancing, I was proud of the fact that I could learn all kinds of dance. I loved every kind of dancing there was: Brazilian dancing, African dancing, ballroom dancing. I loved to do it and my job was to master it. That's how I felt. I loved classical ballet and my postmodern work. I wanted it to be like that for everyone else. I couldn't understand it being any other way.

kraig patterson

from an interview with rebecca nettl-fiol, september 2002

Kraig Patterson danced with the Mark Morris Dance Group from 1987–99. He also danced with Glenn/Lund Dance, the Danny Lewis Repertory Ensemble, Ohad

Naharin, Mark Haim, and the White Oak Dance Project. He formed his company, "bopi's black sheep" in 1997.

rnf Tell me about your early training in dance, noting especially the things that were really significant.

kp The bug came in high school; I had this teacher named Jolene Bryant who taught musical theater. Her daughter was in *Zoot Suit* on Broadway, and she would come in every year, and set choreography for our musicals. She didn't give *tendus* or stretches—I just learned by mimicking. I remember the joy in doing that, and standing out because I always danced as a child. We had dance contests and I would win my little dollar at birthday parties. So that was the bug, and I thought I was going to go to New York to dance on Broadway.

The next significant thing came when I auditioned for NYU, and I was cut because I didn't know the terminology and so on, I guess. I cried and wept and thought I was unsuitable for dance; it totally broke me. I was going from being the featured dancer in everything to not even being accepted in the first cut, so it was a big reality blow. After that, I studied intensely at Princeton Ballet for a year; I got a scholarship and started learning about dance belts and *tendus* and *relevés*. I then went to Mason Gross School of the Arts, the performing arts part of Rutgers University, for a year. All the women at that point were looking to get married and keep their hair like Farrah Fawcett and I thought, "Are they really committed to this? Where will I be in ten years with this?" Now that I've aged a little, I think the curriculum was probably good, but it just wasn't good for me at that time. There were no men in the upper class, for one thing. There was a lot of Laban Movement Analysis, and I think for young people, the teachers have to almost trick us into thinking about aligning our bones correctly. Basically, we just want to run for 900 miles, and sweat,—dance like crazy. And I didn't really discover that kind of information until towards the end of my school years at Juilliard.

rnf Did you graduate from Mason Gross?

kp No, I went there for a year. Instead, I tried it again in New York; it seemed that everyone said I had to audition for Juilliard. I got into Juilliard, long story short. That is where all the heavy-duty training began. The classical modern dance began there. It is a really good program, in retrospect, even if while you are there, you feel more or less imprisoned, as if you have to curtail your expression, which is not exactly true. They do slap you down and clean you up and neutralize you. Then you build on top of that. In my first year there, I worked with Anna Sokolow, which we thought of as going through the dungeon. Actually, it was probably one of the best presents they could have given us. She was just an incredible woman. It wasn't about technique or making sure of our finesse, it was more about courage and going deep within to make an idea happen.

We were required to do ballet every day and at least one modern class every day. If you were really gung-ho some of the teachers would let you sneak into the advanced class. I would finish my lessons, my music, and then beg to be in the advanced Graham class. I don't know whether for good or bad, but it made me a little stronger to be in a big pool, with big piranhas. Juilliard is a really strong program for building performers, more about building performers than building choreographers. At the time Martha Hill was still there; my graduation was her last year in full charge.

Muriel Topaz came in as I was leaving. I remember there were twenty of us in my class: ten that were obvious technicians, then ten like me that were "freaks," without the body type, or the feet, or the weight that they wanted for performing. What we had was a choreographic eye, or some kind of other potential. It almost seemed like they put up a thin screen—some of us went to the left and others to the right. My group was encouraged to take four years of composition, which I did. I'm glad about that because I also learned technique. But those people who really didn't care about teaching or choreographing—who just wanted to be vessels—only took the two years of mandatory composition and could not take it as an elective after that. The other half continued creating, and we were encouraged to do it. Also, in terms of my time at Juilliard, I probably would not have gotten in Mark's [Morris] company if I hadn't had composition and, most importantly, the materials of music.

rnf After Juilliard, did you continue training?

kp Laura Glenn came to Juilliard—she had some company members that were still in school. I was in my second year in school, and she asked me to work with her. So, halfway through school, I was working outside. I was allowed a couple of weeks to work with them, probably partly because they were graduates and very closely connected to Juilliard. Then, in the first year out of school I worked with Ohad Naharin and Daniel Lewis, among others. I had about five jobs, plus working at a restaurant to pay the rent. It was great to have all that experience, but I felt like I was getting nowhere in a way because I had trouble juggling it all. At the time, Paul Taylor was my hero. Mark [Morris] hadn't been noticed like that yet. In my senior year, we dancers talked about "going shopping," which meant checking out companies, seeing where you wanted to get a job. Mark's company blew me away. But the youngest one was five years older than me. I thought, "Okay Kraig, you have to slow down and concentrate on your goals." My goal was to get a mentor and work with him for at least ten years, learning how they choreograph, and having a secure job. I thought it was Paul Taylor, but I was too small to dance with Paul Taylor. I started quitting my jobs. I was at the Graham school, and I got very close to getting into the second company; this was when Martha was still alive. When I got into Mark's company, I had to leave the Graham school, but that was fine. I also studied at [Alvin] Ailey on scholarship, and went to ADF [American Dance Festival] as a performer for the composer/choreographer program. I studied with Viola Farber and Betty Jones; they were my heroes. Molissa Fenley and Doug Varone were also teaching. At ADF you can pick your classes, and I really have a good eye for seeing whom I want to learn from, or who is going to build me. When I was at Juilliard I was still not interested in going to the "avants." I wanted to go to Viola. I was very curious about it, and it opened my eyes about dance. Cunningham [technique] still crosses my eyes to watch, and to take the classes. So that's the place now that's the source of my stimulation as a choreographer and as a technician, so to speak. It's like my second college, learning about craft and learning about movement.

rnf Do you go to class in New York? You take modern?

kp After Juilliard, I went to Jocelyn Lorenz because some of the upperclassmen graduating recommended her classes. It wasn't so much because of her teaching—she's a great teacher—but because all the modern companies that had substance would be there. All the star dancers would be taking ballet for modern dancers. I don't believe that's what she was teaching, but even some ABT [American Ballet Theatre] people would be there, Cunningham dancers would be there, and Paul Taylor dancers; it was almost a social club. So, you would take classes with those people, then they would do concerts and see you there, and you would get invited to do things—that's how I got into all those small companies. I advise students now to do all they can in the beginning, then at some point you have to edit and sort out what is really right for you. Eventually, you have to ask yourself how are you going to take those next steps, and what you need to weed out.

rnf I think it's rather unusual for people to keep taking modern classes in New York. Do you think that?

kp There isn't much there. And modern's such a big word these days.

rnf But you sound like one person that's doing that. I mean you don't do yoga or other somatic practices?

kp I do yoga. I'm interested in yoga, but not to the point of becoming a yoga guru. Now I'm into gyrotonics—I love that actually. I've done Pilates, now I want to do Karate. I don't really want to call anything my own, except me. Whatever I can experience, whatever I can borrow or beg or steal from. Thank God I had Graham, because now I know what tension in movement is, and what heroic or archaic movement looks like. I can draw from that in a piece. I create my own vocabulary, but I like for people to recognize the history behind things. There is nothing wrong with using old movement, or borrowing from somebody, or doing a reference to this or that. You spend so much time trying to create new movement, but you can only walk forward or back or diagonal. You can only curve so much. I'm constantly trying to create new rhythms and new moves. I want to have a structure I can then bend. You can't bend something if you don't know the structure. That's where ballet comes into play. I love ballet. But how can you make ballet strength and ballet lines but at the same time contort it to another thing? For me, the closest technique to doing that is Cunningham, and the only thing that Cunningham misses is swing. Without a sense of swing, you can wind up being very angular. It's very strong, but there's no wind. So I have to counter that with something else.

rnf When you're creating work?

kp I want to be studying everything. When I was leaving Mark's company, I had a dream. I wondered, "What would happen if I really tried to get into the Cunningham company before my days were over as a performer?" And the more I think about it, okay, I don't have to dance in his company. It would be cute, but I don't have to. I know I don't have the skills to figure out how to get in the door.

That led me to thinking, what is it I teach? There is the whole release movement. Some students wind up doing so much release, if you say to *developé* and hold it for three and a half seconds they get upset with you. I want to know what they are releasing from. Do they know the places they are releasing from? Or are they releasing everything until they are lying on the floor like a dead chicken? I'm in the middle. I feel like the middle brother. I respect my dance elders, and I thank God I had the training that I had. I have to watch myself that I am not too passive in my teaching, or too much of "that's good, yes, that's coming." My teachers told it like it was—it hurt, it stung. That doesn't happen so much anymore. And there was always a reverence, a high regard for our teachers. And a high regard for line, which I think is almost kind of fuzzy now. I don't know if that's bad or good. I feel you should know where something came from, time to have at least one beautiful contraction in your young dance career. Or one semester of swing, or a semester of walking in turnout in the Graham form. It's an interesting time we live in, as far as movement.

shelley washington

interview with rebecca nettl-fiol, october 2001

Shelley Washington danced with the Martha Graham Dance Company before becoming a member of Twyla Tharp Dance, where she maintained a career-long collaboration as dancer, rehearsal director, and associate artistic director.

rnf Tell me about your training history, starting from the beginning, including significant teachers or forms of training that had a strong impact on you as a dancer.

sw I took ballet classes like every little girl from the time I was about six or seven, and more tap, and jazz, about once a week. Then when I was about fourteen and I really was interested in pursuing a career in dance, my mom and dad sent me to Interlochen Music Camp. For me, that was a great experience because it was a nonthreatening environment. And the thing that was great about it, and what I feel so fortunate to have had in my early days was an eclectic background. For maybe three months Helen McGehee came in from the Graham Company and we had really serious Graham. And then we would have Louise Burns come in, who taught [Merce] Cunningham [technique]. And then we had ballet class every day. There was a sort of discipline that those guests carried with them, and an artistry, that I got to witness from the age of fourteen or fifteen, this was in the late '60s, early '70s. We also had classes on how to wear make-up; we performed on the Academy stage with the Interlochen orchestra. So I was there learning about music and drama as well.

In 1970 I went to Jacob's Pillow, which was a huge turning point. Because it was there that every week a different dance company came in, so that all of a sudden my world expanded. I was taking ballet from Margaret Craske, Indian Dance from Rita Davies, and Dance Theatre of Harlem came in. Alwin Nikolais and Murray Louis came. Ruth Page came for the whole summer and made *Alice in Wonderland* on us. Edward Villella was there, with Patricia McBride dancing, which really made me want to take more classes, and learn more. By the time I went to Connecticut College in the summer, the sky was the limit. Walter Nicks was teaching jazz, Clay Taliaferro was teaching, and Peter Saul from Cunningham was teaching—it was just amazing! So I would take five classes a day in all of these different techniques. You watch their performances or watch them in classes, and start formulating your own opinions about where you wanted to really hone in.

rnf After Jacob's Pillow and Interlochen, where did you go to college?

sw I went to Juilliard, where again, every day we had ballet, Graham classes, and a lot of Limón. And then I went to the Graham Company from there. In New York, if you wanted to take another class, you could just work it into your schedule, or go on the weekends. There was the opportunity to be around all of these different people, researching, learning, watching, listening, and doing.

rnf How were you introduced to Twyla Tharp?

sw In the summer of 1973 I was at American University, apprenticing with José Limón [the company]. I saw that Twyla Tharp was teaching, and despite the apprenticeship, I decided to take her class during one of my breaks. I hadn't heard of her, but I thought I would go try it. And I really got into what she was offering in the class in terms of the phrases: the retrograding, the inversion and changing front and how we were counting, and how the movement and the space were being manipulated. I had never worked like that before! And I enjoyed those classes so much, I went every day for six weeks, and it was completely different from anything else. I knew then that that was what I wanted to do, but I still had school at Juilliard, so I went back to school, and to the Graham Company from there. Later, when Twyla had auditions and didn't find anybody, they remembered me from two years prior and called me in for an audition. She says in her book [*Push Comes to Shove*] that I'd come in with a strong dramatic kind of energy; that had been from my year in the Graham Company.

rnf What did you do for training after you left the Graham Company?

sw I used ballet all through my years with Twyla, as my base. You know, I'm not a great ballet dancer, but that was where I found "home." And then from there, I would go to Graham, or to Twyla or Cunningham, but I always turned to something simple. Even when I stopped dancing and when I was cycling, I would get on the machine, hit the same program every day: a six-minute program at level seven, for example. And in that six minutes I would know exactly how my back was feeling, my knees, my legs; it was the same thing every day.

rnf You mean that the ritual aspect of it appealed to you?

sw Yes, the ritual aspect of it. It wasn't my ultimate goal to be a ballet dancer or to get my leg over my head. I mean, I wanted to do those things, but the ballet *barre* is home, where I know that *pliés* are first, then *tendus* are second, etc. I like to be able to feel improvement or see it. I can hold this balance, or I can do a double *pirouette*. But not being able to do things wouldn't send me through the roof, because ultimately that's not what I did on stage—stand in *tendu* and do a double *pirouette.* So I just used it as a "getting to know." Maybe now in my life I would use yoga in that way.

rnf But you didn't start doing yoga until after you stopped dancing.

sw I had done some yoga with Twyla in the mid '80s. She brought in Jonathan Watts to teach yoga to our company every day, and I really loved it. I didn't hold on to it, none of us did. And now there are a few of us twenty years later that are saying, "God, if only I had known!" Maybe, like studying Alexander Technique, it was too passive. I wasn't ready yet to figure all that out at that time; I was more into jump, skip, hop, play, run, throw, kick, and hit!

rnf For training then, did someone in the company give *barre,* or did you go elsewhere to take class?

sw We took ballet class wherever we chose, but most all of us took from Maggie Black. She taught a ballet class for modern dancers—this was the '80s, and it was very crowded—sometimes between 75 and 100 people. There were dancers from many companies and choreographers: Cunningham, Tharp, Douglas Dunn, Dan Wagoner. Then there were also professional ballet dancers in the classes at times; it was pretty wonderful.

rnf Did Twyla expect you all to take ballet classes?

sw We were expected to be warmed up. You could warm up any way you wanted. There were a couple of people who did not do ballet, but the majority certainly did. When we were on tour we always did a ballet class, especially the last eight years that I was in the company, which would be through '88. When I was Associate Director, I taught a full ballet class in the morning. After that we would rehearse all day, and then the company would go have dinner, and maybe a nap, and we'd come back at 7 p.m. when I would give the same *barre* from the morning. Twyla had many ballet dancers in the company over the years: Rose Marie Wright was a ballet dancer in the '60s with Pennsylvania Ballet. Billy Whitener, Chris Uchida, Richard Colton all came from Joffrey Ballet. That was in the '70s. Gil Boggs and Elaine Kudo, both soloists in [American] Ballet Theatre, joined us around '87.

rnf Would you say, then, that Twyla trained dancers in her style in the rehearsal process?

sw Yes, in the dance, and in the work.

rnf It's a shift from the old paradigm of training where you study Graham technique to prepare directly for performing Graham choreography.

sw It certainly is, and there are some people who still do that. But you'd have Graham dancers in ballet class, and certainly dancers like Peggy Lyman or Janet Eilber [Graham company dancers] were beautiful ballet dancers. In those days, there were certainly some people who never took ballet. I always had problems with turn-out, and so ballet was a really good place for me to work on my hips and things like that. Also, Twyla was starting to ask more from us technically, with *pirouettes* and things like that, so where else do you learn to do a *pirouette?* You have to go to the source.

rnf It makes sense to me knowing Twyla's style that you would choose to study ballet.

sw But Twyla and I were always trying to figure out, . . . you know, we would be in the studio saying, "Okay let's do this Tharp technique, what *is* Tharp technique?" In preparing for my residency here [at the University of Illinois, teaching *The Fugue*], I was listening to her in a lecture demonstration that must have been in the '80s. She was telling the audience how important *The Fugue* was to choreograph, because without choreographing *The Fugue* she could never have choreographed *In the Upper Room,* and those pieces were sixteen years apart. It was interesting to me that she said that. So when I was coming here to teach this technique-repertoire class, we were very careful. She wanted to know what I was going to be teaching because she only wanted the material that was going to pertain to *The Fugue,* that would help *The Fugue,* since that was what I was teaching here. So if I didn't get a lot of rehearsal time, where was another place I would have time to work on the technique? We decided I would do some yoga warm-ups, because much of *In the Upper Room* was done when the yoga teacher was with us. In fact, one whole section is called "The Dog" because we were spending so much time in Downward Dog [a yoga posture], and so much of the material from that is pulled from the beginnings of *The Fugue,* all the parallel positions, and the use of weight. So, we went back to teaching the things in the technique. Actually, I would say that maybe her technique *was* through her repertoire. And that's what I've tried to teach here.

But going back to my own training, I didn't have great technique, and one of my ballet teachers told me I would never be a ballet dancer because I didn't have the proper turn-out. But it didn't discourage me from taking the class. I mean, no, my legs are never going to be 180 degrees turned out, but it gave me that push to go on into modern dance, something that was a little more acceptable to all body types. And I think this teacher would be shocked to know that I really was a soloist in ABT [during Tharp's tenure with the company]. But even with all this, I wish I'd known more. I wish I'd taken some acting classes, or had some injury prevention information when I was growing up; I never really studied kinesiology, or took nutrition classes, for example.

rnf Yes, and nowadays so many of the somatic practices have come into dance training. I know that yoga has become a popular form for dancers to study.

sw Yes, and it seems half the dancers are doing Pilates, and Gyrotonics. I look at the dancers on Broadway; some of the dancers in ABT are doing Broadway now. They have learned to sing or act, and there is always a need for a ballet dancer who can wear pointe shoes. It's "crossing over." In Twyla's company, there is a dancer, Elizabeth Parkinson who did *Fosse* on Broadway. So it's not just the ballet dancers who don't have the perfect ballet technique or the women who are a little bigger, or don't have the perfect feet. Different types are crossing over. Also, what I keep saying to people here [the University of Illinois Dance Department] who may not have the best technique, but might have the most beautiful voices in the world, is that voice is important in dance, and communication skills are important. And Contact Improvisation—it's huge now.

rnf Right, you have to be able to do a lot.

sw Or at least be exposed to it, or just open to it. Maybe that's what I really learned and I thank my teachers for allowing me to be open to trying all these different things. That's something Interlochen was so good at doing. That was also something so good about being in New York and at Juilliard—the exposure, and the professionalism, which is so important.

contributors

melanie bales attended Interlochen Arts Academy, and studied ballet in New York at the Joffrey School and as a Harkness Ballet Trainee. She graduated Magna cum Laude with a BA from Carleton College in 1976. She subsequently performed both classical and operetta repertoire in Germany, and danced principal duet roles with Douglas Nielsen Dance (New York). She received an MFA in Performance and Choreography from the University of Illinois Urbana-Champaign, where she was a Visiting Assistant Professor from 1982–87. In 1994, Bales completed the course in Laban Movement Analysis through the Laban/Bartenieff Institute of Movement Studies. She is a Professor of Dance at The Ohio State University where she choreographs and teaches technique and courses in LMA. Since joining the faculty, Bales has received support to commission dances for a solo repertoire, including the work of John Giffin, Iréne Hultman, Daniel Nagrin, Tere O'Connor, and Catherine Turocy. She has written and presented papers for various professional organizations including the Council on Research in Dance (CORD), the International Council of Kinetography Laban (ICKL), the National Dance Education Organization (NDEO), Motus Humanus, and the Laban Institute of Movement Studies (LIMS).

rebecca nettl-fiol is an Associate Professor of Dance at the University of Illinois, Urbana-Champaign, serving as Interim Department Head from 2001–5, and BFA Program Director from 1991–2001. She teaches courses in the Alexander Technique, anatomy and kinesiology, somatics, modern dance technique, and composition. She holds an MA in Dance/Choreography from The Ohio

State University and a BFA in Dance from the University of Illinois. She completed her teacher and reconstructor certification in Labanotation in 1985 and then studied the Alexander Technique with Joan and Alexander Murray, certifying in 1990. Her choreography has been supported by the Illinois Arts Council and has been presented in New York, Chicago, throughout the United States, and annually at the Krannert Center for the Performing Arts. She has presented papers and workshops on the applications of the Alexander Technique in training dancers for Journal of Dance Education, the International Association for Dance Medicine and Science (IADMS), the National Dance Education Organization (NDEO), the American Alliance of Physical Education Recreation and Dance (AAPHERD), Motus Humanus, the Laban Institute of Movement Studies (LIMS), the Alexander Technique International (ATI), the American College Dance Festival Association (ACDFA), and the American Society for Alexander Technique (AmSAT).

glenna batson has developed an integrative approach to dance, movement science, and somatics, and has been an educator, practitioner, and performer for more than twenty-five years. She holds an MA in Dance Education from Columbia University Teachers College, MS in Physical Therapy from Hahnemann Medical University, and a Doctor of Science from Rocky Mountain University of Health Professionals. She apprenticed with Irene Dowd in Ideokinesis and is also a certified teacher of the Alexander Technique. She has taught Alexander and lectured on dance science and somatics at the University of North Carolina, Chapel Hill, Hollins University, the American Dance Festival, Bates Dance Festival, and in Europe, Japan, and Australia. Batson currently directs the Contemporary Body Practices curriculum for the Hollins/ADF MFA, and is Associate Professor of Physical Therapy at Winston-Salem State University.

wendell beavers began dancing in 1976 in New York with Mary Overlie after a career as an athlete (football, basketball, baseball) and scholar (economics, intellectual history). He studied every known modern technique, ballet with Jean Hamilton, and improvisation/performance with The Judsons: Steve Paxton, Robert Ellis Dunn, Barbara Dilley. He began performing and creating his own work in 1986 while studying developmental movement and experiential anatomy with Bonnie Bainbridge Cohen. He was a founding member and early director of Movement Research; a founding faculty member of NYU's Experimental Theatre Wing (ETW) in 1978 and a principal architect of ETW's unique physical theater/dance cross training curriculum. He was named Director of Performing Arts at Naropa University in 2003 and began chairing a new MFA in Contemporary Performance at Naropa in 2004.

veronica dittman danced with the St. Louis Ballet before receiving a BFA in Dance from The Ohio State University. She danced for a number of choreographers including Vicki Uris, D. Chase Angier, Joe Alter, and Jordan Fuchs, as well as cochoreographing and coproducing "The Industrial Valley Celebrity Hour" with Faith Pilger. She is a certified dance notator (Laban) and one of the founding editors of the *Dance Insider*. She currently runs *firefly* restaurant with her husband in Dodanduwa, Sri Lanka.

natalie gilbert has been Music Director of the American Dance Festival for over twenty-five years, and was Music Coordinator at The Ohio State University Department of Dance from 1997–2006. Her music degrees are from Oberlin (BA) and Ohio State (MA). She is a founding board member of the International Guild of Musicians in Dance and has worked extensively teaching and accompanying dancers at NYU Tisch School of the Arts, New World School of the Arts in Miami, and CID in Paris.

joshua monten received his BA in Literature and Cultural Anthropology from Duke University, after which he began studying dance more seriously at the North Carolina School of the Arts and at the San Martin Theater School in Buenos Aires. He obtained his MA in Dance Performance and History from The Ohio State University in 2001. After two years of performing with the Tanztheater Irina Pauls, he is currently a member of the dance ensemble of the Stadttheater Bern, under the direction of Stijn Celis.

martha myers is Dean Emeritus of the American Dance Festival and the Henry B. Plant Professor of Dance (Emeritus) at Connecticut College. She has taught and lectured across the United States, in Europe, South America, Asia, and Australia, and has authored articles on choreography and somatic training for dancers in numerous dance and dance science publications. Myers has received honorary doctorates from Marymount College, SUNY/Purchase College, and Virginia Commonwealth University. She was a founding member of the National Dance Association Commission on Dance Science and Somatics, a board member of International Association for Dance Medicine and Science, and a member of the advisory board for the Laban Institute of Movement Studies. She has received numerous awards for "lifetime achievement in dance," among them: the Laban Institute of Movement Studies and the Connecticut Arts Commission.

Index

The University of Illinois Press
is a founding member of the
Association of American University Presses.

Composed in 10/13 Adobe Minion
with Futura display by BookComp, Inc.
Designed by Copenhaver Cumpston
for the University of Illinois Press
Manufactured by Sheridan Books, Inc.

University of Illinois Press
1325 South Oak Street
Champaign, IL 61820-6903
www.press.uillinois.edu